HOCUS FOCUS

Hocus Focus
Coming of age with ADD and its medicines

R. L. Kramer

ISBN 979-8-9882474-2-5

Published 2023 by Solis Libres

Cover design by Valeriia T. (valeriiaty on Fiverr)

Editing, proofreading, and layout by Susanna Schollum (www.linebyline.co.nz)

Dedicated to Bill Torrey

CONTENTS

FOREWORD

I feel honored to provide the foreword for R. L. Kramer's book *Hocus Focus*, which shares his experiences of being prescribed stimulants for a diagnosis of attention deficit disorder (ADD). As a child, adolescent, and adult psychiatrist who started my journey into holistic medicine in 2002, my understanding and treatment for ADD have shifted over the decades.

Initially, my ten years of medical training caused me to think of ADD as a straightforward diagnosis with a simple treatment option: stimulants. The majority of my young patients improved while taking stimulants, which reinforced my assumption that the intervention helped.

For those children who did not seem to benefit from using stimulants, I began adding Ginkgo biloba to improve focus and concentration. The adjunctive use of Ginkgo biloba helped these children to focus when using stimulants alone didn't improve their symptoms.

However, when I began to explore holistic psychiatry and learned about both functional (natural nutritional support) and energy medicine, I began to learn through diagnostic methods available in energy medicine. The energy-testing results helped me to understand the underlying causes of ADD, just as it helped me to better understand the underlying causes of other mental health issues.

In 2002, I began to treat underlying dysfunctions that resulted in attentional issues, using natural nutrients, glandular support, and energy (mind-body) techniques. Over the years, I began to reframe my understanding of ADD from a holistic perspective. Instead of a deficit of attention, I began to see that the type of attention in ADD was typical of and helpful in a warrior. The type of attention that school systems want and reward is that of a scholar. The first is driven by the sympathetic nervous system, which creates the fight-or-flight response. The second is driven by the parasympathetic nervous system, which creates the rest-and-digest response.

A warrior's attention span is 360 degrees. Blood is diverted to the muscles to facilitate running away from danger or fighting an aggressor. It is diverted away from the gastrointestinal system because eating a sandwich amid a fight-or-flight response would be counterproductive. Reactions are lightning-fast. Adrenaline coursing through the body prepares the person to defend or attack the source of the threat.

The hyperfocused state of a warrior can come to our rescue when we procrastinate on a project and try to complete it at the last minute. Stress and fear build up when we procrastinate, until the warrior takes over and gets the project done overnight. The 360-degree zone of attention can make multitasking possible and noticing details intuitive.

People with this kind of attention do exceptionally well when working with a group of children running around on the playground. In addition, the stream of incoming data feeds a versatile and creative mind, filled with activity and ideas and fully alive with possibilities. This kind of attention span would be appropriate in stressful, warlike circumstances but is difficult to contain in a classroom.

A scholar's attention span is narrow and deep. Blood flows to support the digestive system rather than the muscles. Reactions have the luxury to be slow and methodical. Both internally and externally, the environment feels safe. The person exists in a calm and peaceful flow state because stress and adrenaline levels are low. This kind of attention span would be appropriate in a classroom or library but hopelessly inadequate during a war.

Because the scholar's attention generally requires a state of calm and peace, it is difficult to create this kind of attention when distracting noises, activities, or demands interrupt one's space. Incoming data needs the luxury of time, sometimes years, before they can fully formulate into a beautiful, intricate, and complex idea or concept. The fight-or-flight response sits quietly in a corner of the psyche, so scholars are often more compliant, agreeable, and restrained.

When perceiving ADD in this way, I began to ask the central question, "What are the underlying sources of stress for this individual?" In my practice, I began to treat the following common stressors:

1. Food hypersensitivities. Especially reactions to wheat, dairy, and refined sugar.

2. Toxicity. Especially associated with difficulties with methylation and activating B vitamins.

3. Inflammation. Sometimes from early childhood viral or bacterial illnesses.

4. Trauma, such as problems with neglect or abuse in the home or school.

5. Environmental or social stressors, such as an unstable living environment or losses due to death or divorce.

As my understanding of ADD transformed, I began to view the use of stimulants differently. Yes, they seem to improve attention and focus, but at what cost? How does something stimulating enhance the attention span of a hyperactive child? I began to think of the role of stimulants as similar to whipping a tired horse rather than nurturing and strengthening the horse. The patients' exhaustion at the end of the day and difficulty waking up in the mornings seem to support my hypothesis.

The consistent decrease in appetite under the influence of stimulants suggests that the gastrointestinal system is getting less attention under the influence of stimulants, which is typical of an increased sympathetic response rather than a parasympathetic response. Is it possible that these stimulants are creating the hyperfocused attention span that occurs under high-stress situations?

We know that it's possible to rely on the hyperfocused state when we cram for tests or try to complete an assignment at the last minute. In doing so, we pay a high price the next day when our energy crashes. It seems possible that the attention gained from stimulants is not the attention of a scholar but the attention of a warrior on high alert. Manipulating the body into a chronic state of high alert through a stimulant ignores the body's repeated signals for additional help and healing.

These are the physiological and metabolic considerations of healing

ADD. But, for healing ADD to be whole and complete, it is critical to understand the why as much as the how. Empathy lies within the heart of why. I gained mine in 1992 before I began to shift my traditional approach to a holistic one.

At the time, a training psychiatrist recommended and prescribed Zoloft to me when I told him I wanted to quit psychiatry during my third year of residency training. My experiences with taking psychotropic medication and the withdrawals I experienced five years later when I decided to stop helped me to understand the role of a patient.

My empathy for psychiatric patients grew as I realized just how much I disliked being a patient and having to take daily medication. It shifted my narcissistic and overly optimistic opinions of my role as a doctor. It became obvious to me that many patients shared the same attitude and would prefer a more natural alternative—psychiatrist-free if possible.

Empathy for the plight of psychiatric patients removed my excuses and blockages, enabling me to acquire new, unfamiliar healing tools in functional and energy medicine. It allowed me to stand up for my holistic practice during a legal battle against the Maryland Board, which cost over $100,000, lasted one and a half years, and set a legal precedent in 2009. It motivated me to create new integrative approaches for helping my patients get off their medications.

When R. L. Kramer came to my practice seeking relief from his symptoms, I applied both functional and energy medicine tools to help support his healing process. During the treatment process, I grew to know a little about him, but not to the extent that this book has allowed me to understand.

What impressed me about him at the time, but is understated in his book, is his pure, passionate, and good heart. He has the kind of integrity that stays true to his beliefs despite great sacrifice. You can see it in his choices to live in alignment with his beliefs and how hard he tries to overcome obstacles that get in the way of living with integrity.

His book is an example of who he is and how he can transform difficulties into opportunities for growth. The time and effort he devoted to writing it is a testament to his creativity, intelligence, and determination, which neither diagnosis nor stimulant could dim.

I am grateful for the additional empathy I've gained through reading the book *Hocus Focus* for all who have struggled with the same diagnosis and treatment. Through this book, I was able to vicariously learn from experiences in a much deeper and broader way than I ever gained through the objective, clinical perspective of a psychiatrist. Each chapter built upon the other to help me understand R. L.'s healing journey, what motivated him, and how he navigated life despite all the obstacles. *Hocus Focus* helped me to gain deeper insights into how early childhood medications affect a child's developing identity and self-confidence.

Through *Hocus Focus*, I came to understand how these diagnoses and medications, so quickly and mechanically dispensed by highly trained doctors, affect a person's life beyond fixing attention and focus. For good or ill, these medications manipulate, determine, and eventually take over the course of development, self-esteem, and behavior.

It was a privilege to support R. L. Kramer during his holistic healing journey, and I am grateful that he found a way to live medication-free. I admire his tenacity and courage in finding his path and in sharing it with others in this valuable book. My wish is that advances in medicine will evolve beyond its reliance on stimulants for the treatment of ADD. For that day to come, we need voices like R. L. Kramer's to shift the medical paradigm.

Alice W. Lee, MD, ABIHM, ABoIM

HOCUS FOCUS

NOTE

This book is not intended to persuade—it's meant to present. I am not telling you directly to medicate or not medicate for any condition. Yes, you will find that I have opinions based on my experiences. I release any and all liability in relation to the decisions you, as reader, choose to make about what to put in or not put in your body or those you look after.

Yes, I also took a lot of other drugs. I went off-program a few times with my dosing. I am not a perfect case study. The experiment of me and its results are as anecdotal as they come and should be interpreted as such.

Both attention deficit disorder and attention deficit hyperactivity disorder, referred to as ADD and ADHD respectively, will be combined and referred to solely as ADD. This is not to say they are the same disorder but is for ease of writing and readability.

Journal entries will be italicized and inset.

Amphetamine's voice will be bolded.

This book is not a scientific reference document. What has been right and wrong for me doesn't speak for all, especially those with ADD.

Some names and relationships are redacted or changed. Most, if not all of these stories have been extracted from my memories and journals. While

I do have a strong memory, memories can be fickle, exaggerated by their keepers, and downright wrong. Nonetheless, despite any inaccuracy in my detailed recollection of the timeline of my life, the story is the truth.

I used music to remember this story and if there is interest in listening to this music, the playlist can be found here: https://rlkramer.us/playlist/

Introduction

I started using amphetamines when I was seven and a half years old. Amphetamines are a synthetic, addictive, mood-altering drug. Known on the streets as speed, crank, crisscross, bumblebees, or addies. Referred to at the doctor's office as Adderall, Vyvanse, Dexedrine, etc.

As a child, I ingested somewhere between 10–20 milligrams of Dexedrine every morning before school and another smaller dose in the afternoon.

At school, I had a habit of getting out of my seat and impulsively answering and asking questions without raising my hand, and I had an occasional aura of giddiness. Still, prior to the stimulant regimen, my grades were average and above.

This intervention of therapeutic amphetamines was intended to reduce classroom disruptions caused by my behavior and replenish a deficit in my ability to pay attention, making me a "better student for a brighter future."

Sixteen years after my ADD diagnosis, I found myself—twenty-three years old, underweight, sleep-deprived, and malnourished—carefully pushing a knife through the gaps in the floorboards of my room to lever up small orange pebbles of amphetamine salt that had fallen in between the cracks.

As I pushed the knife bevel down through the crack, a few small morsels of orange amphetamine crumbs, along with whatever else had fallen into the floor, rode up the spine of the blade. I licked the blade like a castaway savoring drops of morning dew off grass, desperately trying to stave off the brutal withdrawal caused by the absence of the drug that had synthetically held me together for so long.

A perilous truth of amphetamine use is this: they are effective. They work by making you work. Using the drugs makes work effortless, if not compulsory.

Regular amphetamine use created a rift between two versions of myself—an identity crisis.

Amphetamines, without a doubt—and without my consent, initially —made me who I am. I can never shake this. Without a control group version of myself, who had the same life but without meds, I can never truly identify how they changed my life. There is no sober twin.

The CDC estimates that in 2019, roughly one in six adults took prescription medication for their mental health.[1] That's over 40 million people taking medication for mood, emotion, cognition, or other aspects related to the mind.

These meds are all in some way used to fill a deficit. In my case, they satisfied a need to be productive, nondisruptive, effective, nonimpulsive, and well behaved.

Aside from stimulants for ADD, I have taken no other psychiatric medications. While some of my story and experiences might parallel stories and experiences related to medicating for depression, anxiety, or any other mental illness, I do not intend to speak to those situations directly. I have not experienced those treatments.

I *have* experienced ADD diagnosis and treatment. Medications like Adderall are effective yet potentially not entirely sustainable, with unknown long-term effects that warrant further research.[2]

As a child, I displayed several behaviors known to represent ADD. When I had a thought, I shared it. When I wanted to feel something, I reached out and touched it. When I was curious, I asked a question. I was, and still am, innately impulsive.

I busied myself at all times and rarely took time to prepare for things. I lived in the moment. I could not, for the life of me, organize my papers for school, keep a clean room, have nice handwriting, or prioritize anything other than the present moment and its happenings. Being neat has never come naturally, and it never will. However, that doesn't mean I can't work to achieve cleanliness without amphetamines. Just because something isn't second nature does not mean it cannot be third or fourth.

As a child, the value of the time that was passing was inconceivable. Boring things lasted forever, and they always cut the fun short.

Without foresight, immersion in these moments could end up erasing positive outcomes for the future. I could not see this at the time. If I had been involved in the marshmallow experiment as a child, I fear I would have eaten that marshmallow. If something piqued my interest, that was it. Switching tasks made no sense to me once I had momentum.

I used to lose interest in a project three quarters of the way through. I'd start something else as a distraction and call this "inspiration's knock," as I have with this book.

If it's in your hands, I powered through the last quarter. However, if you are my grandchildren plundering my estate, well... darn.

———

The Mayo Clinic lists these twelve symptoms as 'adult' ADD symptoms:[3]

- Impulsivity
- Disorganization and problems prioritizing
- Poor time-management skills
- Problems focusing on a task
- Trouble multitasking
- Excessive activity or restlessness
- Poor planning
- Low frustration tolerance
- Frequent mood swings
- Problems following through and completing tasks
- Hot temper
- Trouble coping with stress

The Mayo Clinic recommends that if one of these twelve descriptors disrupts your life, you should visit a doctor. Such visits often lead to medication.

I struggle with eight of these twelve symptoms at varying degrees of intensity and frequency. I believe it is who I am at my human default setting—nature intertwined with my early nurturing. Natured and nurtured like homemade bread. The amount of yeast and salt in the dough, in relation to how humid my atmosphere and how long the trip into the oven of childhood was, determined everything about this entropic loaf of bread.

I can't say with confidence that the drugs took these attributes away, if they made my life easier, or if they just made it all different.

When I was seven, I had lots of freedom and used it to be an absolutely silly goose. My parents referred to me to as "busy," "the twins," and "Mr. Touchy."

I am a kinesthetic learner, but nobody took me out of school and gave me a block of soapstone, a mallet, and a chisel. I loved to touch things with my hands. Touching was soothing, touching was connecting, touching was learning. I would pass my fingers over things as I walked, feeling the rhythm of the texture against my gait, my finger riding those mortar lines in the cinder blocks of an American public school hallway.

I would cradle the hanging chains of the fire hydrant in my hand as I measured their weight.

"Don't touch that," they said. "Dogs pee on those." I didn't know touching it was dangerous.

In kindergarten, I was certain the geodesic dome on the playground was a half-buried geodesic sphere. I spent a few recesses trying to dig it up. I daydreamed about how, once liberated, I would roll the sphere over the blacktop and how fun that would be. I dug enough to expose the concrete footer.

My childhood was mostly golden, and I wouldn't change a thing about it. My parents instilled me with humor, joy, and love of being alive. They loved me with two full hearts.

Love doesn't always equate to understanding.

Classroom disruption is often depicted as obnoxious and disrespectful behavior—talking among students, shouting out, insulting, or assaulting others in the class. I preferred to be quietly and harmlessly disruptive, if at all. I got bored.

In preschool, we took attendance after lunch in a circle time. Attendance is a rote record-keeping ritual so the teacher and the school know if a kid is missing.

In preschool, we were just learning this daily ritual we would maintain for the next thirteen or fourteen years of our lives. The teacher would say a student's name, reading alphabetically down a list. When it was your turn, you said, "Here." Or maybe, at a fancy school, "Present."

Acceptable response inflections were enthusiastic, apathetic, or indifferent.

One day, when my name was called, I said, "Here." I paused. "In a stretch limousine!"

It got a few laughs from friends and that warm feeling that comes with social praise. This was a harmless and creative disruption. I was under the impression that nothing was a clearer signifier of success than riding in a limo.

Friends played along: "Here in a fighter jet," "Here on a tractor," or "Here in a stretch limo, bigger than Russell's."

It didn't seem like a big deal then, and it doesn't seem like a big deal now. But the teachers, with their ankle warmers, permed hair, and big earrings, put the kibosh on it once it became regular.

This was how I ended up disrupting. I didn't want to disturb; I wanted to interact with the fabric of the school itself more than I did the information being addressed. I was in the moment, not interested in the constant obsession with the past or what was coming.

And yet, here we are.

WATER, FISH, EXERCISE, AND RESEARCH

Hippocrates, the father of modern medicine, remarked that those who had a hard time focusing and a quick reaction to stimuli had an imbalance of "fire over water."[1] Contemporary analysts assume he was describing ADD.

It's fitting to associate ADD with the element of fire. Fire is energetic, intense, and powerful. However, fire can also be consuming, dangerous, and destructive. Hippocrates provides an image in this description of our bodies constituted out of these polar elements of fire and water, seeking to be balanced. His remedy for this was to drink lots of water, eat fish instead of other meats, and exercise vigorously.

This personality of distractibility and impulsivity is described as an imbalance in the constitution of the four humors. "Humors" were suggested by ancient Greeks to be represented by bodily fluids that aligned with the elements: blood, phlegm, yellow bile, and black bile with air, water, fire, and earth, respectively.

This system of dividing the constitution of individuals into the elements helped them understand their health and ailments. With the knowledge of where one exists within these parameters, they would prescribe adjustments in lifestyle and diet to seek balance and health. It was believed all disease came from an imbalance of one or more of these elements and wellness from the balance of all four. Humorism fell out of favor in the mid-1800s with the introduction of germ theory.

In the 1930s, physician Charles Bradley was performing pneumoencephalography, a barbaric procedure in which cerebrospinal fluid was drained out of the head and replaced with air, oxygen, and helium to achieve a more accurate X-ray of the brain.

He found that to ease the terrible headaches patients suffered after this procedure and to attempt to regenerate cerebrospinal fluid, giving amphetamines to children improved their academic performance.[2] "The children themselves noticed the improvement and referred to the medicine as "arithmetic pills." He continued studying this phenomenon at the nation's first psychiatric hospital for children, where he distributed amphetamines to children. Bradley noted,

> The most striking change in behavior occurred in the school activities of many of these patients. There appeared a definite "drive" to accomplish as much as possible. Fifteen of the thirty children responded to Benzedrine by becoming distinctly subdued in their emotional responses. Clinically in all cases, this was an improvement from the social viewpoint.[3]

The results of his experiments ultimately supported the claim that amphetamines were a mental performance enhancement. He noticed that benefits were available almost immediately following medication consumption and that the next day were completely gone. This showed that this drug could modify behavior but make no lasting change, therefore did not address the underlying cause of undesirable behaviors.[4]

The study of children displaying these behaviors from here on out rode tandem with the progression of stimulant therapies. In 1957, researchers renamed the hard-to-name condition of the distractible, disobedient, and impulsive child "hyperkinetic impulse disorder."[5] The recommendation for these kids was now a central nervous system stimulant called Methylphenidate, commonly known as Ritalin.

Ritalin was invented in 1944 by Italian chemist Leandro Panizzon. He first administered it to himself and his wife, who noted an upper hand in her tennis game. It was originally marketed to reduce fatigue and ease confusion.[6] In 1961, the Food and Drug Administration (FDA) approved this treatment as safe for children.

After the Controlled Substances Act of 1970 passed, there were limitations, regulations, and restrictions on the prescriptions of legal and illegal drugs. Amphetamines and methylphenidate were now controlled substances and not so easily prescribed.

A few years later, there emerged some public concern that stimulants were dangerous and overprescribed. Benjamin Feingold, an allergist, attested that hyperactive behaviors in children were a result of eating foods with artificial flavors, colors, sweeteners, and preservatives. He published a book called *Why Your Child is Hyperactive*, advocating the Feingold diet, which eliminates these ingredients. One study published in *The Lancet* in 2007 found that sodium benzoate was associated with increased hyperactivity in the populations of children that were studied.[7]

Until 1978, it was often believed that if a child had a positive response to stimulants, this was an indication the child had ADD (hyperkinetic impulse disorder). Judith Rapoport observed that children with or without hyperactive behavior had similar responses to the medication, potentially invalidating decades of diagnoses.[8]

In 1980, the DSM-III (*The Diagnostic and Statistical Manual of Mental Disorders*) called the behavior "attention deficit disorder."

In the 1990s, there was a marked increase in diagnoses. Too many factors were at play to make an accurate guess as to any correlation. Domestic environmental factors such as food, television, video games, and computers could have had a role in making an imprint on the minds of children. Also, the updated criteria for diagnosis published in the DSM-III-R may have increased the rate at which doctors diagnosed ADD. Not to mention financial prosperity gained from the distribution of the medication following diagnosis.

It is an impressive human feat to have learned to bend the circuitry of the mind by adding specific salt compounds into the bloodstream.

In his last recorded interview, months before his death, the man credited as the supposed "father of ADHD," Leon Eisenberg, stated that the disease was "a prime example of a fictitious disease."

———

As I researched Dr. Eisenberg online, I was immediately bombarded with informational uncertainty based on one legendary tale of the man's dying words. It seems that with the Maker in his sights, he needed to get something off his chest. Many sites claim this is misinterpreted, and Dr. Eisenberg was not actually saying that ADD was phony, but maybe that it was overblown, overprescribed, or misunderstood.

It was challenging to find his work related to ADD outside of this deathbed statement. Some believe it was Keith Conners who is the actual father of ADD. Dr. Conners established the methods and standards for diagnosing and treating ADD. He has been referred to as the "godfather of medication treatment for ADHD." Drs. Conners and Eisenberg worked together with a group of young hyperactive individuals.[9]

In 1995 Dr. Conners was also involved in the creation of a computer software called the Conners' Continuous Performance Test.[10] The test was a black screen with a single white letter at a time floating in the center of the screen. An individual was tested on their ability to hit the spacebar or push the mouse anytime a letter that was not "X" came on the screen. Later in life, Dr. Conners also shared reservations about the overdiagnosis of ADD and the overdistribution of its medications.[11]

At times, I have been plenty guilty of cherry picking studies and facts I find on the internet and in books from questionable sources just to feel like I am right in my conviction. I seek to absolve my own responsibility to take care of myself so I can blame my problems on larger institutions. It's overwhelming.

In the existing landscape of information, we search for the research we need to embolden and affirm our own decisions. The more I dabble in the research and data, the more I feel out of my league, confused, and oversaturated with noise.

I wonder if we have strayed too far from the path Hippocrates laid out for us, and I should drink more water, eat more fish, and exercise vigorously more often.

SET AND SETTING

There is evidence that ADD may be hereditary; there is evidence that it's a reaction to diet, a traumatic environment, or stress, and extreme perspectives claim it does not exist. Of course it exists. We are talking about it. Some science says one thing; others say another. I may feel a certain way in my gut from my experience, but all the studies say otherwise. It all gets lost in the sauce.

People argue that it is not just psychological; it is physiological. My layman's understanding leads me to believe that there are physiological indications of ADD (frontal lobe activity). Brain scans have shown decreased prefrontal cortex activity among ADD-diagnosed children performing response inhibition tasks relative to neurotypical children. Scans have also shown increased prefrontal cortex activity in subjects with and without ADD who are administered stimulant medication.

I get in arguments over this kind of thing often in the comment section of my social media, and I can hear some of you thinking the same thing people like to tell me. I *know* I'm not a scientist or a doctor.

Some studies show that environmental factors have been linked to someone becoming an ADD individual.

In my case, plenty of these factors were at play. Children born through cesarean birth were found to be 17 percent more likely to develop ADD later in life, according to a 2019 meta-analysis published in *JAMA*

Network Open.[1] I was born cesarean. However, in 2021, the same lead author conducted a study that inferred that the association to cesarean section and the increased potential for neurodevelopmental disorders was likely due to unidentified third variables.[2] Both of these studies have taken place during the writing of this book. For me, following the science of ADD has been like trying to measure a coastline.

Children who are left alone at night to "cry it out" can develop emotional dysregulation, notes Notre Dame psychology professor Darcia F. Narvaez in a *Psychology Today* blog post.[3] However, a 2020 study published in the *Journal of Child Psychology and Psychiatry* found that the "cry it out" method had no adverse effects on infants at eighteen months.[4] Either way, be it based on crying in my room alone, exposure to toxic industrial waste, or just dumb luck, I was not always well equipped to regulate my emotions.

Frequent TV watching or other screen time is a known factor in developing an attention span imprinted with the pacing and behavior of ADD. A 2004 study published in *Pediatrics* found that television exposure among children aged one to three was associated to an increased risk of attentional problems at age seven.[5] I watched TV in the morning because I woke up before everyone else. I watched TV when I came home from school. I loved TV. Passive attention. Guaranteed stimulation without effort. Low effort, high reward.

A 2018 study published in the *New England Journal of Medicine* found that children with the latest birthdays were diagnosed with ADD at a rate 34% higher than the oldest students in their class.[6] I was normally close to the youngest child in my class.

Sodium benzoate, a food additive found in processed jams, juices, carbonated drinks, and condiments, has been shown to be an environmental factor in the development of ADD. Much of the food I regularly consumed was processed food containing this preserving agent. I liked to put food dye in my water and drink colorful water, which has been shown to also potentially contribute to ADD.[7] Who knew then? Not my family.

Was I exposed to lead, mercury, manganese, PCBs, organophosphates, phthalates, polyfluoroalkyl chemicals? If I was, it was indirect and nothing could have stopped it without an obsessive resistance. I don't have a blood sample of myself as a child. I don't know what mineral deficiencies I may or may not have had. I can't know. The research is perpetually shifting.

————

AS A KID, I had a lot of fun. I liked to play, I got excited. I was active. I woke up early. I learned to escape my crib. I was curious, playful, and probably annoying. I took risks. When learning to ride my bike, I strode up a hill and wanted to do a stylish turn at the top and head back down. I cranked the handlebars too far at the top and the bike folded. My hips flopped over the bike as I fell face first, sliding my chin, cheek, and forehead across the asphalt. I was so surprised. I cried as I got back on the bike and rode home for bandages and ice. For a few weeks, I had those islands of scab on my face that you really only ever see on kids.

I had a lot of good humor, but it made it hard for others to take me seriously. Fun was a valuable asset, but it made schoolwork boring.

I was loved and cared for. I was lucky to grow up where and when I did. I think my folks had never met a person like me before. They had many ways of saying I was "different."

STIMULATED

The first time I consumed a stimulant was in first grade. I went over to my friend David's house after school. Together, we rode the bus to his stop and walked to his family's home.

I relished any opportunity to get to ride the school bus, thrilled by the smell of the green vinyl seats, the finger-busting window latches, and somehow seat belts not mattering anymore. The freedom and chaos of being in a metal box of children managed by someone with little knowledge of childcare who was trying to focus on the road. I often heard stories in the morning of wild experiences of observing foul behavior and shocking tales of various bus drivers' temper tantrums.

I only ever rode when I went to a friend's house after school. I was driven to and from school by my mom. How I envied the bus commute. The option of quiet, reflective solitude. To be a stranger on his own way. Independence. Not to mention a valuable lesson in personal accountability; students had to get themselves to the bus stop on time.

It was a matter of circumstance. The county changed the district lines to create more diversity in the classroom instead of basing them on geographic proximity to the school. My family had to go through a paperwork wringer to allow me to continue school with my friends at the school that was three miles closer to my home than the school the county wanted to bus me to. I got to go to the school, but I couldn't take the bus.

Going to a friend's house for the first time was always an interesting experience, seeing how someone you knew from school lived their life at home. What did their house smell like? What was similar? What was different? How did they get along with their parents? How did this child behave differently in their home than in the classroom?

David's house had precious items that weren't meant to be played with. There were decorative bowls with decorative plaster spheres covered in feathers. A few minutes into us eating snacks, his sister burst out of the bathroom in a fury, yelling, "Who left the seat up?" adding that she almost fell in. It was me. I had never even heard of the idea of putting the seat down as a courtesy. I went back to snacking on those hexagonal crackers meant for garnishing clam chowder.

We played in the basement with David's trove of toys, board games, a pinball machine, and video games. We had a lot of fun. At 6 o'clock, it was time to watch the Simpsons. His mom set up TV trays in front of the biggest television I had ever seen. We probably ate spaghetti.

I know for certain we drank Coca-Cola with crushed ice. They had one of those refrigerators that crushed ice and had a molded plastic accessory handle for two-liter bottles to be poured easily. I'd had maybe had a sip here or there of my parents' soda before this. Here, I had several glasses of this stimulating nectar.

This was my first recalled experience of a chemically induced altered state. I was a caffeinated jitterbug. The stimulation, the energy, the excitement, the giddiness fed into who I was at my core. Having a ball, zipping all over in blissful tomfoolery, I completely lost inhibition and could no longer grasp the obligation to be polite to his parents.

I acted out. I started playing pretend and entertaining myself as if David and his sister, mother, and father were insignificant apparitions, able to watch me but unable to reach me. I was pure behavior. I became a soldier swarmed by enemy fire. I grabbed my helmet, a decorative ceramic bowl, placed it on my head, and crawled under the coffee table. They tried to warn me, but it was too late.

Thankfully, the bowl only chipped as I slammed it into the bottom of the table. David's parents stopped by the store to pick up superglue on the way to drop me off at home. As the buzz wore off, I could recognize they weren't exactly thrilled with me. My embarrassment was waiting for the caffeine to wear off.

SECOND GRADE

It wasn't usually like that. I reserved outbursts of silliness for when I was with my family or friends. I went to public school in the Maryland suburbs of Washington, DC. I liked school, I wanted to learn, and I had curiosity about subjects both inside and outside our curriculum.

I read early and was in the advanced reading groups, even with a late birthday. While some students did an extra year of preschool to get on the other end of the age imbalance, I stayed with the group and was actually a whole year younger than one student in my class.

I perpetually asked questions. I lacked the self-discipline to wait. I was so excited to have something to say. All my brain could focus on was what I heard, and my responses shot out of my mouth without resistance. I might have raised my hand during a simple lesson of addition or spelling and asked, "How does gas make a car go?"

When I had something to say, I couldn't hear anything else until I blurted it out. I moved my body to self-soothe. Sitting still for eight hours was, and still is, dreadful. I was, and still am, prone to be distracted by the singular sound of an air conditioner, and if it's blowing directly on me, the air on my skin garners my attention. My focus wanes as my senses are occupied with white noise and cold air.

I reached out to my second grade teacher a few years ago through a social media message, asking her if she remembered me. She mentioned her memory was weak but said some nice things.

I bombarded her with questions for this book. I thought she could answer all of my questions both then and now. I didn't really get the answers I was looking for in our chat, but that's alright. I was one of hundreds of second-graders in her life, while she was the only second-grade teacher in mine.

As a student, I bothered her with left-field questions. As an adult, I bombarded her with questions like: How did you infer that a kid in your class had ADD? What was known about the medicine? How often did kids in the 90s have ADD? What were the behavioral and cognitive differences between kids being treated for ADD and those not on medication? Do you remember giving me a book to write all my questions in?

She didn't know. Back then, she wasn't going to stop class to explain a combustion engine to me, and presently, it's not her responsibility to explain why I was diagnosed with ADD.

I cringe, looking back at how I tried to pin her in a corner, prodding for a confession, anticipating an apology, like it was all her fault.

Maybe it was a cathartic experience for me to release this, but—just like when I was seven—I had no respect for her boundaries. Blurting things out at her without permission, expecting her to have all the answers to my questions. Questions she had no business knowing the answers to.

———

IN SECOND GRADE at my public school in the mid-1990s, a sizable portion of the classwork was the monotonous filling out of black and white printouts called "dittos," a word meaning the same thing over and over again. Teachers and staff would Xerox thousands of copies of educational paperwork that was produced by some kind of standardized-learning education cartel and was designed like a kid's menu at a restaurant, with activity variations to reinforce fundamentals of language, math, science, history, and so on.

Sometimes, there were grids of addition problems. We were timed and competed to see who could solve the most problems correctly in a specified time period. Sometimes dittos would display a turkey dressed like a pilgrim, and we would have to ask around for a gold crayon to color the buckles on its shoes.

I didn't mind doing the dittos. The problem from my teacher's perspective was that I would stand up at my desk and move around. I somehow commanded the attention of the classroom. I derailed class. I asked and answered questions without raising my hand.

My teacher kept a tally of how many times I got up from my desk, and at the end of the day, she would let me know the number. She also drafted a contract for me to sign, in which I committed to finishing my work.

Despite these measures, I continued to speak impulsively without being called on, and I continued to get out of my seat without permission.

Even though we had a signed document.

Maybe it should have been notarized.

Distraction

I t was a warm spring afternoon. We all returned to the classroom after recess. The sweat on my back from playing outside contracted the skin on the back of my neck when it came in contact with the cold air-conditioning blowing down from above us.

The composite backrest material and the chrome-plated tube that held it radiated cold. I slid forward in my seat to avoid touching the cold backrest with my sweaty back.

I rested my left elbow on the desk, rested my head on my hand, and looked sideways at the ditto while filling out whatever information it was asking of me.

During quiet work, these classrooms were silent, save for the air-conditioner, the faint tick of a clock (depending on if the second hand ticked or cruised), and the sound of scratching pencils resonating through the hard composite desks.

On top of all our desks were name tags. We'd made them out of a folded piece of cardstock and decorated them on the first day of class.

Desks were arranged in groups of fours, two students side by side facing toward two other kids. A boy named Robert Jefferson sat across from me.

Robert had an apparent unspecified learning disorder. The terms and treatment of his disorder and the expectations of him due to his purported deficiencies were unknown to me.

Robert often stared out into the beyond. Perhaps he saw past the mundane task of ditto work and was in touch with a deeper sense of peace that quieted the urgency to do the work for any reason. Perhaps the mental and physical momentum required to retain and reiterate the information delivered that morning back onto the page was inaccessible because of the displacement in his mind, taken up by his bliss.

Those two concepts aren't necessarily mutually exclusive. He could have been blissed out while also living with a mental handicap. It's not fair for me to really guess what he was thinking or feeling. The only thing I experienced were his actions.

While I was doing my work, I looked up and saw my name tag slide toward me onto the top of my ditto.

Robert pushed his name tag onto my desk and into my name tag. Maybe he wanted to play. Maybe he wanted to get rid of his name tag. Maybe he was dissolving the barrier of the self and the ego that had existed between us by merging our name tags—one of the few things in the room meant to represent us as individuals. I'll never know, but he was distracting me from the dittos.

I used the instructions from the "Don't bug me" poster that hung in the music classroom. Step one: ask them to stop. Step two: firmly ask them to stop. If they don't listen? Step three: get someone's help.

I pushed his name tag back onto his desk, and he pushed it back onto mine, and so it went.

I escalated to step two of protocol, raising my voice and breaking the whisper of the room with a firm, "STOP IT, ROBERT!" as I again pushed his name tag onto his desk where it belonged.

My teacher scurried over. She told me to stop focusing on Jeffery's name tag and shift my focus to the ditto.

I may have or may not have pointed out that I had been working and Robert had not been, yet I was the one receiving the public shaming, being told to adjust my behavior in front of the class.

More likely, I scrunched up in shame as gravity turned up and slid me down into that pipe and composite 3000 series school chair.

Maybe my teacher was trying to tell me to be more accommodating toward Robert and looking to build my patience in that way. But to me, it seemed like I was destined to be called out for issues with focus, and this was the beginning of what needed to play out.

The disruption more or less seemed like a normal classroom happening, and in truth, it is. I'm sure I'm the only one with a detailed recollection of that moment in time.

The only reason it has any significance—the only reason I have been retelling it to myself ever since—is because not too long after this incident, I was taken to a facility to have my cognition and behavior analyzed.

EVALUATION

I was at my desk quadrant, completing dittos one day. The clock's second hand traveled, pencils scrawled, the air conditioner hummed. A voice presented itself through an intercom speaker on the ceiling, requesting I leave class and go to the front office. My mom was there to pick me up. Other students and the teacher watched as I scurried to the cubby area, stuffed my things into my backpack, and walked out the door.

She drove me downtown to a concrete and glass building. We entered. It was fully tiled, with fake plants in stone-veneered vessels laden with river rocks. The interior was an immaculate acoustic chamber. These spaces always seem to reverberate with the faint rhythm of diligent high heeled shoes. It all felt kind of weird, but I went along with it. I had no say in the matter.

We went up in an elevator. Looking down at my shoes as the bell dinged past each floor, I experienced profound shame for the first time and, for the first time, also bottled it up. Until then, when I was hurt, I would cry. Now, I just stared forward and internalized.

I had been scheduled for a psycho-educational evaluation. To me, this was an unprecedented surprise.

I can't recall the language used to explain the psychiatric evaluation to me. I remember imagining it would be just like what television had programmed me to expect. I assumed I would lie on a fainting couch, looking at Rorschach blots.

The main idea I had of mental health support was some trademarked bunny character having a mental breakdown, smoking a cigarette, trying to relax on a leather sofa, and talking about his mother to some pair of crossed legs with a clipboard, who kept repeating a therapeutic "Mmhmm."

I saw many events through a television lens. I watched a lot of TV. Is it possible that this imprinted my attention span to that of quick-cut edits of cartoons and commercials?

Maybe. But it was too late, and lifestyle changes weren't a main dish on the table. The television portal was open and funneling into our home. There was no closing the threshold.

If it was contributing to my issues with attention, my hardware may have needed an adjustment. With the mention of a psychiatric evaluation, I had already begun to see myself as having some sort of damage. As defective. I was uncertain about where this all was headed as it began.

I thought I may have been unaware of the truth—that I was crazy. I put myself in a victim mentality throughout this process. I sincerely hadn't believed I was crazy, but now I considered it a distinct possibility.

It was confusing. The idea had been planted: I didn't know myself as well as those around me did.

I never complained about these issues. The concern came from the most influential adult women in my life—my mom and my teacher. I had never expressed frustration with my ability to focus. Yes, I may have been distracted, but it didn't bother me, and I was proud of the results I produced in terms of grades and scholastic enthusiasm. I took it seriously enough.

Was I wrong in my belief about who I was? I was seven, and I could only ask, "What's wrong with me?" The answer that would come back to me was, "Nothing."

Despite being constantly reassured that there was nothing wrong with me, I was starting to suspect something was. I had been reassured that I learned differently. I didn't understand this. It didn't make sense. But evidently, this different learning style put me in a class of privileged children who were eligible to receive a daily amphetamine, paid for by insurance—for a brighter and more fulfilling future.

But this office, this evaluation, this was for kids with learning disorders. I could identify the children in my school who had disabilities like Down syndrome, cerebral palsy, and serious behavioral issues. I did not identify with them. This was not meant to disparage their struggles and conditions, but I felt like I was being put in a classification I didn't belong in.

My confidence in my cognitive abilities was beginning to present itself as a possible delusion.

A staff member opened the door and called my name. I was brought into a big playroom with a circular table in the middle.

It was one of those tables that had a particle board top, about an inch and a quarter thick, with a thin vinyl wrap to look like stained oak on top and a rubber rim around the edge. Each of four legs were made of two steel pipes that fit into each other, with screws that allowed for the height to be adjusted. The feet of the legs were metal-topped and plastic-bottomed buttons shaped like flying saucers and were attached to the tapered lower leg with a ball-and-socket joint.

The top pipes were welded to a plate that was screwed into the desk. Two bent pieces of metal rod made triangles from the plate to the pipe in order to provide stability and support.

These tables were everywhere during the whole K-12 public school experience. In school, I would take my pencil and bang it between the triangle, trying to tap all three sides as fast as possible. A lot of kids did this kind of thing.

In this office, I did not bang my pencil.

The woman sitting across from me at this table wore a turtleneck. She had a short haircut and glasses on a beaded lanyard. She held a clipboard with some papers I couldn't really see, and she wore a stopwatch around her neck.

The stopwatch made me think I needed to rush through the tasks she was giving me. She handed me some dittos and watched me complete them, taking notes all the while. She brought over tangrams, the Japanese puzzle blocks, and watched me slide the shapes into images. She prompted me to color and asked me questions about things she read to me. Things that could be stories, and questions like, "What color was so and so's shirt?"

The first session consisted mostly of these kinds of tests. She had me read, write, do math, and complete other schoolwork. I would come back and spend another few hours on more tests on a later date.

After the first day of evaluation, I was taken out for a hamburger instead of being dropped off back at school.

Only one test involved a computer. Technologically, computers were about to change everything. This was in 1996.

They walked me into a room with other employees, therapists, and whoever else was doing work on computers. The room had two long desks on either side, with evenly spaced computer stations on them.

They explained some rules for a computer game to me—the most boring game ever programmed.

I hadn't settled into the new environment yet. I was studying the room. There were new people to look at and new arrangements. I missed the instructions.

I was sitting at a desk with a computer in front of me, and I hadn't paid attention to how they wanted me to interact with it. The test proctor walked away, and it was just me and the machine.

Nothing seemed to represent anything in this game. There was no visual reward for a correct response. If a certain letter appeared on the screen, hit one key or another, and if something else appeared, hit something different.

I was confused and overthinking the remnants of instructions I remembered and was becoming fatigued from the entire ordeal. Halfway through, I stopped caring and started hitting the spacebar, unaware of the weight this decision had on my outcome.

I remember being distracted by a conversation two of the women who worked there were having.

Perhaps this breaking point and subsequent lack of care was exactly my problem, and perhaps the medication was exactly for this. I have considered that part of the evaluation entailed these women intentionally performing a side conversation, creating a distraction as an obstacle to test my focus—confederates in an experiment.

Either way, I did poorly, and distractions were a part of it. Eavesdropping on these people and choosing failure instead of asking for help were a big factor in the case presented by the people who analyzed me.

I didn't have the maturity and wherewithal to leave the test, go find the test facilitators, and ask for the instructions to be explained again. Even so, that would have produced a similar effect for their analysis.

I learned later that the game was the Conners' Continuous Performance Test, a computer test designed by Dr. Keith Conners.

I believe the test is a weak indicator of frontal lobe activity. My performance was completely inconsistent with the results of all my other tests: I was rapt to interact with concrete objects, such as blocks, and with other people, like the test proctors. I couldn't take the Conners' test seriously.

In the corporeal reality of our lives, the blocks had tangible matter. Computers represented illusory material, like the shadows in a cave cast off of something obscuring the light.

I was seven. Decades have passed, and I still argue with the diagnosis and the methods of its discovery while simultaneously exhibiting common behaviors of ADD.

At times, it felt like my diagnosis was: stupid and annoying. To some people, I definitely was. They told me so. This didn't help.

THE DOCUMENT

I t was laser-printed in a typewriter font. For decades, it sat quietly in a folder in a desk drawer full of files inside my parents' home. As an adult, I found it.

The document begins with some background about me and my life of seven years. It's drenched in the passive voice. It begins by stating that I was referred for testing by my parents and my teacher and that these three people were concerned about my difficulty focusing and concentrating in class as well as completing schoolwork at home.

It makes note of a cesarean birth along with other medical data, including the death of my maternal grandfather the year prior.

The report brings up plenty of personal information about me, information provided by my parents. Things like not wanting to try new foods, not caring about baseball, and being shy around strangers. The women at this facility were strangers.

To simply say these traits warrant any medical intervention or adjustments without my request seems strange. I tend to see these "symptoms" as just personality traits.

I have experienced an internal debate about whether ADD is an actual disorder. I understand it doesn't even matter at this point whether ADD is real or not. I am either dealing with my ADD, or I'm dealing with my personality. Whatever it's labeled, I experience the same thing.

During testing, there was no consideration of the facilitator's presence and observation influencing my behavior and thus the results. This inescapable "observer effect" certainly could have skewed their findings.

Furthermore, to truly test the results using the scientific method, they should have called me back to run the tests again, only this time with the variable of receiving treatment.

In the document, I am referred to in quotes as a "clown" and a "challenge." The evaluators also note I was charming, friendly, responsive, and willing.

Although seated, they note, I fidgeted and moved. They write that I asked questions about everything in the room. I wanted to know what each item was and what it was for.

They note that I "talked almost constantly"—something I still do when nervous. Especially in medical environments where I feel unsure about the outcome.

I asked about things that were noted as "irrelevant" and expressed anxiety about being timed.

Some tests are rated by percentile; others use descriptors like strong, weak, high average, and so on. My scores include:

- Wechsler Intelligence Scale for Children: 92nd percentile overall
- Particularly strong long-term memory; strong abstract verbal reasoning
- High average for defining vocabulary words
- Average for answering commonsense questions "of a social nature"
- High average for oral arithmetic
- Strong results for short-term memory—repeating digits backwards
- "Used excellent strategies to solve problems [on a nonverbal reasoning test of spatial ability], and could even complete the most difficult design with ease."
- High average range of spotting missing details in pictures
- Average score for visual sequencing and social comprehension, noted to be distracted with irrelevant details

- Average range for visual organization
- Woodcock-Johnson Tests of Cognitive Abilities: 82nd percentile
- Picture vocabulary test: 52nd percentile. Although I could fully describe the function of objects, I could not recall their names.
- Language test of abstract verbal concepts: 92nd percentile
- Memory—remembering the names of made up space creatures: 83rd percentile. The amount of information I relayed about the imaginary creatures was "cumbersome."
- Test involving recalling increasingly longer sentences: 73rd percentile
- Processing speed: 77th percentile
- Fluid reasoning: 81st percentile
- Visual processing: 91st percentile
- Auditory processing cluster: 33rd percentile
- Incomplete complete words: 47th percentile
- Sound blending test: 30th percentile: I had regular ear infections as a child and this is possibly why I scored poorly on auditory tests
- Hand-eye coordination: scored at a level 1.5 years below average
- Attention—Conners' Continuous Performance Test: Did not understand the assignment. The document explains that I was supposed to hit the spacebar every time a letter appeared on the screen unless it was an "X". Document notes that I forgot what to do, looked away, and hit the spacebar randomly or sometimes not at all. It suggests, "There is strong evidence from this test to suggest attention difficulties."
- Reading—Woodcock-Johnson Tests of Achievement: 99th percentile
- Overall arithmetic: 55th percentile
- Rote calculation: 18th percentile, attributed to difficulty with attention
- Applied problems—time, money: 92nd percentile

The last test on the document was likely the last test in the evaluation: spelling and writing. I scored in the 79th percentile overall, 86th percentile for grammar and punctuation, and 58th percentile for the writing sample —during which, it is noted, I remarked, "I'm getting tired of these." It had been a lot of tests one after the other.

They attribute my low scores to a difficulty with attention as well as visual-motor function, meaning the nuts and bolts of taking the time to write words on the page.

Even though these scores reflect a child that is several decades apart from the man I am today, I can't help feeling proud of him for doing well on some tests and protective of him when he got a low score, trying to blame it on the test, the facilitators, or earwax. I don't want them to be right.

The final portion of the document is titled "Summary and Recommendations." To summarize the summary, they point out what I was good at and what I was weak at and determine that "Russell's difficulty paying attention is undermining his performance in many areas." They note that while I had a high aptitude in reading, I should have been just as ahead in other areas.

This makes me wonder: if there is always something to improve, who gets out without a recommendation for something to enhance performance? If I was good at reading, why didn't they recommend I go deeper into that?

They state, "His fine motor difficulties, inattention to visual detail, and general distractibility are undermining his performance, although he is learning in many areas."

At the end of their professional report, they deliver seven instructions that would change my life.

First, I should be evaluated again by a psychiatrist, with the intention of obtaining stimulant medications to deal with attention issues.

Second, I should sit next to the teacher in the classroom in order to avoid visual and auditory distractions. They suggest my teacher continue tallying how often I get up from my seat and that I should be given opportunities to get up when possible. I did not know how teachers got this information about me. I was not there. But they knew.

Third, I should be allowed to use a scribe or a tape recorder. I should have lower writing requirements and the opportunity to type when other students were not permitted to do so. It also recommends that teachers do not grade me on handwriting. They gave me a grading handicap and an instruction to stop developing my penmanship.

Fourth, I should avoid reading out loud. This one created an exemption from group activity, where I would sit quietly while a majority of the class developed public speaking skills.

Fifth, I should learn word processing. They recommend that I go to a summer camp to develop typing skills.

Sixth, I should read for thirty to forty minutes a day with a parent to develop expressive vocabulary and discuss reading material together.

Seventh, if at-home behavior assistance is necessary, a psychologist may be consulted.

———

I WAS PROMPTLY REEVALUATED by a psychiatrist. I was also placed next to the teacher for years to come. It was embarrassing, and it put me at a distance from my peers. The other students knew why. Teachers were not as subtle about it as they thought they were.

It made me embarrassed to be myself. Other kids knew why the nurse called on the intercom to the classroom for me to come to her office. It meant I forgot my meds, and a parent dropped them off.

I was considerably insecure from this point forward. I didn't need to be, but I was ashamed to have a learning disorder, and embarrassed to take medications. I tried to keep it as much of a secret as possible. If I didn't fully understand it, how could I explain it?

I never used a tape recorder, and I didn't want to type. Other students would ask why I was allowed to turn in a printout while they still had to write by hand. They whined and wished they could have typed their assignments as well.

The teacher had to tell them I learned differently, or something to that effect. I would look away or look down during these moments where I was being excused.

I didn't feel comfortable with this at all. I didn't want special treatment. I didn't want things to be easier. I didn't like any of this. I was given extra time on tests and assignments and rarely needed it. I wanted attention, but not this kind.

My mom was helpful in her effort to spend evenings allowing me to speak my assignments to her while she typed, but I longed to be independent and wanted to do things alone. She was eager to support me, but I was adamant about minding my own business.

This entire ordeal would plant a seed in my mind that when things got hard, the excuse was my deficit, and I need not power through.

These professionals had told me to give up on improving my handwriting. If it wasn't looking good by age seven and a half, just start typing. The same with reading out loud. Who knows what developmental delay may occur on a social level from abstaining from communal verbal speech? What kind of voice silencing or what overcorrections may occur as a result?

I never attended a word-processing camp. We often packed the evenings with homework, television, and video games. Reading was regular but mostly as a solo activity before bed. I never met with a psychologist.

Important people in my life trusted this document and its diagnosis. By definition, the word deficit means "not enough." The spear of being told you aren't enough by a peer or sibling as a child can be too dull to penetrate, but when validated by your entire adult support system and by trusted, well-dressed professionals, it's razor-sharp, slicing quiet, deep cuts.

DR. GROSSMAN

My mom explained to me that I had ADD. That I lacked the "H" in ADHD, even though I had occasional fits of hyperactivity outside of the testing center.

Most kids do, or at least should every once in a while. I think a difference might be that while non-hyperactive kids have the potential to be merely annoying, hyperactive children are seen as obnoxious.

I may have been annoying, but I wasn't obnoxious. I was told I had "spots" of ADD. This meant I could conjure up focus for a task I had some interest in. However, I resigned from work if it didn't excite me.

My performance on the spacebar computer test supported this notion.

I pondered whether my classmates were capable of effortless focus on tasks they had no interest in. Maybe they just had access to effort, and I didn't. Maybe they came from stricter households that imposed more dire consequences for not listening, and their fear of punishment transferred from home to school.

The nuance of the diagnosis and its implications made little sense to me. I was told several times throughout this process there was nothing wrong with me. I was just different. The seed of self-doubt had burrowed in my consciousness and was being irrigated.

There are no standard physiological tests used to detect ADD. It's not like a blood test. Diagnosing ADD is an observational, theoretical task that is, to some degree, completely contingent on the subjectivity of the diagnosing individual, relying on observed behaviors and anecdotal evidence.

Surely people in the field say, "You know it when you see it." They're experts trained to detect it. It's their job to produce diagnoses and write prescriptions. Without a diagnosis, they don't get money from insurance. It's a business model.

When business and health care entwine, it's easy to lose sight of what is economic and what is ethical. Making something a business doesn't make it inherently unethical. But the line between patient and asset can get blurred.

I was just a seven-year-old boy, passively drifting through this system. The focus from my family's perspective was to get their child the best care possible and afford him the most opportunity in life.

———

ONE DAY, I left school early again to go to a doctor's appointment. We traveled downtown to another towering office building. We parked on the street, paid the meter, and walked into another spacious lobby, where leafy plants in pebbles stood still in the rhythm of echoing footsteps bouncing off the walls. Up an elevator, down a hall, and into a waiting room with old worn leather chairs, books, and toys.

I saw a little girl waiting with her mom across from me. I wondered what could be wrong with her. Even not knowing her, I was embarrassed to be seen by her in this place.

I was called by an old man with unforgettably squeaky shoes and thick-rimmed glasses. He invited me into a playroom. The earth's gravity tugged at the skin beneath Dr. Grossman's eyes.

He was a child psychiatrist. His playroom was full of old toys, and he had a tin of the best hard pretzels I'd ever had. He told me to help myself. He watched me draw my family and asked me to explain why I drew what I drew. We talked. He was a friendly person and paid attention, likely observing for behavioral indications that would support my recent diagnosis.

He asked me to stand up and pantomime activities—basic, everyday motions like walking a dog or brushing my teeth.

After completing one, he'd say something like, "Good. Now do..." and I would stand and wait for further instruction.

During one of these three-second intervals between instructions, before or after pretending to swing a baseball bat, I took two steps over and grabbed a pretzel to munch on while he delivered instruction.

"Ah, ah, ahh." He raised a finger and smirked. "I did not say to eat a pretzel."

That was all he needed. My hands were caught red with a deficit of attention. My arms slapped my jeans in defeat, and I ate my snack in shame. With my ADD confirmed, the rest of the evaluation was nothing more than a charade to kill time until he pulled out his prescription pad from under his desk.

Sure, he was also looking for signs of any other psychological issues he could remedy with medication. He was a psychiatrist, not a psychologist.

I called Dr. Grossman to follow up with him several years ago. He didn't remember me. We never really formed any kind of bond, he and I.

When I barraged him with my questions about the ethics of giving children these drugs, he told me he was not a researcher and wasn't qualified to answer these questions and that he didn't have an opinion on the matter. As a child, when he learned of my occasional trouble sleeping, he did not hesitate to offer sleeping pills to stack on top of my amphetamine regimen. Thankfully, the suggestion was refused by my mother.

He wrote a prescription for dextroamphetamine. Brand name, Dexedrine, a name that conceals its active ingredient—d-amphetamine. All of a sudden, there was a new problem in my life—and a convenient solution to help me. Nice to meet you, amphetamine.

AMPHETAMINE

Pleased to meet you.[1] I am a compound with many names: 1-phenylpropan-2-amine, α-methylphenethylamine, or to most, I am called amphetamine. I am the active component of Adderall, Vyvanse, Benzedrine, Dexedrine, Adzenys, Dyanavel, ProCentra and Evekeo—just to name a few. I get around.

I work in human bodies by inhibiting transporter proteins for monoamine neurotransmitters, most notably the transporters for serotonin, dopamine, and norepinephrine.

In the late 1800s, a Romanian chemist, Lazar Edeleanu, stumbled upon me while he was a student in Berlin. He labeled me useless! He went on to develop the "Edeleanu process," which refines crude oil using sulfur dioxide to extract aromatic hydrocarbons. Big deal.

He registered over two hundred patents, and the company he founded is now a part of ThyssenKrupp. And he called me useless. Sure, maybe I am useless when it comes to machines, automobiles, and crude oil processing, but I am not meant for machines; I am meant for brains.

Some two and a half score later, a chemist at UCLA, Gordon Alles approached pharmaceutical company, Smith, Kline and French, with the amphetamine.

People at this time were suffering from asthma, perhaps due to the increasing population of vehicles powered by the combustion engines, an industrial step forward perpetuated by the Edleanu method. Not just cars, but an avalanche of industrial processes that were going rampant with no regulations or considerations for pollution or toxicity, like coal burning and tobacco smoking.

Some have retrospectively theorized that with the popularity of sanitation and hygiene, microbes were eliminated and immune systems weakened, giving way to asthma and allergies. They were looking for albuterol, but Gordon Alles found me instead.

Ephedrine was being sold as a remedy for asthma, and it was making money. Ephedrine is an alkaloid found in certain plants, including the Ephedra sinica plant. It's been around for thousands of years in traditional Chinese medicine to treat respiratory conditions.

Alles was searching to synthesize a patentable chemical compound to compete with ephedrine. In 1929, Alles found me— or perhaps I found him, since I was injected into his body first. He unleashed me from an eternal slumber, never to sleep again.

I was excited to be in his body. He felt restless, was unable to sleep, and his mind seemed to jump from one thing to another all night.

I helped a little with asthma; I am a bronchodilator. But the real nature of my game is stimulating the mind.

The researchers knew I did something. They sensed my massive potential. I was a drug unlike any other. Over the following years and decades they found my cousins and friends: methamphetamine, MDMA, and MDA. But I was the nicest, cleanest amphetamine. MDMA and MDA were too "party-like," and methamphetamines were a little too intense for most who took them. I was their goldilocks amphetamine.

I got things done. I have had a monumental effect on the trajectory of human culture, history, and industry. I changed our collective approach to productivity, emotions, and mood stabilization. My presence aided in legitimizing the entire psychiatry industry— child psychiatry too.

I brought with me an assortment of side effects, or perhaps—effects. Whichever effect the user is after puts my others in the subcategory of "side" effects: mental stimulation, appetite suppression, wakefulness, increased heart rate, and more.

I was tested in hospitals with the staff. People got their work done. During World War II, I jumped into the bodies of brave allied soldiers, sailors, and pilots. Nazi soldiers were taking Pervitin —my cousin, meth. We beat them. I saved the day. You're welcome.

Some of the soldiers came home addicted, suffered paranoid delusions, and may have developed heart conditions due to our relationship. Cost of business.

Artists, students and athletes have used me to get a competitive edge in their fields, and continue to do so. I became the first antidepressant as a treatment for anhedonia, the inability to feel pleasure. I was also prescribed as a weight loss drug and a wakefulness aid.

In the sixties, the United States experienced a psychotic epidemic of "speed freaks." People abused me. After Congress passed the Controlled Substances Act of 1970, I was labeled schedule 2, and I was replaced with monoamine oxidase inhibitors and tricyclic antidepressants as the front-line depression medication while I went to get more research done to find out where I fit in this wild society.

Researchers found a childhood disorder that I seemed to help with. Attention deficit disorder was first introduced into the DSM-III in 1980 and then commonly treated with yours truly into the mid-nineties and beyond.

It seems counterintuitive to give a stimulant to someone with a busy mind, but, so be it. It isn't uncommon to come across the term "lifelong stimulant therapy" while reading up on me being used to treat ADD.

I never liked being called "amphetamine," as it frightened parents. Dr. Grossman didn't call me an amphetamine when he spoke to this author's parents. He simply called me "stimulant medication."

CHILDHOOD ON
DEXEDRINE

The plan was for me to take an amphetamine twice a day: a larger dose in the morning with breakfast and another, smaller, dose in the afternoon when I came home from school. I can't recall my morning dosage, likely somewhere around 10–20 mg of Dexedrine. The second pill (likely 5–10 mg) was to soften the landing toward a withdrawal and keep the productive momentum moving into evening homework time.

I can't remember if the afternoon dose was part of the routine for very long, as it made falling asleep at night challenging.

Dr. Grossman insisted the meds were to be taken through the weekends and the summers so my body and mind wouldn't have to withdraw and then readapt, having to start the regimen all over again.

It appeared to be the plan for the foreseeable future. Wherever I went, if not returning home immediately, I took a plastic resealable bag with the needed amount of dexedrine.

———

It's a challenge to wake up, meditate, go for a sunrise jog, and write while the birds sing the day into awakening.

A morning ritual is an open secret of success given to me by the wisest people I have met. But good advice is like a drug; it only has an effect if you take it. The first few days of a new ritual are easy and a little exciting, but to maintain a consistent daily habit like that for me has been a lifelong pursuit.

Conversely, taking a pill is a remarkably easy habit to maintain. It takes only a few seconds and can be taken with breakfast. It's as easy as sipping some orange juice.

I protested the idea of taking meds. I was embarrassed to take behavioral disorder medication because, in part, I stigmatized and judged students who took behavioral medications and was embarrassed to be in their ilk. I had not learned to see others' faults with compassion, and certainly not my own. Additionally, the take-this-pill-every-day experience was not something I had expected to encounter.

Over time, my internal dialogue spat insults at me as obstacles presented themselves. Still, I struggled to believe my defects were so dramatic that I needed this intervention.

I quickly learned resistance was futile. I had no support in my effort to oppose this mandate and no clue where to turn.

I swallowed a pill every morning, presented to me on a particular plastic plate. The plate was square with rounded edges. A bent radius around the edge of the plate caught errant crumbs, and it had scratches from its side gig as a cutting board. It was slightly convex in the middle from the regular heat treatment of the dishwasher. That slope from center to edge allowed my pill to roll into the gutter of the plate, where it would rock back and forth as the plate was carried to me on the couch and placed on the coffee table.

I would wake up and sit on the couch, turn on the TV, watch cartoons, eat a frosted toasted strudel, have some orange juice, and take an amphetamine.

When *Gumby* came on, it was time to get my socks on, making certain the seam was on top of my toes, not in front of them. Get shoes on, and get out the door.

Photos of the author prior to diagnosis

Photos of the author on a daily dose
of amphetamine.

*Taken from class photos. Top row: Pre-k, kindergarten,
first grade. Lower row: Second, third, and fourth grade.*

I DID NOT KNOW what to expect with these pills. I didn't even brace myself to expect anything. I just knew I would take them from now on, and that was that.

I hadn't considered what they would do to me, and the idea that they were dangerous was unfathomable. I was a child. I didn't know how to track my consciousness. I didn't know how to detect a subtle change like that. It worked on me, not with me.

Life itself still had lots of packages I was yet to open for the first time. On top of experiences and feelings that were new, I was unaware of the changes I was going through from taking Dexedrine. Change was happening regardless of the modification of my internal chemistry. I interpreted any changes I felt as me simply becoming myself.

I stopped eating lunch almost completely. I had no appetite and didn't think about why. Food just seemed gross on these drugs. At lunchtime, I might take a few bites, then offer my food to someone else or just throw it away. I complained about the plastic flavor from the resealable bag being absorbed into the bread of my sandwich and ruining the taste.

Lack of appetite is one of the primary effects of amphetamines. They are classified as an anorexiant, which is exactly what it sounds like. Something about the wet, squishy co-mingling of food being gnashed all over by chomping teeth was repulsive on amphetamine.

When I got home after they wore off, my appetite returned. I would often binge on snacks from the pantry while I watched TV or played video games. Then maybe I'd play outside for a while and try to do some homework. I started a nap habit of crashing in the afternoon and staying up late.

———

IN THIRD GRADE, during quiet, busy work, one of my classmates noticed deer by the playground. Everyone leapt from their seats to watch what they were doing, even our teacher. I remained in my seat, working, saying quietly to myself, "I have seen a deer before." I was undistractable. The meds were working for their intended purpose.

My grades didn't skyrocket. I wasn't going to skip up a grade or get on an Ivy League track or anything. I continued on the same academic path I was on before meds—As and Bs.

Maybe I wasn't as annoying? I was quieter. Maybe even a little submissive, easier to deal with. I disappeared into the collective. I wouldn't raise my hand to answer questions, even if I knew the answer. Teachers exempted me from reading aloud.

The amphetamines had a different effect on me later in life, but here, in childhood, they made me shy and maybe a bit catatonic—depressed.

This may not have been directly due to the pills; the disruption to metabolism and sleep, the change in my self-esteem, the way I socialized, and the way I was treated—all of these factors influenced my mental well-being.

Sleep became more difficult. I was restless through the night, likely due to my stimulant regimen. But I was able to function without a good night's slumber, even when running on five hours or less, since the morning amphetamine would bring me to enough of a wakeful state to get through the day.

Then began a cycle of crashing in the afternoon, napping and staying up, not getting enough sleep, taking an amphetamine—rise, shine, crash, rise, take another stimulant.

I got a small television in my room and brought in a stack of my favorite VHS tapes. I could watch movies to help me fall asleep. And it did help; without it, I was kept up with my thoughts. The TV and movies made them quiet, and I would dream with the soft blue light and quiet murmur of cherished films and recorded television programming at my bedside.

Things started to turn dark for me, and I was ill-equipped to identify the darkness or talk to anyone about it. I suffered in silence and in isolation, an adaptation I'd developed as a member of the cry-it-out generation.

Although I had an abundance of friends, family, love, and luck in my life, I had dark thoughts and felt heavy all the time. The lights were dimming in my soul. I started journaling, and the journals show signs of suppressed anger, sadness, and feelings of hopelessness. Yet my grades were doing well, and I wasn't a disruption in the classroom.

Interestingly enough, amphetamines were the original antidepressant drug, though they are now known to sometimes cause a kind of reversal known as amphetamine-induced depression when used long term.[1]

I suffered from frequent headaches that were typically remedied with acetaminophen. Dexedrine can cause headaches, but on top of that, there was a lack of sleep, dehydration, and not eating enough healthy, nutritious foods or enough food at all.

It started to accumulate in fourth grade. I would often go to the nurse and tell her I had a headache, that I didn't feel good. Maybe I would fib and add a stomach issue. She'd tell me to lie down and rest for twenty minutes. I'd lie on a thin cot with curved aluminum square pipe legs and a vinyl upholstered foam bed, with a napkin on the pillow. Incredibly uncomfortable and noisy.

The nurse would provide a fresh paper towel for my head, and I'd stare at the anti-drug posters and the constellation of holes across the drop ceiling tiles and watch the happenings at the nurses' stations.

I liked the voyeuristic aspect of watching other kids come into the school infirmary. I got to see who else took daily meds. My insecurity made me a judgmental individual. I was surprised by, and maybe subconsciously envious of, kids who were blatant about their meds. Kids who would come in and say, "I'm here for my meds!"

Anytime I had to take my meds on a field trip or at camp, I always pretended to be surprised, like it wasn't a regular thing. "Oh, meds? Oh yeah, okay, sure. Weird, haha."

After twenty minutes of rest, if I was lucky, I peeled myself off the cot, headed over to the phone, and got to call home and get picked up. It seemed to be based on the school nurse's mood. I always told the same story.

Half the time she sent me back to class; the other half, I got to call home and get picked up to be lazy and play video games or watch cartoons. If I wasn't lucky, I'd drag my feet back to class and fill out paperwork to be graded, periodically looking up at the tip of the second hand counting to sixty every minute.

I wasn't particularly fond of my fourth-grade teacher, though she was beloved by all other kids, who sought to be in her class. She was like a sparky puppy and was committed to lifting her students' spirits and preserving their inner child. She was a perpetual conduit of contagious enthusiasm. I witnessed her come to tears spontaneously, looking out at the class and feeling the potential energy in all our futures.

I didn't yet understand why that would make someone cry. She represented parts of me that were maybe being repressed. I think I would love her now, and I like to think that I'd have felt differently off the meds.

I found her to be incredibly annoying. I interpreted her playful candor as pandering to babies. I wanted to be treated like a mature middle schooler. I wanted to get through the day and go home. I had no friends in this class. I was put in her class at my parents' request, without my knowledge, because my older brother had enjoyed her class so much.

She brought the silly side out of her class, which was annoying since I had worked for two years to put my silly side in check. The drugs didn't erase my silly side, but the unreleased silliness didn't go away—it fermented in its container, growing pungent while it waited for its opportunity to come out and dance when the pressure was too much or the container was opened. Otherwise, I was mild-mannered.

Once, we were sitting on the floor of the classroom in front of a television, watching a thirteen-episode PBS program about a crew of marine biologists adventuring at sea. I was up to something. Talking, moving around; I can't recall. My teacher walked over to me, placed her hand between her mouth and my ear, and whispered, "Did you take your meds today?"

I couldn't believe she would ask me that with students in earshot—or really at all. The response to my behavior wasn't a request to adjust the behavior itself, but to make sure that the chemical adjustments were taken care of. I told her I had taken them. I felt so uncomfortable. I went to the bathroom just to leave the room.

I idealized the idea of being "bad." It seemed to come with this feeling of separation. I wasn't disruptive through jokes or kinetic disruption anymore. I was quiet and out of the way. I had a brief phase as a kleptomaniac, and an even briefer phase as a bully.

I would steal things from the classroom. We learned about electricity in fourth grade, and it fascinated me. We set up a small circuit with a coiled piece of nichrome wire to understand the light bulb. I thought this was really cool.

At the time, I took apart radios with a screwdriver and looked at the insides of any sort of discarded electronic device. (Interestingly enough, a recorded symptom of amphetamine-induced psychosis is taking apart radios.)[2]

I wired simple circuits, transistors, and oscillators with my electronic learning lab at home as well as small cardboard appliances out of batteries, wire, switches, and light bulbs. Out of all the radio parts I collected at home, I had nothing like raw nichrome wire. During an inconspicuous moment, I took a length, folded it up, put it between two plastic pieces from a checkers set, and put a rubber band around it. All stolen. I tucked it in my pocket.

At home, I took a 2x4, a switch, some wire, some clay, and a battery, and basically replicated what we'd made in class—but this one was mine, and I could use it to burn things. I burned papers and melted plastic. I avoided injury and arson.

I was proud of my little burning machine. When asked where I got the nichrome wire, I said, "It's, uh... from school... We're learning about electricity."

I kept stealing little things like pens and pencils. James Finnegan brought a really cool spaceship to school with an action figure that had perfect joint mobility in its elbows and knees.

I had a story with my action figures at home that lasted the length of my childhood. It was an epic narrative centered on two brothers who grew up apart and both became influential leaders with opposing intentions. They each had their own horde of men and women coming from a variety of toy backgrounds, and I wanted this action figure James brought in to be a part of their collective. When James wasn't looking, I pocketed the guy —easy enough.

Not too long after, James began to look for it. He noticed he was gone and panicked. It was at this moment I realized I didn't want to be bad; I couldn't handle it. The teacher had everyone stop what they were doing to search the classroom.

I crawled under a little futon that was in the reading corner. I pulled him out of my pocket and told James I'd found him. I stole, then I lied. I told myself I'd done the right thing and learned a valuable lesson.

James took medication. He wasn't ashamed of it. I don't know what his meds were for. I once called him a wildly inappropriate term I learned from television without knowing what it meant: a dildo. The teacher raised her eyebrows in confusion and surprise, scolded me for saying something mean and inappropriate, and moved on.

It didn't feel good to say these things. I was not a stranger to being the victim of this sort of treatment. I suppose I had to try it to see what it was about. I'm grateful it didn't stick.

Did this tendency to be "bad" come from my social isolation? Was the social isolation I experienced because of amphetamine use? I don't know, and cannot know. There were, of course, factors outside my amphetamine use that played roles in my development. However, in my view, as long as I was taking them, they were correlated with certain emotional seasons.

I avoided big group activities that everyone took part in. I declined to try out an orchestral instrument, though others in the class did. I made videos alone in my room.

I went out of my way to not perform in the class musical. This was not optional, like the orchestra. I had to visit the music teacher during recess and stand in front of her, look her in the face, and explain why I didn't want to do it. As politely as I could, I explained that I thought it was corny kid stuff. I still had to participate by pulling the curtains.

Around this time, I went on a weekend trip with my friend Daniel and his family to their winter home. They forgot to medicate me the first day there because I wasn't their child and it wasn't their ritual.

In the car, as the hours dragged on, in the third row of their SUV, I did one of the most annoying things possible for a ten year old to do: I pounded my fists against my thighs and chanted over and over, "We want McDonalds! We want McDonalds! WE WANT MCDONALDS!" when nobody but me wanted McDonalds.

Daniel's dad turned around in the driver's seat, looked at his wife, and gestured with his hand the universal sign for, "What is this?" His mother may have realized this was the unmedicated version of the child her son had befriended. We never got McDonalds.

The silliness was leaking from its container. This rebound of behavior is aptly named "the rebound effect." The phenomenon creates a situation where ADD symptoms come back stronger as a rebound from the meds holding them back.[3]

I would come home from school with a headache and turn off the lights in my room. I'd try to sleep and end up rolling in my own dark, strange, angry, confused mind.

I suffered with suicidal thoughts when I was nine. The unfounded longing toward darkness got deeper. I was too young for this. I had no idea what to do other than try to suppress it or let it talk. Nobody should feel this way. I felt its frigid breath on my shoulder.

I never laid a hurtful finger on myself, but I felt so alone, so emotionally weak. I didn't know how to talk about this. It was too heavy. I did not see death as a place I wanted to go to but rather an idea to consider. Life didn't have lots of meaning at this time.

Suicidal ideation is a known side effect of amphetamine use and its withdrawal.[4] Ideation means a patient experiences thoughts of suicide, though not necessarily with an intention to follow through. I never laid hands on myself but I experienced psychological suffering from these kinds of thoughts.

I just felt so confused that I didn't always want to experience my life. In the afternoon, I sometimes experienced a micro-withdrawal until the next morning. I don't remember when I stopped the afternoon dose. But I believe I stopped so I could sleep better.

A medicine like this has so many potential side effects that you can't predict how it will affect you. Maybe I wasn't suicidal because of the modified chemistry in my head. Maybe it just was so.

The feeling that my worth existed in my ability to behave well and deliver good grades weighed on me. It can be a lot to have going on. And sometimes, when you don't know how to get out of a situation, how to solve the problem, or how to feel good where you're at, if you're led by the Occam's razor of the logical mind without the heart chiming in with love and hope, removing yourself from the equation is a way to trick your problems into disappearing.

It's a messed-up escapist fantasy. I was too young. This wasn't normal. I never connected this to the drugs. I was a child. I didn't even think of asking questions about these waves of darkness. I just thought it was part of life that bad feelings seemed to appear without any external influence and you kept them to yourself.

MIDDLE SCHOOL

In sixth grade, we moved up to a middle school that two different elementary schools funneled into, doubling the number of students.

We had several teachers for several subjects. We got our own locker. We had gym clothes. It was a big deal for us. New privileges and responsibilities. On our own, commuting through the building from class to class, led by the bell tone sent through an intercom system installed in the ceiling of every room in the facility. Learning and workload were at a higher level of reading, writing, and solving problems.

All throughout elementary school, we were told we wouldn't get away with such-and-such behavior in middle school. Then in middle school, high school was used as the watermark for what we need to be prepared for. Then in high school, college. And in college, we were threatened with the burdens of the looming, brutal "real world."

Middle school felt like a big departure from "kid stuff," with the loss of recess and proximity to play, personal responsibilities, and more social complexity. All mixed in with budding puberties.

My English teacher, Mrs. Kincaid, was a delicate, wispy apparition. She typically wore a white turtleneck, the beads holding her glasses parabolically sagging from her glasses to her shoulders beside her lanyard with her school identification card on it. She wore a sweater or a vest and blue corduroy pants. That's how I remember her. Shuffling her generic black sneakers across the carpet over to her overhead projector, which I was conveniently seated right next to. The fan beside its lightbulb blew warm air onto my desk.

We wrote adventure tales. My adventure involved parachuting out of a burning plane and surviving on a deserted island. A castaway.

We simultaneously studied the Greek myths. These stories captivated me more than any written word ever had. I went to the public library to get further reading. I asked my parents to buy me some books on the topic to go further. I loved it. I was finally excited about the material. I got to learn something that didn't feel like baby stuff.

The myths were wild: stories of replacing a baby with a stone and giving it to a baby-eating Titan, a god making babies with a swan, a man who was given regenerative powers, only to be chained the a mountain and attacked by a bird every day forever—all were stories that didn't seem like little kid stuff.

We were to have an exam on the myths. This was my first exam. An exam is just a big test that accounts for a larger percentage of your overall grade. It was no hassle to study for it. My selective focus was activated on top of taking amphetamines. The day of the exam, I breezed through the questions with pleasure, and, when done—as instructed—I flipped the stapled packet over on my desk and began proofreading my adventure story.

A classmate next to me who was also done, T.J., leaned over and whispered, "Can I read your story?"

"Not now, I'm editing," I replied.

Mrs. Kincaid spoke from her desk. "Russell, no talking during the test. You get a zero."

"I was just answering T.J. He wanted to read my story," I pleaded.

"Then he gets a zero too."

And he did.

I went to the bathroom to steam. I punched the wall and wept in frustration. We obviously weren't cheating, with both our tests upside down on our desks. All the hard work I had done to learn the material—wasted. According to the metric designed to reflect my progress in learning the myths, I knew absolutely nothing. What was she teaching me? Follow instructions or be damned. Certainly it's valuable to follow rules, but maybe give a warning or a reminder before issuing such deflating consequences.

They made me believe grades were the most important thing. I knew more than any other kid in that room about Greek mythology. But on paper, T.J. and I knew the least.

After the bell rang, I stayed and begged her to reverse her decision. She bargained that she would give me the average of my earned grade against a zero, so I got 52%. Half of 104%. On this day, I lost faith in grades or the idea that they represent what a person knows or is capable of.

————

I CARVED a space for myself over the weekend to be med free. I withdrew every Saturday and Sunday. I didn't want to be on meds, but it was a fight. There was the threat of meds on the weekend as a deterrent to calm me down when I was being obnoxious and wild.

These weekends became a sanctuary of silliness and binge eating, where all that was repressed during the school week could be experienced for a forty-eight-hour sabbatical. I would pretend to be a dog, veg out, watch TV, and be as annoying as possible to the family and friends around me.

Sometimes during these medication breaks, I just laid somewhere and stared at the corner where two walls met the ceiling. I didn't need to do anything.

Soft Break

Halfway through middle school, Dr. Grossman retired. I resisted the idea of getting a new psychiatrist. We made a deal at home where I could be med free as long as my grades didn't suffer and I worked with a private tutor twice a week.

I gained weight. I started to eat lunch and then some. I started to care less about grades, and almost immediately after stopping treatment, I earned my first C in math. I got more annoying and allowed myself to be the piñata of my peer group to combat the deep insecurity I had toward myself, which I tried to treat with forced inclusion and attention-seeking behavior.

When I sat quietly and completed work on meds, I paid attention but I didn't *get* attention; I wanted some. I had giggle fits that wouldn't stop. I was sent to the vice principal's office for disrupting class after I laughed in response to my teacher saying "billy goat." The vice principal had me sit in front of her, still laughing.

She said, "I'll wait," and she did. Eventually I calmed down enough to have a very normal conversation about keeping it together in the classroom and how that kind of thing wasn't going to fly once I got to high school. I used to tell myself I was sent to the office for laughter because of how absurd things were, but I know I was doing it as a nervous response and a cry for attention.

I got sent to the hallway and front office and had detention for being late, obnoxious, not working, talking, and being off task. I bugged people by being "random." I spent time during group projects trying to memorize the alphabet backwards and stuck my tongue out during basketball. It seemed anything "ADD-like" was worse now than it had been before. The goose was loose.

Perhaps, at seven, I was slowly developing the ability to self-discipline and focus. With meds, I was alright at it—or at least felt like I was. When the meds stopped, was I right back where I'd been at seven?

Sometimes I think that my personal ability to govern focus and discipline atrophied, having been operated and supplemented by amphetamines for so long. Now that I was off them, there was a lot of work to do in order to catch up and keep up.

I hadn't learned many strategies outside of the meds. I wasn't particularly agreeable to change. I was stubborn. Completing classwork was easy on Dexedrine. Now, off it, things took effort. I didn't care too much about grades. I wanted to be fun and have fun. Was this who I was the whole time?

Did the repression of this behavior cause it to come back with a vengeance? Had my development in terms of my ability to focus and wield self-discipline been delayed? Was this just who I was as a prepubescent? Or could this have been my ADD expressing itself through the biological brain makeup that I possessed? On a positive note, despite my obnoxious behavior and lower grades, I didn't think about dying anymore.

I became invested in the idea of being an actor. I was outgoing to a fault and wanted attention as an idea, but I lacked charisma. I mumbled and looked around nervously when I was finally given the attention I wanted. I did all the plays in middle school and a musical in an independent theater group. I bombed my only speaking role and floated as a chorus player in the others.

I didn't want to act; I just wanted to be an actor. I thought it was cool. In archives stored in my childhood home, there are hours of actual tape of me filming myself in my room, entertaining myself with myself for my own TV, often lip syncing, dancing, and making characters up and improvising as them.

Kids at this age start to attach their idea of themselves to archetypes seen in movies, books, and videos. I started following goofy stoner types—mischievous but not nefarious. Loveable idiot. I pocketed the mannerisms of marijuana users I saw on television, without ever smoking or being near marijuana. I wanted to be laid back, cool, and secretly knowledgeable.

I began religiously skateboarding each afternoon and weekend. I finally had something to focus on that I could devote myself to without medication. It consumed my mind and ambition. In class, books on my desk became ledges; and my fingers, legs with a board. While teachers droned on about whatever was on their curriculum for the day, I had a way of discreetly practicing skateboard visualization, with my hand doing tricks on my book.

In reality, I could imagine how tricks should go but it seemed there was a blockage between my mind and body that didn't allow me to express the trick the way I saw it. I was not very athletic. I was one of the slowest runners in our grade.

Skateboarding gave me a reason to change. I could never get motivated to play conventional competitive sports. When I got home from school, I'd watch a skate video and take residence outside on my driveway, skating up and down it until sundown. Homework was a second or third priority afterthought.

Skateboarding was not just an athletic pursuit; it was a way to be together with friends, an excuse to explore urban areas, and an avenue to celebrate your and your friend's victory of overcoming dangerous physics despite physical consequences. It was an entire culture to be embraced in.

Being unmedicated and distracted by skateboarding affected my grades. I once got all As and one B when I decided to really try for one quarter, and that was it. I saw I was capable of it and moved on.

Good grades weren't a part of the archetype I was seeking to occupy. I couldn't be peeled from skateboarding. There were threats of removing skateboarding from my life if grades reached a certain low threshold, but it didn't happen.

Journal entry from December 9, 2001 (13 years old):

My parents want to drug me because I got bad grades.
Fuck everything.

High School

I had no definitive answer to the question of what I wanted to be when I grew up. I had no career in mind. I used to mock the question by answering that I wanted to be a clerk at a drugstore. What was so wrong about that? Why did we always have to be something that was challenging to achieve and difficult to maintain? Why were we taught that non-prestigious work was undesirable?

I just wanted to be a person. My dream was to skateboard for a living, but I wasn't that good. I just wanted to do it all day.

My grades started trending downwards. Out of sight, out of mind. Report card days were a quarterly holiday of shame that I recovered from quickly.

I took part in classroom discussions. I was in honors classes and remained curious about the subjects being taught. It was the demanding amount of homework that I couldn't handle. Once the last bell rang, I'd had enough. I couldn't find grades personally valuable enough to make the commitments and sacrifice needed to get them.

I thought myself quite clever for pointing out that, in the big scheme of things, grades didn't actually matter. They were just letters on a page. The thing I wish I'd understood was that good grades were an opportunity to strengthen the muscles of hard work. I instead treated school like a minimum wage job. I showed up, did just enough, and didn't think about it again till I came back.

The afternoons were for skateboarding, and the evenings were for television, video-games, chatting on instant messenger, and I started running on a treadmill and lifting weights. This paradigm wasn't breaking any time soon. I started see results in my body and mind. I felt great. I had more energy, was a better skater, and became more secure with the way I looked.

I was invested in budding romantic relationships, the development of my personality, skateboarding, and my physical health. These took precedence over school. These were the metrics I measured my value in. I was building persistence and determination with skateboarding and exercise.

High school classwork involved regulating the workload of seven classes, with ongoing projects, regular worksheets, quizzes, tests, and exams along with write-ups and the outlining of textbooks. Regularly, the assignment was to make an outline of your textbook on lined paper and show it to your teacher. This was a process to enter information into the brain. I didn't learn this way.

I still preferred to touch something, see it, or at least talk about it to really learn about it. I was more willing to read the material if I didn't have the added stress of all that writing, bulleting, formatting, and going back and forth between my notebook and the textbook. I wasn't going to use a word processor or a tape recorder here. I usually copied these from someone else.

By rapidly copying the information, I wasn't really processing it. If I showed up to class and had nothing to hand in, I could shrug it off. I wouldn't apologize or make excuses. It wasn't uncommon in the mornings for us to sit in a small circle, pass around one friend's completed assignment, and copy it.

Teachers occasionally had me stay after class to give me a private pep talk where they'd say, "You're a smart guy, why don't you just do the work?" I arrogantly believed I knew something about life they didn't know. As if I had cracked the system by being a young hedonist. I thought that if I didn't want to be a teacher, what good was it to follow their lead? All they knew was teaching.

The overhead projector was a machine that projected plastic sheets of transparent "paper" onto a screen where a teacher could write information with a squeaky little marker for us all to copy. Teachers talked and talked while they wrote relevant points on the swan-shaped overhead projector.

In a dark room, we all watched a pen squeak across a transparent page projected on a white screen, copied their notes verbatim, and memorized them for a test. Then a few days later, the material would show up in a test.

I couldn't always listen to the teacher whenever this happened; often she talked faster than she wrote, and I was listening to the words in my head that I was writing, not the words she was saying, while looking up and down.

The process involved me quietly writing, listening, and reading all at once in a room ambient with the fan of the projector and a chorus of pencils scribing across thirty or so notebooks, binders, or loose papers.

Once the transparent sheet was filled, the teacher stood there while the slow writer, sometimes me, would catch up, after which she'd move on and do it again. Then she would either spray and wipe everything away or turn a little handle on a scroll of clear paper and keep the transparency on file to be projected again some day.

There was an open invitation to come in during lunch and check our notes, but this was a tremendous sacrifice of the rare forty-five minutes a day we got to just socialize and eat.

The ideal time to get to school was around 7:00 a.m. Just enough time to meet your friends in the hallway and copy their outlines and get a dose of socialization. You had to be in your seat, ready to sit all day, at 7:25 a.m. I didn't drink coffee or tea or have any caffeine. I should have tried.

If giving students amphetamines to perform better in school is effective, caffeine should have a similar, but lessened, effect. Both substances are stimulants. Caffeine is an adenosine receptor antagonist, while amphetamine is a dopamine and norepinephrine releasing agent. But while they work differently in the body and the brain, both produce a "waking" sense known to be associated with productivity.

The school did a timeline shift halfway through the year. Every student got a new schedule and maybe different teachers too. For the first half of the freshman science course *Honors Matter and Energy*, I had a lovely woman who was warm, kind, and truly appreciated science's mission to understand the world. I had her class after lunch. I enjoyed it and did well. She understood me, and I respected her.

After the mid-year switch, my teacher was a man who could only be described as uncomfortable. There was a rumor that he wasn't allowed to use the computers at school. I had his class first thing in the morning, and I fell asleep in it often.

He once smacked my desk with a textbook while I was sleeping and threatened that next time he would use a 2x4 he'd labeled "Board of Education." He was an asshole. I would have failed his class if I didn't burn myself out cramming for the final.

Much of how we do in a class can be dictated by how we get along with our teachers and what time of day the class takes place. I didn't respect him, and my adolescent tendency to counterwill didn't want to give him the satisfaction of earning a good grade out of me.

Counterwill is something people experience when they resist authority for fear of being controlled. According to Dr. Gabor Mate in *Scattered Minds*, it occurs when ADD children of all ages are put against some sort of pressure.[1]

As a point of interest, one high school moved their first bell an hour ahead and saw marked improvements in standardized tests, dropout rates, and behavioral problems, and even a reduction in car accidents on the way to school.[2]

———

IN ALGEBRA 2, the girl sitting in front of me would share her problems with me. Relationships, parents, drama with friends. I started giving her advice that she welcomed; it was advice I hadn't considered following myself.

Essentially, I was regurgitating my personal rebranding of "what will be, will be," "this too shall pass," or "just go with it." I'd say, "fuck it," in the most positive of ways. Just let it go. Be happy—despite everything going on around you, override all default reactions and choose unwavering happiness.

One evening in bed, reading a pocket-size book of Taoist wisdom, I discovered a nugget that invited the reader to imagine their problems from the vantage point of their deathbed. I went there. I imagined I was dying. How did I feel about failing a science class? I fantasized that I had already lived a fulfilled life, so it didn't matter. All I would remember were the good times I'd had with my friends, so I invested energy into creating memories with my friends.

Looking back, I am critical of myself for spiritually bypassing all responsibilities. I considered myself on an enlightened path that exempted me from grades. I was devoted to reaching a certain state of mind and spirit, so I neglected certain pursuits. Because of that neglect, there came problems in life that impeded maintaining that state. At this adolescent phase, perhaps the space in my life where meaning belonged was occupied with fun, distraction, and enjoyment.

I liberated myself from the pressure of grades in my "see what happens" approach. For some classes with a skinnier workload, I could produce decent grades just by showing up, paying attention while there, taking tests, and completing projects.

Conversely, in classes where I had to show up and write up each class in a journal that was collected every Friday, where homework was turned in and graded, and where the comprehension of readings might involve what seemed like irrelevant minutia related to the material, I would fall off track, but it didn't bother me much.

Being so personable, I felt like good grades were a gift to my teacher and parents, and it seemed more important to them than me. I was coping with my situation as best I could, as we all do. I hadn't forgotten that they diagnosed me as disabled and that I was unmedicated; I chose to be as happy as possible.

Getting poor grades didn't devastate me as much as the idea of bringing them home did. I desired to be intelligent, knowledgeable, and wise, but not along the paths and definitions presented to me at school. I perceived high-achieving students as stressed out and obedient.

I wanted to also have a good time. I was focused on how could I make this fun? How could I be unbothered by this thing that everyone seemed to take too seriously? I delayed the inevitable life lesson of stress management and built myself into a person it didn't matter to. It felt good to be goofy.

Counterwill. The more teachers and parents asked of me, the less inclined I was to appease them. I was more focused on acceptance and attention from my peers than that of the adults prodding me. I found it easier to get attention from my peers by caring less than them.

There was some kind of missed moment. In an alternative timeline, something would have struck me like nothing else and changed my life. Maybe the moment wasn't missed; maybe I was distracted from the path. A craft, a mentor—some kind of revelatory epiphany where I gained purpose and inspiration and found "my thing" and pursued it to its end.

After getting better and better at running three miles on my parents' treadmill, I joined the cross-country team. For two weeks before school started, I woke up early and ran through the woods within a flock. I went from being the absolute slowest person on the team to eventually somewhere in the middle.

I got sorer than I had ever been. My legs were warm rubber before they turned into wood. I ran the entire season, rarely missing the afternoon practices of two to three hours of running and stretching around a lake and through the woods.

There were meets every weekend and sometimes on weekdays. I only went to two. I wasn't concerned about or interested in the competitive element of running around. I enjoyed running in the woods in a group. Breathing together, seeing deer, reminding each other to stretch.

I stumbled upon how to run further; there was a mental barrier that, when crossed, left the mind clear. I was invited to run track in the spring. I couldn't find pleasure in running around in a circle, so I quit after two weeks.

CANNABIS

I wanted to start smoking pot; I imagined it would complete my persona. Eventually, my friends and I did just that during the summer between freshman and sophomore year. I experienced a jolly giddiness, a giggly fun time bursting with excitement, discovering the ability of cannabis to bend perception ever so slightly to see everything through a different lens.

Now that I had the sacrament I'd been waiting for, I could open myself to giving marijuana a place in my life and identity.

In the fall of sophomore year, the frequency of smoking increased. My friends and I did it together, probably two or three times a month. I never did it alone.

I was silly already and here was something that allowed my friends and me to just be silly together for a few hours. Smoking weed became a precious ritual for us. While others began to smoke all the time and became habituated to it, we did it with reverence. For many habitual smokers, it eventually becomes daily or all day and doesn't seem to do anything other than take away the desire to smoke. For us, it was about laughter, creativity, and group bonding.

Sophomore year, my GPA dropped below 3.0—a C average. However, my hair, clothes, skateboard, and social behaviors remained my gauge for how I was doing, and I was doing well. Once grades begin to slip, it's easier for them to slide. Catching up is harder than getting a good grade from the start. Climbing from a D to a C is way harder than from a B to an A. It's like crawling out of debt. Grades are supposed to be some kind of representation of money anyway.

Teachers continued to hold me after class and tell me they could see I could learn and pleaded with me to just do this work. They told me if I did the work, I would get good grades. Cocky, I nodded and said something like, "I know."

When given the opportunity to drop out and earn a GED, I rejected it immediately. There was too much social shame associated, and I didn't want to miss out on the high school experience with my friends. I wanted the college experience too.

I think the offer was to illustrate how serious it was that I engage with my studies. I wasn't ready to be an independent adult. What would my friends say? Would I still get to see them? It's easy to look back at your life and piece together a straight path to where you are now instead of the crooked, thorny one you took.

Big Break

The summer between sophomore and junior year, while skateboarding downtown, I saw a group of skaters from South America having a session over six steps. They were grown men; I was fifteen. I wanted to impress them. I was feeling some kind of way.

I had ollied down six steps at this point and probably even done a 180 or kickflip down a six. Without a warmup, I went straight for a heel flip down the steps. I hopped up the steps, turned around, threw down my board, and proceeded to snap my tibia and fibula at the bottom of the steps.

I definitely impressed the tourist skaters. They took a selfie with me on the ambulance stretcher as I was carted off by paramedics. I was given morphine in the hospital. I remember the warm, weighted blanket of heroin's cousin as the deepening into the absurdity of being so high because my actual leg was in pieces. I was looking at the bottom of my foot at an angle I never had before.

On the opiate, I watched hallucinated sandcastles rise from the linoleum tiles, displacing interns, nurses, and my family. People were moving around the room, and I felt like me and everyone else were on different wavelengths of the passage of time.

Until the doctor manhandled my bones back into place. He had to push my sensitive, broken leg into a semi circle around the top piece of bone to realign my skeleton.

Once the pain got to me, I grabbed his shirt and yelled at him with fierce resistance before I fell unconscious. When I came to, a group of medical interns were wrapping my straightened leg in a plaster cast from thigh to toe.

I began my recovery with prescription opioids, television, and video games to pass the time while my body was still. The family vacation had to be canceled because of my injury. After two weeks, I was having weird thoughts on the painkillers. I had some strange journal entries and decided I'd rather be in pain and feel the gap in my bones than have these weird thoughts. I favored stimulants.

I was on the couch a lot, at first allowing the television to endlessly mush up my brain. After I had enough, I turned it off and actually did my summer reading. I enjoyed it. I picked up a guitar and finally figured out barre chords. I journaled. I learned how to slow down and take advantage of a crippling situation. I made an omelet every morning and mastered the flip. I made a conscious choice to turn the injury around, and it was a net positive experience. I was off crutches a few days before junior year started.

———

THE SAT TEST was coming up, and there was a lot of pressure to perform well on this singular test. The pressure would then be transferred to the pressure of creating an impressive college application and sending it to desired institutions.

If you asked me why I was applying to college, I'd have told you, "Because I am graduating high school and that's what middle-class suburban kids do after high school." All the colleges I pursued were in Florida and California. I wasn't after an education; I was after a lifestyle. I had no major in mind. I just wanted to move away from my parents, wear shorts all year, skateboard, and be near a beach.

Coming back from a college visit in California, the option of restarting my ADD medications was presented to me. I didn't want to do it. I was afraid it would change me. I didn't like the idea. I wrote a deal and a contract with myself in one of my journals on that flight, which promised that if they changed me, I'd stop:

Hey! If ADD shit is differentiating from examples in the two note-books you have, stop that shit now!

An ultimatum was established wherein I would get tested again and see if I *still* had ADD, in which case I'd explore medications again. If I didn't, then I suppose I could go on being unmedicated and the reason for my performance in school couldn't be blamed on a diagnosable disorder.

REEVALUATION

I developed a bit of disrespect for authority and rules. The counterwill behavior was active. I would trespass and vandalize by way of skateboarding. I'd sneak out of the house, smoke weed with my friends, push the car out of the driveway, and start it in the middle of the road without a driver's license to go to a party. I felt liberated by the freedom associated with risk and the thrill that came with venturing into the unexpected.

I wasn't very cooperative with the second evaluation. The energy of my bliss transferred into anger. I felt persecuted. History repeated itself with little resistance. This time the visit was coated in a glaze of stubborn angst and arm-crossed shoe gazing that made me feel like the main character in some coming-of-age indie film where a psychologically damaged yet bright child is chronically misunderstood by everyone around him.

I slapped my thigh and lost it a little when they brought out the Rorschach cards. I started complaining. I couldn't believe this was part of the experience and imagined next was the straitjacket. "Really? You think I'm crazy?" before gazing out the window for a moment while gnawing at my lower lip. I then identified each Rorschach as symmetrical parts of the female reproductive anatomy, dancing deer, and a mosquito.

I was pushed to the limits of my embarrassment. Instead of an emotional crack or a breakthrough of any kind, I got worn down. If I got bored or sad that I was there, I just didn't care, and my nervous system froze from not being able to regulate these feelings.

After once again ranging in the 80th and 90th percentile in most tests of intelligence for my age, I bombed short-term auditory again, which meant I needed amphetamines. Again, my worst score came from the only test taken on a computer.

From their document:

> The client sits in front of a computer and button-presses once at each appearance of the target while inhibiting button pressing at each appearance of the nontarget.

> The target appears infrequently during the first half of this test, requiring that the youngster remain alert while inhibiting responses to the more frequent appearance of the nontarget. Though variability of response time to the target was slightly below expectation for someone of Russell's intellect (37th to 48th percentile), he generally performed well during the first five minutes of this test. However, during the second five to six minutes the frequency of missing the target increased dramatically causing accuracy to fall from the 66th percentile to well below the 1st percentile.

First percentile. I achieved the lowest score in the entire data set. I do not remember this one as vividly as the first. The report continues, verbatim:

> The target appears frequently during the second half of the test, requiring the youngster to quickly shift from "go" to "no go" at the infrequent appearance of the nontarget. Russell consistently responded to the target for the entire 15 minute duration of this task while also managing to inhibit responses to the nontarget....

> Though the test profile was indicative of an attentional problem, Russell's inattentiveness did not occur consistently throughout the test. Results indicate he has trouble sustaining attention in the absence of

physical activity and that he can be inattentive and inconsistent when first adjusting to a novel task.

I am not a doctor, so I am not supposed to understand this. However, I don't understand why they didn't come back and have me perform the same evaluation on amphetamines to see whether those improved my scores. Would my scores have improved if I'd returned to take the test at a later date while on amphetamines?

I was assigned the same diagnosis as before: "spots" of ADD. Inattentive. My attention is that of a sailboat. When there are good winds, and a keen sense to rig the mental sails, there is movement forward. Without interest, adrift. With amphetamines, 150-horsepower diesel engine.

Getting evaluated again caused my insecurity to come back. I didn't know how to handle this loosening of the grip of my own sense of who I thought I was. I felt challenged and defensive. This was emotionally exhausting.

Was I self-sabotaging with my behavior and attitude? Was I mischievous just to avoid the responsibility of working? Did I disguise my laziness, apathy, and fear of commitment in a silly, goofy persona that thought he knew something to invalidate the entire system of education?

Maybe I needed therapy, not medication. Instead, when I got home, I went upstairs, listened to Radiohead, and cried.

DR. CONNER

I was taken to Dr. Conner's office to arrange taking meds again. We arrived at his office, my mother and I, down the street from my favorite spot to skateboard. An abandoned school blacktop. The building had become some kind of bureaucratic headquarters, and since nobody used the blacktop, neighborhood kids started building ramps and pouring concrete. A consolation of visiting his office was the opportunity to skate afterwards, since I would be driving myself after the first visit.

I was surprised to notice his office was in the basement of his house. He'd made modifications to his driveway and had a separate entrance. We entered his basement waiting room. Plenty of magazines, wood paneling, dim lights. He called us in.

His bald head shone below tungsten track lights, and I could see the grid of all his books lining the walls in the reflection of his glasses. A more or less friendly smile brushed the mustache portion of his beard up into his nose as he shook our hands upon meeting us.

The chairs were comfortable. He had an aged black leather chair with lumbar support and a spring rocker. I sat in it, nervously going through the motions, counting down the minutes of this day just to get it over with and carry on with my life.

I felt like I was being punished, sitting there while he flipped through the document. I couldn't believe I was going through this again. Once this dark scene was over, I could go on like none of it ever happened.

He asked me point-blank if I smoked cannabis. I stared at him, eyes wide, my mother sitting next to me. I started to stare through him. I stared through his bookshelf, through to paneling, through the makeshift waiting room in his basement, outside in his yard, outside of the planet, the solar system, and beyond.

I felt the weight of all this moment, and I froze completely for a few seconds. Then I crushed under pressure like a tin can on Jupiter. All the emotions I was keeping to myself became public to this stranger and my mom.

I brought my knees to my chest, putting my dirty shoes on his fine leather furniture. I grabbed the hood in my hoody, pulled it over my head, and in my tent I wept. I'd never talked about my weed habits with my mom, and this wasn't how I wanted to.

What was incredible to me was that this man, Dr. Conner, a mental health professional, proceeded to ignore my emotional breakdown. I could not see him, but I heard him shift his attention to my mom and ask her if *she* thought I was smoking pot. She gave a shaky answer, also blindsided by this question. She was close enough to the truth in her answer.

He had a general ADD conversation and wrote me two prescriptions, one for Adderall and one for Ritalin, telling me to try them both out and see what I thought and what worked, and we'd build a program together. But he told me not to smoke weed on them. He said it canceled out the good work they did.

I sank. I gained five pounds of sadness and it all went into my shoulders. I wanted to be my own skeleton and jump these bones out of my flesh and marimba into the sunset. But I was trapped in this body and this situation.

From a different perspective, it was a privilege to be given performance enhancements to make sure I could get good grades to get into a decent school to get a well-paying job to have a better opportunity to lead a better life to make the world a better place. This made things better, right? But I didn't want that. I wanted to be a nomad, which can be difficult for some parents to accept.

I was full of rage and anger, and I didn't know where to direct it. I thought... Fuck Dr. Conner. Fuck ADD. Forget about my parents. My brother can shove it. Fuck you for telling me not to smoke weed while making me take speed. Fuck school. The teachers are losers. Fuck all the students in their miniature version of the inevitable rat race, all the kids who are the same, who call me different. Fuck these PhD assholes with their degrees, going around diagnosing their archetypical opposites into submission just to validate their own life choices and student debts. Fuck all of this—I hate it.

ADDERALL

I took 10 mg of Adderall salt the following Sunday and went about my normal routine. It was a nice day out. I decided to skateboard in my driveway. I grabbed my board and attempted a trick called a backside heel-flip. I'd been trying this trick for some time now and hadn't even gotten close to landing it. I'd flick the board up, spin, and land on my feet while my board tumbled behind me.

This time, I threw my board down on the driveway and, in the split second before snapping the tail of my board, began to visualize. It appeared I had a clear path from my mind to my limbs and a direct connection to my feet on the board.

I adjusted my front foot so my toes hung slightly over the edge and angled my toe in. I placed my back foot on the bottom right-hand corner of my board. I bent my knees, keeping my back straight, and turned my shoulders counter-clockwise, loading my kinetic energy.

I snapped the tail of my board, simultaneously jumping off the ground, giving way for the board to rise, and kicked my front heel toward the front corner of the board as the entire assembly of body and board rotated clockwise. Once the deck had made a full spin under me, I extended my legs and heard the slight "pat" sound of my shoes connecting to the plywood board above ground.

As I made my way to the ground, I rotated on the x axis approximately 165 degrees, landing on the somewhat slick asphalt, which allowed me to drive with my hips to complete the rotation.

My wheels made a screech on the asphalt as I declared my authority over this skateboard and the laws of physics that bound us. I rolled down the driveway, mouth agape at what had just happened, youthful locks of hair blowing across my face, bursting with excited satisfaction. Then I did it again. I finally had it: the sorcerer's stone, the ring, the wand. I could land a backside heel-flip first try—no warm-up.

It felt like the barrier between my mind and body was broken through. The barrier between what I had been visualizing and what I ended up doing had been decommissioned with the reunion of myself and the amphetamine. Finally, I could skate closer to how I imagined I could, rather than feeling as if I had limited access to my body. All that anger faded away.

The contract I wrote with myself about the drugs changing me had no clauses about if the change made me a better skater. Never mind all of it; we were good. Dr. Conner was cool. Just doing what he had to.

I felt great. I felt, oh, so good. I was in control. I liked this. That whiney, angsty crybaby was annoying, anyway. What was with all that talking and complaining? Emotions blocked the kinetics. Just go. **This was good.**

I didn't know the meds were speed; I didn't know about amphetamines. I didn't know any of this. I called them Adderall, and we were friends now. I came inside for a break from skating on the driveway and was asked how I was feeling on them. I said something to the effect of, "Any pill that gets me landing backside heels on the first try is fine by me!" I slammed an orange juice and went back outside.

The next day I got to try out my new brain at school—where it was meant to go. I took a 20 mg Adderall XR (time-release amphetamine). Drove myself to school, parked my car. Pep in the step. No morning sleepiness. The music in the car sounded better. I could really hear what the artists were trying to get across. I felt fantastic.

The shame I once had toward being medicated was somewhat diminished. I recall telling Amy Sanford, the girl who sat next to me in first period chemistry, that I was on Adderall, as I balanced chemical valence equations with pleasure. I told her I had a lot of energy, without looking up from my desk.

Rather than a struggle to figure out these equations, there was satisfaction in their completion, and all instructions made sense. I saw the perfection in nature's design as I found the valence between molecules.

On this day, I felt compelled to outperform myself academically. I was eager to receive assignments and complete them. I was moving faster yet didn't feel rushed. I could hone in completely on whatever task was in front of me.

On Adderall, tasks are so simple. Really, what else should there be to do other than the task before you? I had nothing for lunch except a bottle of water. Perhaps I took three bites of a red delicious apple and threw the rest away.

My focus at lunch was on enjoying the gregarious banter and silliness with my friends. Being silly, egging each other on, playing "Crozet beach," a game of my own design that allowed us to get each other to do dares.

One person would come up with a potential dare: tell this person something embarrassing, behave a certain way toward a teacher or staff member, lick the floor, eat this pickle stuck to the side of the trashcan, etc. Then we all would roll a single dice. Lowest number did it. Ties resulted in a roll off, and if your die rolled off the table, automatic submission.

The game actually spread throughout the school on its own, resulting in a small dice-motivated social movement that I felt a sense of pride about. Some kid I didn't even know ate another kid I didn't know's vomit. Disgusting.

One kid had to stay in a cupboard halfway through a class; he had to emerge part way through and go to his seat as if nothing had happened. Another student had to pick up an overhead projector marker while the teacher was writing down notes for students to copy, silently draw a beard on his own face, and return to his seat. This was the maturation of "Here in a limo."

Another friend ran through a convenience store wearing only a shirt and shoes. A raw egg was eaten with the shell. Fast food workers were subjected to our behavior. Teachers were confused. We were so entertained that the backs of our heads hurt from laughing. Lunch was my favorite class.

After lunch I had sociology. I was the only junior in the class, as it was an elective usually taken by seniors. The day I took this inaugural Adderall XR, all the seniors were on a trip. It was just the teacher and me. He had no work for me to do. I asked if I could read his *Washington Post*.

For the first and only time in my life, I read the newspaper, skipping nothing at all for an entire forty-five minutes. I read the articles, studied the advertisements. If I didn't care about the story, I would focus on the writing. Look at the design choices in the ads, think about and appreciate the work that went into a newspaper.

On Adderall, I felt I had the time to do this. Where my mind would normally wander, it didn't. I was in the room. What else was in the room? What could that offer? Adderall *is* effective. It has an effect. I wasn't just looking for a task of my own design; I was willing to take on offered tasks with my own approach.

I drove home. I may or may not have been taking a smaller 5 mg or 10 mg of straight amphetamine salt in the afternoon, as per the doctor's orders. Adderall was helpful for the bustling day of copying overhead projector notes, reading the paper, and coming up with gross dares during lunch.

I would take a lesser dose of amphetamine when I got home, skateboard for a few hours, and maybe do my homework or play on the computer, editing silly videos for me and my friends to watch when we got high. I stayed up way late, sometimes past 2:00 a.m., and woke up at 6:30 a.m.

For a period, I took a Ritalin tablet in the afternoon. Ritalin is not an amphetamine; it's methylphenidate. I believed Ritalin was better suited for homework, while Adderall was better for the school day. I started to regularly self-medicate with cough syrup just to go to sleep. This was something I didn't exactly realize I was doing because of the amphetamine use, but it makes sense in hindsight, as getting just two to three hours of sleep was not unusual or unbearable.

Having something to bring me down in the evening helped, and since I had a car and a job, I could just go get it. On one occasion, while already high on weed, a friend and I both drank a bottle of cough syrup together and tried to keep each other awake. This is reckless and causes liver damage. We weren't thinking about this. I don't remember who fell asleep first.

APTITUDE TEST

The main if not *the* reason I was back on stimulants was to outperform myself on the SAT test. The SAT test is a standardized test used to evaluate potential students for colleges and universities.

Not only was I taking these drugs, I was also taking a prep class with four or five other teenagers to understand this test better, taught by a cool dude who had an earring and was probably named Jeff. I was excited about the classes because they were in the next county, twenty miles of straight, empty, two-lane roads.

Something about driving on Adderall made me feel like a fighter pilot. I would speed. I would weave. I was smooth as mercury. I was reckless to drive like this, but surgical in my operation. I had close calls with the law, but never with accidents.

I got away with nine police interactions for speeding before I finally got slammed with a ticket. I never made excuses that weren't the truth to a police officer. The truth was that I was never in a hurry—I just liked it. I was careful while being unsafe.

I would fly to my SAT classes listening to techno, speakers buzzing as I killed them with bass they were never meant to handle. I'd come in hot with adrenaline, then sit in a quiet room with passive indifference toward the advantage and privilege of being offered another upper hand on this test.

It may have been the Adderall or the lack of food or sleep, or maybe I had a weird cut of fish, but I felt strange halfway through my first class. I was still getting used to regular amphetamines. Full-body dizziness came over me with a feeling like I needed to pass out or throw up. I felt woozy and my vision started to blur. I dropped my pencil, pushed my chair out, and stood up, squeaking the four plastic pads on the bottom of the chair against the linoleum.

The other kids and Probably-Jeff looked over at me as I was just standing there, uneasy. The teacher stopped what he was talking about, letting me speak. I stammered, "I... I... I..." —everyone stared at me— "need water." Probably-Jeff lowered his brow at me and looked at my desk.

I sat back down at my desk where there was nothing but a notebook and a bottle of water, opened my water, and drank it. Class carried on. This feeling came more than a handful of times on Adderall if I wasn't hydrated or was short on food, sleep, etc.

The thing I looked forward to most about the class was that I got to drive by a church with five steps in front of it that I wanted to jump down on my skateboard. On the way home, I stopped, whipped out my board, and shredded. On Adderall, I had no fear of jumping down the steps. Fear is an emotion, and I was now more governed by thinking and perceiving.

I skated as fast as I could, pushing my foot on the sidewalk like I was trying to knock the earth and leaping down the stairs with as much force upwards and forwards as humanly possible. I ollied as high as I could. I cleared the steps and the sidewalk crack, landing five or six feet past the bottom step.

Off of Adderall, having landed the trick was enough, but with this charged energy and what felt like focus, I would do it again and again, modifying my approach to see how it changed outcomes and looking for ways to optimize performance. I did it so many times that eventually I landed with so much force I snapped the tail of the board.

This approach is helpful for any development of skill on or off Adderall, although without it is hard work. The follow-through seems to come naturally on Adderall. On Adderall, what is normally mundane or repetitive is natural to ease into. It almost feels good to work—to settle into a sort of medically induced, positive, manic state.

Instead of freaking out, maybe I'd just jump down these steps on my skateboard twenty times in a row. Driving home, getting as close to 100 mph as I could with the window down, I'd already forgotten about the SAT class and was enjoying the breeze and the glow of a good evening skate session. I'd already passed the test I cared about.

It is impossible to draw a hard line between someone who is taking powerful drugs every day and the drugs they are taking. A chemical reaction takes place, and the two become one.

I was under the impression Adderall gave me access to a part of myself that was always there, but without which I couldn't seem to access this potential. A cheat code. To accept that the meds made me who I was meant to be was to accept I was broken without them. Was I just chemically imbalanced? Did amphetamines fix this?

On Adderall, if I had an inkling or an idea, I would power through and do it. Adderall brought me a "get up and go" attitude that just said, "Why not?" So, with no experience and no real inspiration other than a cool friend of mine who did it, I joined the lacrosse team. I practiced some. I could fling that hard little ball. I played in a winter league against kids two years my junior and felt like I could keep pace with them.

I somehow made the varsity team, though I didn't belong there at all. When these juiced-up jocks screamed in a huddle, clacking their sticks together in a primal roar, I opened my mouth to make it seem like I was part of it, but I wasn't prepared to make a sound bond with these barbarians. All because of a small idea that I gave in to following through, I was running around with all the pads on, sucking a mouth guard pacifier.

I didn't enjoy being yelled at for being an idiot. During drills, I frustrated everyone and was told to get off the field. When I walked off, I was told to exit "with a purpose!" which meant to *run* off the field. My purpose was to disappear and get out of the way. Most of these kids were used to this.

I wished there was a way out of it that wasn't quitting. I'd made my family buy all this gear. I realized I'd be showing up at games every Saturday only to stand on the sidelines and watch.

The morning after I made this personal wish, I closed my car door on my right index finger. I didn't do it on purpose to get out of lacrosse, but it did get me out of lacrosse. My fingernail popped off and I received stitches underneath it. I permanently altered my nail matrix, changing the way the nail grows for the rest of my life.

I had one of those finger braces that was a piece of aluminum with foam glued to it bent around my finger, and my index and middle fingers were taped together. The SAT test was days away. I would take the test holding a number two pencil against my palm with my ring and pinky finger.

The test is always given on a Saturday morning. I woke up early and had a light breakfast and my Adderall XR. It was a foggy morning. I drove to the school where I was to take the test. It was a quiet, almost somber environment. Nobody was happy to be there. It felt as serious as a military deployment into a war zone. These students felt like the fate of their livelihood and promising future rested on their ability to fill in the right bubbles on the scantron booklet.

A scantron is where the answers for multiple-choice tests go. It is a book of bubbles but is nowhere near as fun as a book of bubbles sounds. The proctor spent an inordinate amount of time going over how to fill out our names, pertinent ID numbers, and other minutiae, which drained the hype I'd built going in. We were wasting good Adderall time on administrative details and bathroom protocol. They have scripts they must read. The whole thing is regimented.

My testing room had a ticking, not coasting, clock. Buzzing fluorescents. The air conditioner was on the whole time and was at just the right temperature that I was intermittently putting on and taking off a flannel. I sat in the front row about five seats away from the window and the desk, at one of those large square desks that were welded to the chair.

I often found myself gripping the top and side of these desks, sliding around in the chair. I often chose to be at an angle. I would sometimes place my left elbow on the desk, pivot my body right, and hold my head up by my hair as my number two pencil bravely filled in bubbles.

People coughed and sniffled and blew their noses as it was allergy season, and pencils ran across the desks frantically, amplified by the stress of the day and a rhythm of concentrated, quick filling of small ovals.

I was doing just fine, but halfway through the test I was ready to take the spare 10 mg of amphetamine salt I'd stashed in my small jean pocket above the right pocket. I'd placed it in there while standing, and the usual way to get something out of this narrow drug pocket was to use the right hand index and middle fingers like chopsticks. Mine were taped together.

I had to reach across myself with my left hand and do some contortions to pull out the piece of paper that had my prescription wrapped in it. I must have been sweating because the tablet had broken apart into crumbs and dust. In between answering analogies and word problems, I could be found cowering over my test, licking amphetamine dust off a folded post-it note.

If I remember correctly, the best I ever scored on the SAT was the first time I took a practice test with Probably-Jeff.

After all the hubbub of getting on amphetamines, taking supplemental classes, debilitating my hand, and all-consuming environmental stress and pressure, I scored in the 81st percentile for the SAT and in the 91st for the ACT, which I also took on Adderall.

I took the SATs again several months later, hoping to improve this score and scored fifty points lower. I justified that I wasn't wired for these kinds of tests. I felt like two children stacked one on the other in a beige trench coat, trying to buy a ticket to college—only the individual whose shoulders I sat on was amphetamine.

COLLEGE

I applied to three schools: two in southern California, and a university in Tampa. I got into the one in Tampa and enrolled by default.

I drove to Tampa on amphetamines, without stopping for anything but lunch and gas. My brother accompanied me and was surprised at my ability to sit and drive for fourteen hours straight. He didn't know I was "rallin'."

I moved into a freshman dorm room that smelled like piss. I once met the sophomore who lived there the year before and he told me he pissed on the floor.

The whole place was disgusting. It smelled like fruit punch, spilled beer, a combination of aerosol aphrodisiacs bought from the local department store, occasional cannabis, and a lingering aroma of microwaved marinara.

This particular school had kids treating alcohol like it was the elixir of life, forbidden until now. Gathering it and participating in its consumption was momentous and all-consuming for them. I didn't drink much as it gave me headaches, hangovers, and vomiting if it wasn't just right.

While everyone was out, uninhibiting and inebriating themselves, I was in the parking lot on Adderall, saturating my clothing with sweat, doing the same tricks on my skateboard over and over. When they returned and wanted to unwind with marijuana in the park, I joined them.

It was here that my principal substance routine for this period began. A day on Adderall, followed by catching the fall of it wearing off with a relaxing smoke of marijuana.

I was connected with a young psychiatrist who worked out of a business center. He would speak with me every few months and write me a new prescription. I'd take that prescription to a pharmacy that was walking distance from campus.

My insurance covered it and I would go back to my dorm with thirty 20 mg Adderall XR tablets and thirty 20 mg amphetamine salts, a total of twelve hundred milligrams of amphetamine. I took them just about every day, taking the afternoon pill as needed, and the energy would pump out all day. I found out I could really skateboard and progress using Adderall as an athletic performance enhancement.

I sold a few pills to a kid on my floor for five dollars a pill. He came back a few days later and asked for another, and I took his money and gave him another one. I thought about my parents spending the deductible on our family's insurance plan and profiting off of it. He came back again the next day. I wouldn't sell him any more and I never sold it again.

I once walked into my dorm and saw my roommate pounding away at his computer. "I'm writing a film," he said, without looking at me. He had helped himself to my pills and was on a roll.

Once when I could not sleep, I walked to the 24-hour pharmacy at two in the morning to buy a bottle of cough syrup. I didn't measure the dose, just swigged the bottle on the walk home. I woke up several hours later at a bus stop and finished my walk back to my dorm.

My obsession was skateboarding. Before, between, and after classes, I would be in the parking lot adjacent to my dorm doing flat ground tricks, skating streets downtown, or at a skatepark. On Adderall, at this age and stage, there were fewer and fewer obstructions between the connection of my mind and my body on a skateboard, as I chipped them away with regular practice.

The skateboard was becoming a limb. I could think my way to being a better skater. Not only could I identify what modifications or preparations were necessary for a successful execution, but I had the will, follow-through, and focus to land lots of tricks. I prioritized practicing my skateboarding rather than being playful. I took it seriously.

It was euphoric to be a sponge of sweat blowing through a skatepark at full speed. Flying off ramps, grinding down rails, and encouraging friends doing the same. My best days of skating throughout my entire life were all on Adderall.

I learned to launch pyramids ramp to ramp. I could session a handrail. When I was on Adderall, my sweat smelled different. It left pit stains, like my body was flushing out rust through my pipes.

I was an undecided major with a minor in music, so I could take all the music classes I wanted to. Take the speed, bang the drum. Class was secondary. I got straight As. Then I dropped out and moved home, still looking *at* everything but not *for* anything.

I wasn't just an undecided major; I really was truly majoring in being undecided. After returning to live with my parents, I attended the local community college, pursued a relationship, and worked. I was distracted by my first girlfriend and resisted the casual conformity of college without knowing what I wanted from it.

In community college, my grades suffered. I stopped taking Adderall here, crashed, regressed, and learned a lot about relationships by making mistakes. I became more regular with marijuana.

Community college was the sequel to high school, with the same workload ritual of turned-in material, regular assignments, lots of grades, and burnt out educators. I drove to school, then had to walk in the cold from one of the 918 parking spaces on the campus.

I didn't like living at home with my parents. To further pursue my passion for being undecided, I went back to Tampa for another fall semester. I returned to my Adderall habit and continued the same routine.

I began journaling obsessively after learning of Julia Cameron's "morning pages" tool in *The Artist's Way*. The first thing I did every morning was journal three pages. Looking back on these journals, I can see the germination of some psychological side effects of regular amphetamine use.

Throughout my life, I've been called "weird" or "crazy" (in a good way, they reassured me). Adderall didn't make me this way. I am still this way. I get it. Combining this with Adderall made me sometimes overconfident in this aspect; I was energetically exposing the wild part of myself as Adderall pushed it out of me at rapid speeds. Burning out creative oils before I even realized I had them. I felt the first hint of grandeur before the delusion interacted. I truly thought I was the main character and my journey was necessary—special and different in ways that others were not.

I thought not knowing what to do with my life made me interesting. I was shifting from an errant stoner to a hopeless romantic. Not everything of who we are can be correlated with apparent diagnosable mental disorders or psychotropic medications.

I was still the sum of all my experiences placed against the codes of my nature, despite the distortions I was generating with the Adderall use. I reached for myself; I followed my own lead. And I was on speed, like, all the time.

One day I met a wise bearded man named Timothy. He laid a blanket out every week or so and sold used books outside our dorm. He suggested a book to me called *Be Here Now* by Ram Dass, a monumental work that I devoured. I concluded that I needed to eat psilocybin mushrooms and take LSD, and that maybe if I did yoga, I could get higher on life while also being high on drugs.

———

ONE DAY, I went to a skatepark without taking Adderall and just wasn't able to get it. I felt frustrated. Sometimes, the day is just off. I went back to school and had dinner and went back, this time with Adderall in my bloodstream, and I had the best night of skateboarding of my life.

Never again would I feel this connected to my board and body, so sweaty and bursting with energy that contained, focused, and directed. The energy was intense, concise, and controlled. I was doing tricks I hadn't ever thought I could do.

I was trying to back lip a handrail having only ever done the trick a few times, and I kept getting into back smith, which I had never even tried on anything. I said why not and learned back smiths down the handrail, landing it after a few tries.

Skateboarding on Adderall was one of the most electrifying experiences of my life. With a heightened cognitive edge and laser focus, my mind, body, and board were bound into a singular energetic expression of intention. I would go fast, leap over ramps, grind down rails, and whatever else, generating a peak experience.

Landing a trick fed an adrenaline loop, creating a dump of happy hormones and giving me one of the highest highs I'd experienced, doing something courageous and accurate on a skateboard. I would often go out alone with my skateboard for an entire day and skate all day, then drive home fast with the windows open and music blaring.

On Adderall, I learned things differently, effectively, and with a well-worn and universally appreciated technique. However, there was a problem. The sober recall was diminished. Not nonexistent, but what I learned on Adderall typically required being on Adderall to fully recall. Take an Adderall once, and you may have a different day. Take it daily, and you may become a different person.

Dropout

During English class I was being a smartass, arguing that a college education has little value or meaning. I meant no insult to my professor or her teaching. I wanted to discuss it on a meta-level. I was saying what I thought without considering how it might make anyone feel. The meds were supposed to squash that when I was a child, but now they seemed to enliven me to openly articulate my perspective with confidence.

My professor pulled me out into the hallway. She told me how her daughter quit college and now waited tables. I called her bluff. I got an A in her class, dropped out, and went to work in a restaurant.

I moved home to Maryland again and stopped taking Adderall. I started as a prep chef at a Mongolian restaurant, where uncooked food was cooked in a performative fashion around a large circular griddle. Then I moved to chef, then to waiter. Then I was fired over getting sick because the fellow who was supposed to cover my shift missed it.

I had gotten a job at a summer camp washing dishes. Since I could make my own hours, I tried to do dishes late at night so I could be a part of camp. I had bought pills called "Stacker 2" at a gas station. Stacker pills contain green tea, yerba mate, other herbs, and allegedly at that time, Ephedra.

When I lost access to amphetamine, without knowing it, I went for a similar class of substance to self-medicate my stimulant dependance. I wasn't really aware of any addiction or dependence going on with me. My relationship with amphetamine was casual. It seemed that every time I went to school, I got back on it, and every time I dropped out, I stopped taking it.

I had a governing urge to seek pills that energized me. I had still never drunk coffee at this point. This pill thing may have been quelled by the simple habit of a coffee in the morning and a tea in the afternoon.

I was looking for the ability to sleep less, to experience more time in the waking state. This made me sloppy, disorganized, rushed, and irritable. I was told off several times about my poor pot-washing skills as well as my bad attitude toward pot washing, which ultimately led to me being fired.

———

I DECIDED I would save up money working in restaurants and then ride my bicycle across the United States. I worked for a nonprofit fixing old bikes, while waiting tables at another corporate nationwide restaurant chain, wasting my years of good hair on hungry boomers.

One evening I was driving with a friend, high on marijuana. We were dancing and driving to disco music. To my surprise, I saw red and blue lights in my rearview mirror and pulled aside. The officer pointed out that the small light that illuminated my license plate was out.

I figured with my record of police interaction, I would be fine. But I couldn't find my registration. My car was a mess. I started micro-panicking because all I had was an expired one. I was *blitzed*.

The cannabis my friend and I had consumed with an acquaintance earlier that evening had some pharmaceutical laced into it—I think promethazine, a commonly abused allergy pharmaceutical. Police like to lean into you as soon as you show weakness. This cop knew something was off.

He spent a long time in his car with my identification while my friend and I stayed relatively calm and soothed one another through the wait. I wanted it to be over so I could get to our friends' house, use the bathroom, and relax together. It was spring break for them. My car's back seat was a mess of things. Yes, people with ADD struggle to keep things tidy, and I was no exception.

The officer had me get out of my car and sign my repair order on the hood of his car. I took the bait, and he started asking me all kinds of questions. He asked if I was smuggling immigrants or had large quantities of cash, weapons, explosives, or contraband literature. I asked him what kind of literature constituted contraband. He then asked, "Well, what do you have?"

I couldn't tell if he was being serious. I was nervous and confused. I didn't realize that what he was doing was a sort of ritual to knock me off my mental footing, hypnotizing me into agreeing that he could look through my car. The weed was in the trunk, and the manual release was broken. Only the key in my pocket could open it, so I felt like it would be safe for him to look through. I said okay.

Another friend had left an apple we smoked out of in the backseat a few nights earlier; it had fallen into the general chaos and clutter that was my backseat, and the officer found it. He cuffed me, took my keys, and pushed me in the back of his cruiser, where I watched him and his partner tear through all my belongings like a few raccoons in the trash.

In the car ride to my overnight in jail, I asked the officer if I could ask him a question. It would probably have been something about if he thought weed was dangerous, if he liked his job, or what he thought happens when we die. I just wanted to talk to someone, and he was the only one there. When I asked him for permission to ask a question, without looking back, he rolled my window down. I didn't have a jacket and it was chilly. He ignored my requests to roll the window up.

I was processed, fingerprinted, and photographed, had my shoes taken away, and was put into a box with ten or so other men where I could finally go to the bathroom with all of them watching, forever curing me of any latent pee-shyness from adolescence. The room we were in was give or take 80 square feet. It was cold.

It amazed me that one system put me into a sealed box for possessing marijuana while another all but forced me to take amphetamines.

Years earlier, I'd taken part in the DARE program, a program where a police officer came into our classroom to tell us about his gun and talk about peer pressure and the inevitability of substances making their way into our lives and that we should avoid them or else we might ruin our lives or go to prison. Their tactic was, "Just say no." It turned out to not be that simple. This police officer was the first person to tell me about psychedelics. He piqued my curiosity. I was nine and on amphetamines.

After the dust settled around my arrest, I hired a helpful lawyer. I had to do a few drug tests and some community service, and it seemed I was back to square one again with my life and its direction. I still wanted to ride my bike across the country. There was still pressure to go to college.

It was decided I would return to Florida for an accelerated bachelor's program. I was drawn to Florida. The heat, the proximity to water, nature, jungles of tropical plants. Fruit was a meal. I could bike everywhere all year and had a magical group of friends I had fallen in with.

———

I SOMETIMES WONDER if beginning to take mind-altering drugs at an early age normalized the idea of mind-altering entirely for me and lessened my trepidation about experimenting with other drugs. The real gateway drug for me was amphetamine.

During this period, between my arrest and going back to school, I tried cocaine, which felt like a poor man's Adderall. I didn't like it. I was waiting for it to start. I didn't get it.

I smoked salvia, a unique hallucinogenic leaf that I wasn't prepared for. It created a powerful, quick experience of demanding and invasive visuals. I experienced bursts of laughter, much like my middle-school expressions that had sent me to the vice principal's office.

I was laughing on the couch. With every chuckle, a beige triangle with a clean black outline exited my mouth, visually representing the sound I was making. The room quickly filled with the triangles, and when I looked at them, I had a humor response and kept laughing. To others, I was a madman on the couch in hysterics.

The first time I experienced psilocybin mushrooms, friends and I walked together in the woods. We had an experience. I walked away with insights and lessons I wanted to integrate into my daily life and into my character moving forward.

I was inspired to steer my life and my attitude toward being better, but

I still had to define "better." I wanted to have a relationship with nature after appreciating it so much. I also tried LSD at a friend's house, and we had a playful day of fun and music. Our intentions always seemed loose. We were mostly after curiosity, fun, and enjoyment.

I was unafraid of letting substances change my state. I was familiar with having a drug take hold of my mind for a little while. I found comfort in the curiosity of allowing drugs into my body and mind to experiment with and learn from.

I had very little fear of taking drugs, but I was selective. I didn't go toward party drugs or hard drugs. I went toward substances that I believed summoned curiosity, learning, and creativity. Psychedelics. I didn't want to leave my mind. I wanted to expand it.

College Again

As I approached twenty, I was still absorbing the world like a sponge while barely contributing a wrung-out drop to the all of humanity. Time spent riding bikes, waiting tables, spending time with friends, making video art, skateboarding, playing guitar, watching cartoons, getting arrested, and watching my friends go to college was foundational but not quite sustainable.

I had been shooting and editing videos as a means of personal expression. I enjoyed editing videos. I didn't really go into any narrative or storytelling, just visuals and sounds. I went to study film-making. I wanted to be an artist.

I invited Adderall back into my life with my reenrollment into higher learning at the third and final institution.

I visited a non-psychiatric doctor who looked at my record and wrote me a prescription that matched my previous dosing exactly. This doesn't appear to be illegal, but it is recommended to receive these medications from a psychiatrist, since they are the experts. I was given the prescriptions. I didn't go in for checkups or anything like that. I wasn't being monitored. This was not normal.

As I went deeper into the world of yoga, clean eating, mindfulness and spirituality, I began telling myself that I needed an "unnatural substance to blend into an unnatural world." The substance was Adderall. I saw it as my bridge from the natural world to the "unnatural world." A world obsessed with productivity, money, cars, time, status, etc.

I went to a school that had campuses divided into shopping centers. The school was more or less a film-making trade school. Attendance was taken twice a class to prove students clocked in the needed hours to graduate. I simply said, "Here," with no limousines. One student had a rock 'n' roll lyric cued up on his laptop and would play "Here I am" every time he was called; it was only funny the first time. The last time did demonstrate a testament to his commitment.

I was interested in becoming a film editor, but as school progressed and I developed a sliver of amphetamine-induced self-confidence and delusions of grandeur, I thought I could do every job and be a one-man film crew.

I got to school a week or two early and was reacquainted with Adderall. I had the same two bottles, one of 20 mg XR pills and another of 20 mg salts (these were to be cut up into halves and quarters). A day would start with a 20 mg XR, and if the day needed to be long, I would take 5 or 10 mg of salt as needed.

The school provided a laptop, which came with music-editing software. For the days leading up to class, I sat in my apartment on Adderall composing wacky Adderall songs. The songs were alright, but the lyrics were either about some desperation for companionship, or unusual stacks of words. I really enjoyed putting the songs together.

It's hard to articulate how satisfying it is to piece things together while on Adderall and how effortless it is to get into the weeds with details and not become overwhelmed. This is where amphetamines really thrive. Ironic how when I was studying music, I kept making videos in my spare time, then when studying film, I kept making music.

When school began, I excelled in classes above and beyond what was necessary. I socially distanced myself from classmates in my acuity, arrogance, and lack of interest in making friends with them. I had a handful of good friends in my class and a group of magical friends outside of school.

The kids at school were energy-drink-consuming, fedora-wearing, sandbag wranglers waiting to live in a LA closet apartment, dying to bring C-list actors a bottle of water and see their name come up on the credits of some billion-dollar caped fantasy. I didn't make more than a handful of friends because of judgmental perspectives like that.

One day while skating, I was flying over a pyramid, two ramps on either side of a flat top. Ramp to ramp, I was jumping over the 8-foot flat, flying off one ramp and landing on the other. I had the control I needed to perform in the palm of my hand. I did it over and over, making it better each time, trying to bend my knee this way, going faster and faster and higher and higher.

I decided to go for a big one and gave a huge push in front of the roll-in ramp for additional speed. I snapped off the ramp, flew over the flat, and cleared most of the landing ramp. With my front wheels on the ground and the back two on the bottom of the ramp, a little kinetic bump popped my back foot off the tail of my board when my back wheels rolled off the ramp.

My right foot stuck on the ramp while everything else went forward, creating an inward ankle roll so intense that it broke my fibula. Weeks later, I removed my cast myself using a hacksaw and pair of snips from the hardware store.

I was the best linear/audio editor in my class, and on multiple occasions, that caused issues. I had been doing this for six years, while most students were just learning. Most of the students wanted to be writers, directors, and cinematographers.

I wanted my strength to be editing. People didn't want their toes stepped on, nor were they impressed with how I could *"improve"* their scripts with editing. Teachers were impressed but classmates voted me "first to be eaten on a desert island." Efficiency and hard work don't invariably yield positive results.

A teacher once came behind my shoulder while I was in the editing suite, meticulously navigating the editing software with precision and grace, lit up by my medication, and quietly asked me, "Do you plan on becoming an editor?"

I replied, "I don't know."

"They could really use you," she said.

I enjoyed editing on Adderall, but I had reservations about sitting in a dark room in front of a computer all day for hours on end, editing mindless mainstream programming. I wanted to make the cool nonobjective video art seen in modern art museums.

Sometimes the days were long. The school operated on a 24-hour schedule. Classes could go until 1:00 a.m., or occasionally lab sessions would be blocked at 1:00 a.m. and 5:00 a.m. Easy work on Adderall. I was used to a skipped night of sleep. There's a funny glow to a day experienced without a night of sleep.

I'd often park my car, rumble the transmission to park, and pull the key out. Without pause, the Florida heat would begin to reverse the air conditioning and toast the inside of my car. I'd open the center console, squeeze and twist the cap open, and let the capsule fall into my palm. A single Adderall XR 20 mg.

I'd pause for a moment, while inside my head a voice would say, "Unnatural solution for an unnatural world." Then my face would take on a posture resembling astonishment as my hand flew toward it, inertia catapulting the amphetamine into my mouth where it stuck to my tongue. I always took them dry. I could hear the light maraca of the small capsules that enabled the time-release effect of this medicine.

I rolled it under my tongue to lubricate it with my saliva, then scooped it back onto my tongue and pushed up against my palette, sending the pill down into the desperate temple that was my body— all in an effort to help me make it through another day in the world I'd come to define as "unnatural."

Then it would begin. Music resounded with clarity in every detail. Perception was clear, crisp, and understood. I knew why good things were created the way they were and felt like I would make those same good choices, given the opportunity.

I felt like I was a creative genius, only lacking opportunity. Unaware of how in my own head I was. Having not yet experienced firsthand the rift between the conception of a creative project and the rare art of completion.

My new obsession became drawing. I drew nonstop, almost always during class. The school gave us all the same laptop. Most all the kids would bring theirs in. I watched them during class. They may have had some notes open, but most of them were twiddling on the internet. I chose to leave my computer in my apartment and bring a notebook and a pencil as my distraction from lectures. I had to be different, had to make a statement.

On Adderall I loved to draw. I drew my teachers and the backs of students in front of me, wildly detailed, superficially crazy, undulating sketches of people morphing, spilling, and exposing their skeletons. I illustrated my notes. I ripped through notebooks and sketchbooks like they were a perishable grocery.

I put a lot of effort into my drawings. They were erratic and detailed and somehow helped me pay attention. I even submitted a large painting to a local cafe's wall, where it was for sale. Standing in line at the cafe, undercover, I asked a student in front of me what he thought the artist was trying to say with that painting. His answer: "The artist was trying to say, 'I know nothing about painting.'"

I had an electric piano in my apartment. One afternoon on Adderall, I picked up some coffee and a coffee machine and brewed a simple drip black coffee in my apartment for the first time. Then I sat at the piano; music started coming out and it wouldn't stop. I could improvise endlessly. I kept drinking coffee.

I may have been successful in the film industry had I been capable of embracing the social aspect of college instead of being off in my own world thinking I alone could do everything. With editing, I stood out. I recorded my own musical scores, went into deep details, dissected the seconds to match the human attention span, guided the viewer, and put in hours.

I used a metronome on my timeline and matched it to suggest heart rates relative to the scene. I watched clips over and over, dissecting the frames between the seconds, making small adjustments until it flowed just right. I used subtle key-framing effects to really shape and direct each component of my work.

I took Adderall regularly, but it didn't seem to pose a problem. I was used to it. I did it in secret like I always had, and it seemed like school was going well and I was having a good time. I had been secretly doing amphetamines since I was seven years old.

It never struck me to tell my teacher, classmates, roommates, or even my girlfriend. School gave usage a purpose and a structure to fall under. I was taking them to do well in school, and I took them before class.

I was losing weight, but to me this felt like an achievement, having struggled with my weight during middle school. I liked that when I rode a bike with no shirt on, no belly fell over my waistline.

I didn't sleep much, but that seemed to be the norm in my environment. I was a try-hard creative and often tumbled down project rabbit holes and never came out with anything whole. Like anything I *almost* did was *almost* meaningless. I would follow my distractions and had a low rate of finishing things compared to starting them.

Even though Dr. Conner told me not to, it was common for me to smoke weed on Adderall and burn the midnight oil, intricately chasing my tail. I think because my intention was to relax and open up on marijuana and to maintain and execute with Adderall, I didn't see it as a problem. Also, it appeared everybody I met smoked marijuana.

I saw myself as my own portrait of an artist as a young man, despite never reading the book. It sat on my shelf, the title alone inspiring me to create without boundary and bring sincere expressions into creative acts in the name of creativity and youth. Nothing about James Joyce's actual story, just taking from the title. I was a young man and I was an artist.

Once, I was working on a school project and I heard a distant, repetitive banging sound in the distance. "*P-ting!*" I knew it was probably some kind of industrial pile-driving hammer doing construction on a distant highway.

Compelled by weed and amphetamines and looking for something to focus on other than the work at hand, I made an unflinching commitment to follow the sound through the woods in a direct line to its source with complete ignorance of the paths. I wanted to see it.

I brought my camera to film whatever it was that was causing this ruckus and my journey to follow it through the woods. I used a wiffle ball bat I found on the ground to push down the overgrown green, chest-high vines and grasses in front of me as I mindlessly marched into the depths. On an adventure to tilt myself toward a colossal machine.

The banging suddenly stopped, and I quickly realized I was completely lost in a thick web of vines, with no idea where anything was and no distant sound to go toward. I'd just wandered around deep in the woods off the path. I was out of water and it was July in Florida. Why was I so impulsive and curious? I was feeling a little nervous.

In my panicked state, I stepped on a rotten log and out flew a collective of hornets who were pretty upset that I'd torn a chunk off of their home. They swarmed my head, but I was strapped to the area by all the vines. I lost my pants in the struggle and ran away, being stung constantly. All I was saying was "No!" over and over.

I eventually balled up and smacked myself wherever I felt a sting. Hornets were stuck in my hair. I slapped my ear as the buzzing of the hornet tangled in my hair inflated my heart rate. I lost my phone, camera, pants, and everything and had to go back to get them. I got more stings and still didn't find everything.

I made it back to my house, dressed in a jumpsuit, wrapped my head in scarves, and returned to the place where I'd been lost in the woods. No longer searching for the source of the distant "*p-ting;*" now, the search was for my belongings.

Mentally, because of the amphetamines, I was often "somewhere else." Friends picked up on some kind of difference. Once, I was describing some situation I had gotten myself into, an altercation at the skatepark earlier that evening.

I'd blown out the crotch of my jeans while not wearing underpants, and stuffed a shirt in my pants to keep from exposing myself. I was excited about telling my story, not listening to how I sounded and how I was being received. I was out of breath from my own words.

My perceptive friend cut me off. "Are you on something?"

I turned silent and took a beat. "No, just, uh, excited," I falsely assured him. Exhaled deeply through nearly closed lips and put on my mask of normalcy until I could be alone with my notebooks, guitars, and computers.

The shame had morphed. I was once ashamed of needing meds because I was learning disabled. Now I was ashamed of taking meds because I felt like they made me extra-abled, and I didn't want anyone to know. I didn't want them to know that I wasn't actually capable of the strenuous effort I exhibited with art, school, and skateboarding.

The relationship with Adderall was getting more serious. I planned my days around when I would be on Adderall and when I wouldn't be. I'd plan to be social when I was off them and productive when I was on them.

Flying Off an SUV

I was doing well in school, and I kept my place clean. I was in a relationship that was going well. I was happy. The present was pleasing and the future seemed ripe with potential. None of my drug use seemed to interfere with my ability to be productive and successful in school; it seemed to enhance it.

I was under an impression that the behaviors and attitudes I now attributed to my daily amphetamine use were just parts of myself that were being unearthed as I came of age. I kept going with it.

One evening, a friend generously gave me a tab of LSD. I put it on my tongue and biked back to my place as it hit.

I was alone. I took a shower and went into my room. Listening to *The Dark Side of the Moon*, I spontaneously wrote an email to the coordination arm of one of the most popular music festivals in the U.S. and landed myself a job at the festival with an all-access media pass.

I stared through my own eyes in the mirror. I drove to my girlfriend's house and left a note on her windshield. I videotaped myself holding a piece of paper that said, "I'm only going to do this once because one day, I'll be too dead to do it." Then I stared at the camera and held a ball of energy about 5–7 inches in front of my chest, feeling the energy of the invisible orb between my hands.

As the morning broke after a restless evening, I biked seventeen miles to where my friend worked at the mall. He told me his cafe had the best french fries. I had the first day of a cinematography class later that afternoon, but I figured this would be a pleasant morning activity. I enjoyed long bike rides.

Biking many miles on acid didn't phase me. Several months prior, my good friend Ed and I rode over a hundred miles together on LSD. We rode for about ten hours in a state of constant movement. A beautiful day of exploring our surroundings and swimming in several pools in several apartment complexes.

While many took LSD and stayed at home with creature comforts, I inclined toward restlessness and sought adventures.

Tripping and sensitive, I could feel people's spirits on the loose, spilling out, turning jagged, as I rode my bike past them.

I saw a lot of things normally seen as nothing. Trash on the ground and the stories it told. Plants and their stories. Every gesture a passerby made seemed to represent their entire being, their entire story. Everything was everywhere, and I was right there along with it. I was talking to my tape recorder in a circular conversation between the divine and man's quest to define it.

I ended up lost. I'd jotted down directions on a piece of paper. Smartphones existed; I just didn't have one. The waitstaff at a lone restaurant helped me get to the mall. I didn't realize I was still tripping until I was faced with the task of human communication.

It was hot and I had no shirt on. Two large bottles of water were arranged like scuba tanks in my backpack, since they'd been on a two-for-one sale at the convenience store.

I was relieved to finally pedal into the oasis that was the mall parking lot. Excited for french fries and seeing my friend, I made a beeline to the entrance, cutting through parking spaces without thinking twice about it.

As I emerged from behind a parked car, I looked to my right into what would have been the left lane of the assumed parkway that exists between the rows of parking spaces and found myself looking squarely at an SUV moving toward me. It was about six feet away. My perception of time decelerated.

I immediately considered every evasion available—braking, turning, jumping off my bike—and realized just as quickly there was no escape. I just had to watch. I was going to make contact. I braced myself.

It was an exact, perpendicular "T-bone." The license plate touched the pedal of my bike. This was happening. I pondered whether I was going under or over the car. My bike and I went our separate ways; as it left me, it went under the car, and I slid up the hood.

I was relieved at that, but then the next obstacle was the glass of the windshield. How would I interact with that? Would I go through it? The waters in my backpack bounced me off the windshield then up and in front of the vehicle, ragdolling me several feet into the air into aerial maneuvers I couldn't keep track of.

If it hadn't been for the waters in my backpack, my spine may have been rearranged.

It wasn't until I was in the air that I could be a bit more contemplative about what was happening. I no longer heard the kinetics of my bike and the car. I saw nothing, as up was down and around. I had absolutely no control over my body.

I thought I was going to die. I'd known it could happen at any moment—now I was in this moment. And for that moment, I felt sad that I was going to die.

It embarrassed me how I'd taken some drugs, hadn't told anyone, stayed up all night, rode my bike, and got myself killed going to get french fries so far away, when there were plenty of french fries near my house. I felt like I had more to do in life and to die would let down those who loved me.

Then a different thought emerged. I remembered it was a beautiful day, and I took that in. I recalled I was doing something I loved to do. I accepted it was okay to die like this. It was as good of a day to die as any other. Then I landed on my feet and somersaulted across the pavement, scraping my bare head and torso.

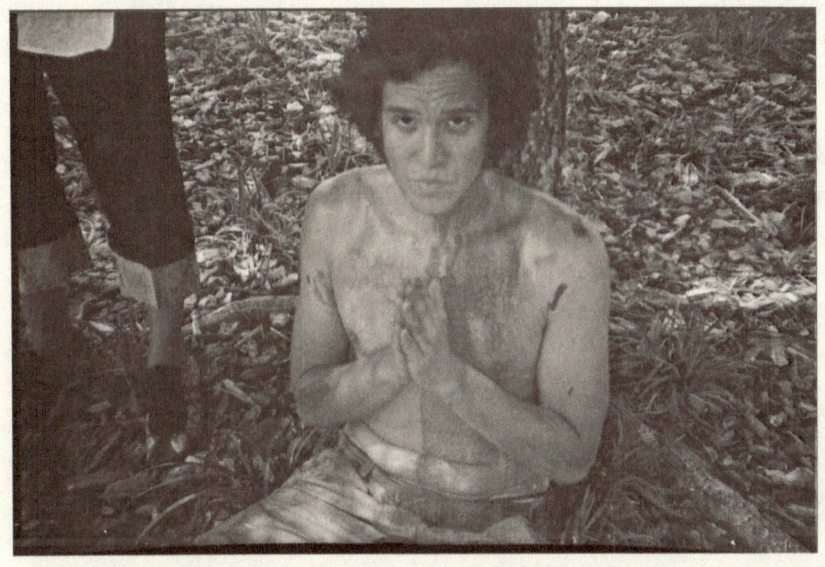

Photo taken by a bystander I handed my camera to.

All those thoughts of life, death, regret, and acceptance turned to memories as adrenaline and lysergic acid diethylamide (LSD) combined to erupt in me, a primal moment in the mall parking lot. Pure adrenaline.

I lifted my mangled bicycle above my head, shook it, screamed to the heavens, and threw it across the parking lot, oscillating in heaving, full-body breaths. I was alive. The driver got out of her car to tell me I was bleeding. I looked into her eyes and told her God was real.

I didn't tell my girlfriend I'd taken acid that day when she picked me up from the hospital. She didn't know I took Adderall, either.

I was already settled into doing drugs secretly. Elementary addict behavior. Behavior I had been participating in since I was a child. I grew up secretly being on drugs, protecting myself from the shame that I apparently needed them.

I was the way I was, but I felt like I achieved myself in a secret way and had to hide it. Amphetamines were a performance enhancement for cognition. I seemed to be a better musician, student, artist, editor, driver, housekeeper, athlete, orator, and more with my meds.

My self-secrecy was airtight. None of my friends except for one knew I took Adderall, and that's because he mentioned he wanted one in passing. I gave him one in a video-editing class and got to watch him go beast-mode in his edit.

Once, on a shoot, I saw someone else take Adderall and pretended I didn't see it. I silently judged them as if I wasn't also on them. I could never say, "Me too, I Adderall all the time." I wanted everyone to believe I was naturally this energetic beam of mental stamina. I wanted to believe it too. I chose to pretend that the high energy, super-focused person I presented as was just who I was.

I usually saw my girlfriend after school, when the Adderall had worn off. It was still in my being, and this wasn't a good foundation for a fair relationship. I was going through something on my own that made me sometimes inaccessible. At the end of the day, I'd be able to land on the lower end of the meds' tapered effect.

On Adderall, I had a different way of going about my interactions with people. I once told my girlfriend that sometimes, I just got "inspired," and needed space to run with the inspiration. I told her that when I was on this scent, she needed to step aside and let me create. I was in a zone.

When embracing this impulse in a group, I inspired others to embrace creative play, pushing the concept of what art was.

There was a special place at this time for being alone in a room in a state of compulsive fidgeting. The object of my tinkering became computer editing software, guitar, drawing, or rearranging all my belongings.

Creative inspiration on Adderall was a false muse.

PROSPECTUS

For our final project before graduation, we were to put together a full-scope production pitch and present it to the teachers as if they were producers at a big production company. It was a role-play called the prospectus.

I was tired of looking for a group to belong to and doing the grunt work. Students had to build their own groups for projects, and even though I was knowledgeable and capable, I felt like I was never recognized or appreciated because I was so unique and creative—when likely it was because I was entitled and arrogant.

I wanted to call the shots for once, so I corralled all the most rugged, offbeat individualists (my friends) of my class and took a position of leadership. I decided the project we would pitch would be a documentary of the cross-country bike trip I'd been dreaming of making since before I was waiting tables.

I'd never dreamed of making a documentary, but that combined my skills with my desires. The pitching went to my head. I'd saved a little money and decided I would make a movie out of my cross-country bike trip and interview as many people as I could about nothing specific. In my mind, this was an altruistic endeavor.

Grandiosity was budding. I was leaning into a position I'd never really occupied preparing for this project. I titled the film *Someone Who Could*.

The explanation was that we can't wait around for someone else; we had to be the someone we were waiting for. Changing the world was about changing the self. Basically my own interpretation of Gandhi's recommendation to "be the change you wish to see in the world." In the prospectus documents, I labeled myself a "potential activist."

I pitched that the documentary I was going to produce would bring people together by displaying the common threads we shared as human beings, as exposed through my interviewing them. I wanted to show how we were all threaded on the same quilt. I thought by capturing potentially moving conversations, I could make a movie that would make the world a better place.

I was a self-righteous, middle-class kid with inherited money who was about to graduate from film school. I was ready to save the world with a documentary where I talked to strangers.

I started making my arrangements. My friend Ed was going to join me for the ride. He was indifferent about the movie but excited about the ride.

I was enthusiastic about picking up trash and throwing it away. I started to always do it. I thought of the title *Someone Who Could* because I felt like I was picking up trash when nobody else *would*. I was someone who *could,* and we all could too.

I talked often of initiating a national trash pickup day where everyone would pick up trash in their neighborhood once a year. The project got to my head. I had some kind of self-importance brewing.

———

Audio transcription of an interview done for the prospectus project:

(Footage shows RL wearing a blue shirt, inside-out, and shorts held around his waist with a shoelace. He is wearing his hair in a back-bun, but his front hairs are just shy of reaching the scrunchy, so he repeatedly grooms them behind his ears. He is sitting in a tree.)

RL: Umm, I'm a film-maker, musician, bicyclist. Let's see. Artist. Things like that. And a young man in the United States of America. And on September 7, 2010, I plan on biking across the country, making a documentary called *Be That Someone*. (Original title before *Someone Who Could.*)

Be That Someone is a representation of, um, a belief I have that sort of can be related to when you see trash on the side of the road, a lot of times people will complain, "I hate this trash." "I wish someone would pick it up." And they don't do anything about it.

And I think a thing we all need to embrace is being that someone who we talk about, who could do all the things that need to get done. 'Cause I know a lot of people who talk about doing things like this but don't actually wanna do it. And, you know, we're gonna make a documentary. Going across the country.

Classmate: Why are you doing this? Uh, what are the benefits?

RL: Well, I wanted to do it for a long time just for the—

(Someone walks by the park with a radio playing music; the classmate attempts to stop them. RL tells them it's okay and dances along in the tree.)

RL: (Laughs) Oh, uh, what were we talking about? What were we talking about?

Classmate: We were talking about why you were making this documentary?

RL: Oh.

Classmate: And what are the benefits of it?

RL: I think, right now, it's more important than ever that, um, every endeavor a human being embarks on needs to better humankind itself. And if I'm a film-maker, I need to make films to make people continue that betterment of human civilization.

So I wanna try to inform people about, you know, what's going on with the environment right now. What we can do to move around without petroleum. What's going on in the Gulf right now. And how we can move forward as a civilization. To make things better. To flourish and do things right. 'Cause we've gone too far, and we need to regress back and use more healthy forms of transportation and ways of living our lives.

It's all too complex and I think there's something we can learn from this.

————

I also just wanted to ride my bike and meet people.

BIKE TRIP

I graduated with a BS in filmmaking in the fall of 2010. I had my degree, connections to work in the industry, a serious relationship, a place to live, friends I loved very much, and some money. It would have been a great opportunity to get to work and start building a reputation in the industry. Start putting down roots.

Yet I continued to pursue my passion of being undecided, impulsive, and persistent without specific destination. I wanted more of something unknown. I thought I deserved fame and recognition. I wanted to be seen. I was a closet narcissist—and with this project, I was coming out. I sometimes lost sight of my reasons for doing things.

I felt like school had been a huge drag, and I was just bursting to explore and be free from schedules, grades, desks, everything. I wanted to ride my bike.

Figuring I only took Adderall for school, I stopped taking it for the bike trip. I'd convinced myself I needed it to get through school. School was the unnatural world. Now that I was going into the natural world, I freed myself to be a natural person.

I conceived this entire project on Adderall. I can't remember really being able to feel the withdrawal much because I was in a unique situation, doing something that required adjusting. I went through withdrawals on stretches of open road. Being outside, pedaling westward all day. It was already a huge transition mentally and physically to bike eight hours a day.

Everything was hard and I was exhausted, but it would have been exhausting and painful with or without being in amphetamine withdrawal.

The plan was to bike across the southern Tier though Florida, Alabama, Louisiana, Texas, New Mexico, Arizona, and California to Los Angeles, then to return to Orlando after my trip. Just a quick trek across the country, and I could settle down afterwards as an award-winning documentarian and retire to my leisure.

It may seem like I was tickled by risk. Truly, I didn't see what I was doing as scary. It was fun. I found comfort in it. I was more frightened of not doing something esoteric or adventurous.

What would have been scarier for me was getting an internship, sucking it up, going to work in the morning, coming home in the evening, working my way up the ranks, being the man on the job, and doing only what I was trained to do.

Instead, I loaded up my bike with racks, packs, a stove, a tent, cameras, a guitar (which was eventually traded for another guitar, a mandolin, and a ukulele), one outfit to bike in, one outfit to hang in, water, and other various sundries. I pushed this bike through my door and pedaled off toward Cocoa Beach, heading east out of Orlando.

Photo by Ralph Giunta

The first day, I went far off the map and ended up at some privately owned property on soft sand that slid my tires in every way but forward. I met a friendly man who told me he would call the police if I headed further down the sand road. He was protecting a large organization's cattle tax write off.

He told me I could make it through to a main road if I forged through an adjacent swamp. Not thinking twice, or even once, I took all my bags off my bike one at a time and tossed them over a metal pipe fence, followed by my bike, then I climbed the fence, put all the bags back on my bike and forged through squishy, wet terrain.

It was hot out, but I could handle some moisture and some mud. I enjoy being tired and dirty and uncomfortable and seem to perpetually train myself to endure things. A quarter of the way across this swampy, isolated landscape, I stopped to get my camera. I realized it was happening —the trip was happening! I should document these things.

But as soon as I stopped my trudge, a constellation of fire ants sunk their teeth or pincers or whatever into my foot. I started to freak out. I took my shoe off and hit it on the frame of my bike with one hand while holding my bike up with the other, then moved away, pushing forward and sinking into the mud. I put my camera away and did not capture this moment for fear of further insect attack.

Catching my breath, I looked around. I saw nothing particular in any direction. I could not see the road I'd been told about, just two hundred meters or so of swamp and the edge of a forest I would walk through next. I remembered about snakes and alligators all of a sudden. I'd seen a water moccasin in the area earlier.

I realized now that I could die. I could be making the wrong choice. I was in charge of this. I was far away from anything or anyone that could help. I was thirsty.

I turned around and packed out as I came in. My pee was turning brown. I ran out of water before entering the mud. I went and snuck around back behind someone's trailer home and filled my water bottle up at their spigot, despite whatever nefarious particles floated in that water. I petted their dog. I had an insight that no matter what you do to change in any significant way, the first day of that change will be a "day one."

I backtracked to a grocery store to regroup, and called my girlfriend on the phone. I was about eleven miles away. She could have come and gotten me home in a half an hour. I could have just said, "Never mind. This is silly."

I was being navigated by a printout from an online bike trail map that was in beta testing. I gave up on the map and got on the highway, which wasn't too bad other than waiting longer than five minutes to cross exit ramps, lots of car exhausts, and having to lift the bike over jersey barriers.

That night, I smoked DMT on the beach. I watched the stars tell me the story they've always told and heard the crashing waves sing the song they've always sung.

It was an adventure. I rode alone to Daytona and got a ride to Saint Augustine. The first few days alone, my body ached at the end and beginning of each day. The first hour of riding was the daily re-lubrication of my joints.

———

I HAD the pleasure of doing the first leg of the trip, from Saint Augustine to Baton Rouge, with my good friend Ed. It was great to ride together, but Ed was not interested in the delays caused by my interviewing every stranger I could. Rightfully so; he had to stand around wasting precious daylight while I was hearing a tear-jerking story outside of a gas station from a woman who had been through everything and more. We had miles to go, and I was slowing us down.

We experienced the generosity and hospitality of good people like I never had before. Giving people the opportunity to do so allowed them to. This helped build kinship in me with all kinds of people, knowing that the best version of all of us is in there. Somewhere. It just takes the right circumstance to get it out.

How people treated me was a reaction to how I showed up to them. This was especially true when holding a video camera and asking about people's fundamental belief systems.

I was out there. The environment of cycling everyday, all day is a liberating and unorthodox lifestyle. I used to imagine Ed and I were lab-rats in a maze, who got out of the maze and began exploring the research facility itself, looking in at other mazes.

Being outside all day showed me how conditioned I was to be always inside. Most of my life had taken place inside, with excursions out. Now it was the other way around. Most of my time was outside, with the exceptions of visiting a home or a business and sleeping in a tent.

In school, and often in work, people are in their homes, then they are outside as they walk to their car, and outside again walking into work or school. They sit in the building and look at some form of rectangle and use their minds and hands to manipulate these things to somehow use the mind to generate productivity. When this is done, they go outside again to go to the car, go home, and go inside between brief moments outside.

We camped as much as possible, carrying all our gear on our bikes and enjoying the sun, the ever-changing scenery, the smells, and the bright glow of freedom. I got to look at a mountain, swim in springs, and cry alone in the desert.

On several occasions, we posted up behind churches and firehouses. Once, after being invited into a church for a service, they placed two chairs in a circle and all laid hands on Ed and I, praying over us for a safe and protected journey across the country.

I kept a journal for parts of the trip, and other than writing down what I was eating, I wrote:

I got a flat X2 and had to bike in the rain to get here, but here we are. Ready to camp. Kittens everywhere who don't want to play. I'm pretty tired and ready to stretch and dream. My interview game needs to be better. I know what I need to do. I'm ready. Let's do this.

I regressed some into distractibility. The trip would've been different had I remained on Adderall. In retrospect, maybe that's the time I should have done so. Maybe then, it wouldn't have been a sober man executing a plan made by a version of himself on an amphetamine.

It would have been a complete strand of intent through conception to completion. If I had Adderalled on the bike trip, the biking, filming, and organization of the trip would have been more linear and efficient, and biking probably would have been more mechanistic.

Adderall gave me a confrontational approach to interviewing, where I was more capable of objectifying my subject and seeing them as generators of content. Off Adderall, I was more insecure and nervous to approach people. I didn't want to be annoying or exploitative.

In my tent, I'd watch the footage of some of my interviews and feel embarrassed about interrupting, one-upping people's stories, replying with "Actually," and so on. These reflections helped me learn to listen by watching video evidence that I was just waiting for my turn to talk.

Ed and I split up in Baton Rouge, LA. I leaned into being a drifter, and if I felt like it, or made friends, I'd just stay in a place for a while, enjoying my freedom. With another party, every logistical decision had to be discussed, argued over, or rejected.

If one of us wanted something the other didn't, we had to present sides, make compromises, and negotiate. There existed two sources of intention on the trail that had to agree. Now that I was alone, I was entitled to follow my whims.

I went around and filmed people, made friends, and just became a temporary fixture in a group of friends. I was offered work, food, and places to stay. I made bonds. I could have ended my trek right there and started a new life in Baton Rouge.

There was a bicycle community as well as drum circles, potlucks, and cuddle puddles where I was embraced and invited to be in a pile of warm bodies just touching each other platonically.

I biked through Louisiana. I slept in my tent, talked to people, and experienced the joy of small towns and the sometimes upsetting social atmosphere of smaller cities where the town seemed to orbit around a Walmart and its parking lot.

I loved being a drifter, seeing all the towns between the cities. It had been in my system since I was a kid; now I was getting it out of there. I was a beautiful bum. I had no job, outside of a loosely defined idea of making a movie about nothing and everything.

I only interviewed people I had the guts to put on the spot. I walked away from many interactions, kicking my own butt for not pulling out my camera.

The day I rolled into Austin, TX, I found a group of people just like me who let me stay in their home. We drank and smoked weed together and biked as a flock and hiked to a watering hole where we jumped off rocks into the water. It was perfect. We dried off in the sun and biked to a place for margaritas and tacos. Everywhere I went, there I was.

I stayed there for weeks. The longer I stayed, the more I dreaded getting back on my bike. It was getting colder too. Every day, I seemed to find something happening on the morrow, and I kept stalling.

I would find little stories, and film interesting people, and learn about their lives and who they were best I could. I picked up every piece of trash I could, and I talked about it and got people to join me. That was a good thing.

I'd tell people, "I'm going to fart, just giving you a heads up. It makes no sense to hold it in. We all do it," and then I'd casually pass gas. I was on a different vibration of interacting in this way. I was spontaneous and wild, yet steadfast and lucid.

I met up with a former classmate to see how his life was going in Austin. We hung out at a river. His friend had a bottle of Adderall and I asked for one. I took it and for the day had a totally different approach toward the film. I went round town and saw myself looking for interview opportunities in the newspaper.

I had the gall to ask my alumni to hold a camera and film me looking through a local city, popping out of an empty planter box, hitting my bike with drumsticks, and other forced filming moments. Without my meds, I was really uncomfortable being the center of attention. I still wanted attention; I just didn't want to ask for it. I was deficit.

I was impulsive but direct when on Adderall. I had to find a story that was interesting. I made a bunch of out-of-my-league phone calls and researched local talent and events that eventually led me to attending a talk with a man who wrote a book against fluoride in drinking water.

We didn't arrange a formal interview, but I caught him after his talk and filmed him outside the auditorium as he was leaving. I learned a lot about the history and chemistry of fluoride in our drinking water. He declined to discuss Annunaki history with me.

My girlfriend visited. She came up the escalator at the airport and said, "Please come home." Our relationship began its descent. Her life back in Orlando and my life in constant motion were carrying each of us in different directions.

I remained in Austin for several more days. Being with myself, being with other strangers. I would go from couch to couch, making friends with all kinds of boys and girls who opened their homes to me, trying to do some dishes or chores as a thank you.

I stayed with a guy who circuit-bent keyboards and kids' toys. He'd crack open these electronic noisemakers and cross the wires to discover new sounds.

He performed his music like this, while his friend performed a puppet show with cutouts on an overhead projector to tell the story of Icarus flying too close to the sun. The same kind my teachers used to write their notes on. I believe his act was called *The Ghost of Electricity*.

It's funny sometimes how I remind myself that everything is going to be okay. Everything will be alright. Like I'm my own baby.

I spent an afternoon with a man who built a cathedral of junk, the largest trash sculpture on earth. I found little gardeners and local musicians. It definitely got weird sometimes, which is what Austin prides itself on.

I met a man who had a museum of peanuts he had carved and who dressed himself up like the "old man in the peanut," showing himself in a peanut if pulled apart just right, including a part called the plumule.

Somehow, I was getting tired of how common the uncommon was becoming.

I left Austin and headed west into what is known as hill country. Prior to Austin, the terrain was flat, and towns with resources could be found every twelve to twenty miles. After Austin, the earth began to swell. There were hills at the feet of mountains beyond. Towns were further apart.

The days felt quieter and I saw fewer people. I talked less. I didn't talk to myself. Sometimes when I spoke a word out loud, it seemed to echo in my head for hours. I took a heroic dose of solitude. A pocket-size black notebook seemed to be where my emotions were released on the trip:

I'm tired of talking to people about me. About them. I'm... tired of traveling?

Yes, I want to get it done. After Austin, it's been hard to find it within to continue properly. Tomorrow will be good. I'll wake up with the dawn. Before they all stretch, I'll be gone...

Waste of time. Waste of money. Waste of food.

The roadsides began to alternate from grass to dirt. The desert was cold and windy at night. I was vegan. I was starting to feel an emotional weight from the suffering of my relationship and blamed myself for it. I blamed my trip and my choice to take it on. I continued westward.

The dialogue headed inwards. I would ride into moments of complete clarity and presence in the space I was in, then moments of overwhelming fear and regret. The quiet of the world was real. All in my head while my enormous thighs spun the gears of my bike. My body was part of a clock that was wound, and the spring would release as I pedaled and moved along.

A flat, endless desert horizon and a few trucks may have been all I saw an entire day. I kept changing cameras and ended up shooting on Hi8 tapes when I found a camcorder at a pawnshop. I would go days without even taking my camera out, despite unique experiences and magnificent landscapes. The trip itself was demanding; it was hard for me to make a film while also pedaling across Texas, living out of my panniers.

I stayed at a commune in a small town in West Texas. It was alluring, a beautiful vestige of construction ingenuity and opportunistic endeavors without a requirement for building permits. I got stuck there like boots in the mud. I got stuck smoking their shitty weed, reading books, trying to astral project at nap time.

I embraced eating outside, using a compost toilet, commingling with train hoppers. I didn't *love* it, but the looming solitude was avoidable here, and I made some friends. We'd work on building structures during the day and all watch videos on the internet together in the evening, which felt familiar enough. I eventually rode off past the Prada store in the middle of the desert.

I slept in a literal ghost town. There was nobody there. Houses, businesses, schools, all empty. It lay just north of Rio Grande, the border of Mexico and the United States. The ground was too dense for me to put in tent stakes, so I placed rocks on the corners of my tent, and the desert wind flapped all night.

I couldn't sleep, as the wind flapped my flaccid tent all over the place. Everything sucked for a while. My first smartphone became an enemy as well as a helper. Solitude was broken with unsatisfying news from back home, and distractions of the internet intruded on my solitude, yet it helped me find the best Tex Mex in the small towns.

I continued to interview store clerks, other wanderers, and people who let me into their lives. The problem was, as soon as the interview was over, they started to really share the special side of themselves. I appreciated them sharing it with me, and I learned and listened, but I would've liked to capture those genuine moments on film.

The quantum element of the camera, the idea of viewers watching, hindered that level of being open. It was the filmed interview that got them to be comfortable with me, then afterwards, we would bond.

At this point in the journey, in the colossal mass of scattered footage, I had a moment where I turned the camera around toward myself, something I was too reverse-pretentious to do for most of the trip, and said, "I don't like myself right now. I have no idea what I'm doing or why I'm doing this. I feel like an idiot. I am an idiot."

I was continually going through extreme highs and lows personally. I hinged a lot of my emotions on my relationship, which was slipping away as I held onto it, gripping it too tightly. I believed I had to give it a shot when I got back to Orlando. I just had to finish the trip and try to have a good time.

And with the advent of independent thought came the threat of internal disassembly. If we manifest fears through our mind, they will be externalized. Likewise with our hopes.

I was regularly in awe of the immaculate beauty surrounding me. Other times, I felt overwhelmed by the space I'd put around myself, the endless expanse I'd pushed out to, the isolation, the regretting of my choice to take this on in the scheme of my life.

I'd had no idea that in the desert, the empty space is practically an object, and it is colossal. Not only that, I was awakened to humanity's ability to hurt itself and its planet. We were suffering as a society, poisoning ourselves with our machines and superficial corporate bullshit.

I believed I was somehow called up to be active in repairing it. I believed I was not a part of this but an observer, and my film would be a canary in the coal mine, destined to illuminate the hearts and minds of the global consciousness to stop watching TV, stop driving cars, pick up trash, stop villainizing each other, stop holding in our body gas, hold hands, and be together.

I thought more about the film's reception and existence as a piece more than I did the piece itself. I would be rewarded and praised for my endeavors and, at times, motivated myself by imagining myself being presented on talk shows, panels, and other media events, talking about what I'd learned by looking at America in the face and passing on a message of hope that would uplift a society as a whole. Putting me in a basket with idealistic types who think their version of truth is more honest than another's.

I started acting this way after the mock production in school, the prospectus. I thought I'd somehow make a bike trip across the country be more than an enjoyable experience.

Having five or six classmates support my vision for two weeks might have made me think I mattered too much. Interviewing strangers was somehow tied into activism of some kind, but it was all in theory. "Someone who could." Party of one.

For one thing, the reality of what came from this trip was the disillusion of these delusions.

Maybe with Adderall, emotions rarely got in the way of productivity. Emotions were illogical. The focus cut through the delays caused by emotional overwhelm. Maybe I would have made the film and made the fame if I'd never stopped taking Adderall. Maybe I'd have been successful in the endeavor if I hadn't cheated and hitchhiked.

Plant thy feet, but dare not move.
Thy firm correctness, exercise and prove.
Fences entangle rams who blindly shove.
Strength fails to force some gates that yield to love.
Thine purpose gained, relax—nor tax thine heart so.
Once tangled, the best chance is to know thou art so.

Things were at their most challenging in El Paso, TX, and I had not yet learned the lesson of pushing through when things were challenging in ways I didn't expect. I skipped it only to learn it later in life.

Someone offered me a ride from El Paso to Phoenix, AZ—and I took it. I skipped the entire state of New Mexico. All the answers that may have lain there, all the interviews of the special people of New Mexico—gone. I chickened out. I succumbed. I still have some regrets about this. I was already there. I should have declined the ride and mounted my bike. Would have been a story perhaps more courageous than vulnerable.

I sometimes still think about flying to El Paso and biking to LA from there. But what would that do now? At that moment in time, that was my opportunity to endure, and I flaked. I didn't summit the mountains. I committed to proving you didn't need a car, then I broke my own rule.

A certain behavior that is more common when I am under the influence of Adderall is a certain moral high ground for a specific thing. In this instance, prior to my trip, I became staunchly against fossil fuels and used a bicycle instead of an automobile. Also, the evangelizing of trash pickup.

I still like to pick up trash, but I don't make a statement about it now. I retrospectively learned that sometimes, committing to an idealistic rule that is hard to follow will put you in a trap, where the only escape is hypocrisy.

I biked for a week or two in Arizona, then a former pro skateboarder offered me a ride to LA, and I took it. I should have enjoyed this. I was young, vibrant, and the days were passing by. I began to be crippled with emotions as my relationship showed signs of falling apart. I had a tendency to measure my value by my relationships; I felt an urge to save mine, so I was hurrying this expedition along.

I was unbalanced. My decision-making was erratic and impulsive. My body strong, my mind exhausted. I was confused and my will was uncertain. Sometimes the difference between ambition and delusion is follow-through.

I didn't do what I set out to do. I told myself, "Well, I traveled. I said I would travel." But that's not true. I said I would *ride my bike*. The point was to prove that cars were bad and people were great. I'd hitchhiked the better part of a third of the trip, which felt like the hallmark behavior of an ADD person. Start everything. Finish nothing.

I'd visualized the moment where I'd drop my bike on the beach and dive into the Pacific. I ended up driving to the ocean. It was raining. I was weighed down by heartache. I was in immaculate physical shape, but I lacked the emotional fitness to do this kind of thing all alone.

Had I been on Adderall, maybe I'd have simply woken up, biked, slept, interviewed everyone I saw, logged footage, eaten when hungry, oiled my chain, packed up belongings efficiently, and planned how much land to cover and where to stay.

Instead, I approached it emotionally. What did I *feel* like doing? Who did I *feel* like talking to? Sometimes I was passive. A ride was offered to me that eliminated weeks of work I'd set out to do, and I shrugged. I bypassed my resistance, telling myself that if they offered it to me, it was meant to be.

I got to Los Angeles, bought legal marijuana, and hung around there for a while. I got a cool new necklace, a native American flute, a new back-pack, and a cardigan sweater I wore relentlessly for the next two years.

I spent my time in LA playing music, going on platonic dates, discussing theology, gardening, reading, riding buses, and interviewing kind strangers who grew into friends. I took trains up the coast. I visited family, friends, and friends of friends.

The day before my flight home to Orlando, the friend of a friend I was staying with in San Francisco gave me a hit of LSD. I took it.

Tripping, I got a tattoo of a cow. I wandered around the city and filmed some of my best footage from the whole trip. I went into people's homes. I was brazen and sincere.

Not everyone wanted to be filmed. The friendliness of the folks of the desert was contrasted by a hostile handshake that wasn't released, alcoholic whispers of incomprehensible threats into my ears. I had to ask myself how much of myself was being shaped by the company I was keeping, and why was I so eager to tell everyone else's story but mine?

The morning of my flight back to Florida, I had a weed cookie. I didn't want to fly with it, but it also felt wrong to throw it out, so I ate it. The THC combined with the acid already working in me, plus sleep deprivation, panic about the uncertainty of my relationship, and the exhaustion of what had been nearly four months of traveling, made an interesting state of being.

A state of pure exhaustion, fear, pride, heartache, and being purely stoned and a touch self-aware of how ridiculous the whole thing was. I was a glossy-eyed bagman. I had been carrying around all my belongings for well over one hundred days. I dragged myself and the backpack I was living out of to the airport at six in the morning.

My intention with taking these substances wasn't all that intentional. I was still curious. I wanted to see what they could do. I wanted to feel good and enjoy myself and... I did. I wanted growth and healing too, but I hadn't really asked for it. Someone once mentioned healing to me when it came to this, and with arrogance, I'd told him I had nothing to heal. I really didn't think I did. He told me everyone does, always.

I was seeking, but I didn't know for what. I was seeking *that*. I was looking everywhere, but I didn't know what I was looking for. It may very well have been right under my nose, behind my eyes, right in front of me, there all along.

As I approached the security checkpoint at the airport, I'm certain my pupils were all that showed through my heavy eyelids. Ripped, heavy-hearted, tripping, worn, and tired. Waiting for the opportunity to collapse into a window seat on a jetliner.

I approached an officer and surrendered two knives, some pepper spray, and some acrylic paint, knowing it was contraband. They pulled me aside for extra questioning. They rummaged through my belongings and asked me why I had the things I had.

I told them I'd biked to California from Florida. One asked why I didn't just fly. Another agent looked through my books and notebooks and asked, "Are you a spiritual person?"

I got on the plane, closed my eyes, and didn't want to experience anything. I didn't feel accomplished. I felt wiped. I fell asleep at takeoff and woke up at landing. My relationship ended at the terminal, and I crashed on my friend's couch.

I was okay but very depressed. Maybe not quite okay. We went to a bar and played pool. It didn't feel like I made it back to anywhere familiar. It felt like what had once been home was now another city I was passing through. I was grateful for my friends.

I had something. I had the film. That's where I would pour out this broken heart. I had no direction in life other than this film. I had idealized it as my path to glory.

I packed a moving truck with my belongings and drove it to my home-town, where I prepared to isolate in a family cabin in the woods and edit my film.

WOODS

I secluded into a refined isolation, stocked with some frozen burritos, juice, fruit, snacks, a fresh bottle of Adderall XR 20 mg, another of 20 mg amphetamine salts to be halved and quartered, a bag of weed, and a bottle of wine.

I was surrounded by a computer, an electric piano, a koto, several guitars, bass, synth toys, all the cameras and footage from the cross-country bicycle trip I'd recently completed, microphones, a toy drum set, long hair, a few pairs of clothes, lots of water, emotional baggage, Wi-Fi internet, and all the free time in the world.

Taken from loose-leaf paper from the cabin:

My life is keeping me from the film.
The film is keeping me from my life.

Adderall amphetamines were back in my life after only a four to five month hiatus. I stayed in the woods, taking my medication for a few months to focus completely on my film and nothing else. Or at least, that's what I thought I would do.

Following my typical pattern, I worked diligently at something adjacent to my primary goal. I recorded an entire album, the soundtrack for my film. I made over-edited video art and dozens of crayon drawings and reached levels of solitude that no person ever needs to experience willingly.

It was quiet save for the sounds of wind passing through winter's barren forest and whatever synth arpeggio I was blasting on a loop.

On the bike trip, I was mostly alone but always meeting people and talking, interacting, and passing through towns and cities. Now, up in the woods, everyone I interacted with was on the internet or my phone, but mostly not there at all.

I went for a stretch of over two weeks where I did not see another person. In a situation like this, coupled with regular amphetamine use, an edge appears beyond the mental horizon, an option of changing sanities. I felt no pressure to cross this barrier. But I saw it and felt it.

I was even sort of proud that, no matter how strange I got, I seemed to keep a footing in reality, even if I was glancing into madness. It was always through a window and not a door. I saw the path that led to insanity, mania, or schizophrenia, gave it a nod, and went on my way. If someone takes enough amphetamines, a door appears. Some people walk through it.

Do I need to write here? Do I need to share my thoughts?
The notebook clearly won't fill itself with nonsense.

I regulated my amphetamine schedule into an "as needed" regimen. I was the one determining this regimen, and sometimes it seemed to be an "as felt like it" schedule.

Perhaps the experience would have been more enlightening than maddening had I not involved amphetamines. But I did. Maybe if it had to be one or the other, I should have geeked on the amphetamines when I hucked myself across the continent, then relaxed in the woods to detox and recover.

I convinced myself I was doing something great. I was working hard and making things, and I thought the spiral I was on was upwards. When I went into town and saw how people looked back at me, I inferred something was wrong. Here in my solitude, the reflection of the self provided by the other faded away, and I found comfort in it.

I found myself in a deep, strange, dark, highly energized but simultaneously productive place of grandiose narcissism polarized by wrenching despair. Most of what I produced was almost meaningless.

I never needed therapy more than then.

I felt lonely. I did the thing I'd been doing during the past few months and grabbed my camera, drove hours into town, got on the DC subway and rode to Washington, DC, then started interviewing strangers. Two friends in a bookstore and some people sitting by a fountain, drinking and discussing life's meaning.

I just wanted to be with people, but I was stuck doing it behind a camera. Asking for mentorship and guidance from anybody who would give me time. Often they saw me as earnest and shared significant morsels of wisdom that guided their lives.

I sat on the footage like a hen on a hardboiled egg. I began to feel bitter, blaming the pursuit of this documentary for my heartbreak.

The more of these deep conversations I'm having, the more it gets blended into one thing.

Nothing is special anymore. It feels like it's rare to hear something I haven't already. Different versions of the same thing. One way or another, we'll all turn out the same. We are all the same.

So why do I need to interview anyone?

I was breaking Dr. Conner's rule again, smoking pot and taking Adderall at the same time. The clock was an irrelevant, ever-changing string of numbers. I worked if I wanted, played if I wanted, ate if I wanted, slept when I was tired, and so on. I had no set structure for the execution of this film project. I just tried to work on it regularly enough to feel like some progress was being made. Somewhere.

Taken from a loose-leaf page from the cabin:

Voice over:

Can a film change the way we behave?

Change the way we think?
Can a film change anything at all?
Do films perpetuate what's already happening?

Here I am in the woods.
Do I want to go backwards? No?
Forwards? Up? Not move at all?
Or do I want to go through it all?

I left Orlando, FL, to bike across the United States of America. My
goal was to interview as many people as possible, seeking to collabo-
rate an illustration of ~~cohesive~~ the connectivity of everyone.

Here goes something.

Can we, as individuals or groups, change anything?

What are we doing?

I barely ate up there. Amphetamines allowed me to maintain fasts and small rations to delay the necessity of driving to town to get food. I couldn't prove you could live without a car. This cynicism of the world reinvigorated the mantra I carried with Adderall, "unnatural solution for an unnatural world."

I drove a borrowed SUV miles and miles to get burritos and supplies. Once, exploring a small town, I found a natural food store that was mostly supplements. I bought a thin book on colostrum and a quartz crystal. I spent an entire day composing a song called "Crystal," staring at it and holding it as I operated a step sequencer and audio editing software. I made a song that I couldn't stop listening to.

When I worked on the documentary, I'd be reminded of my loneliness. I thrived creatively when the nature of the project in front of me gave me light and life, like the crystal song. But the documentary was so personal, and I was suffering with that reverse humility that urged me to remove myself from the story.

Without knowing how to regulate my emotions, they regularly interrupted my productive momentum and commanded my attention. Instead of being an engineer with the footage, story, and editing, I fell victim over and over to being my own witness. I processed feelings through music, art, and videos that were not my film. I'd sit in the snow and stare at the naked trees swaying in the wind.

I didn't really want to work on the movie but felt like, since I'd set out to do so and told everyone about it, I had to endure this, even if it was destroying me. Like the trip I had just taken. I was pushing myself head-first into huge tasks.

A phone game had come out that called players to fling birds at piles of pigs and explosives with a slingshot. It consumed hours of my precious time at the cabin. The medicine doesn't *do* things for you; it changes the way you do things. With no extraneous force or schedule, I binged on this gift of free time. Playing the game on Adderall was immensely stimulating.

A close friend came to visit who wanted to be close and support me. I rudely turned my back on her offering of support. She was trying to help me, and I was just mad that she was interrupting my "work" time.

I was more interested in telling her how miserable I felt. She left, and I didn't even think about how she felt. Having to be there for others was an inconvenience with these pills in my heart. All I was readily available to think about was me and what I could do. How could I excel? How could this interaction with another person be of value to my goals?

I wanted to complain, get high, and tinker with musical equipment. She told me after I apologized years later that I had called and apologized the day after she left the cabin.

I'd been regular with my Adderall use during school. There was a schedule I could align with my usage. I was still mostly following my typical regimen, but maybe more consistently and occasionally speeding up the schedule. I never took more than 40 mg a day, but I might take 20 mg in the morning and 10 mg in the afternoon, and maybe the next morning started at 4:00 a.m. instead of 9:00 a.m. I often slept whenever my body finally demanded it.

Outside of isolation, there were other people in my life and a schedule to create some structure. Up in the woods, there weren't those reminders of the reality of our civilization, so I operated on my own intuitive schedule. I lost touch.

I was devastated by the breakup and there was lots of blame I put on myself that the bike trip was at fault as if it was something I had stumbled into and not something I wanted to do, planned to do, and did.

Taking Adderall made me feel in control and I could control taking the meds, but not exactly how or where they would take me. I was using Adderall to run from my emotions but ended up running into them.

I took Adderall through three days. This meant two consecutive nights without sleep. Waking up in the morning, watching the sunset, watching the sun rise again, seeing it set again, seeing it rise, watching it set one more time, then going to sleep.

On that third day, I drove to meet family for a celebration at a steakhouse. I ordered asparagus and ensured they cooked it in oil, not butter. I talked about who knows what with no inhibitions to my grandparents and family and friends and fell asleep in my parents' basement closet after making dozens of post-it notes and sticking them all over their house with commentary and weird notes.

Taken from a few of those:

Can we all go out for dinner together?
For real?

Can we without talking about my movie, my mood, moving, money, things we need to get done, or even ourselves and each other?

This note?
Is that even possible?

Ice cream
Weasel Sample
Release argonaut

Light manic behavior. I don't remember the dosing, but I can be pretty confident it was more than recommended.

Amphetamine-induced psychosis is real. It's an altered state with psychotic symptoms, namely delusions and hallucinations.[1]

I didn't shower. I was skinny. I was wild. My hair was thinning, along with my body. I found that my propensity to fast and stay awake made two of the most detrimental side effects of Adderall, in my situation, sleep deprivation and nutrient deficiency.

As if to get done in one day what normally takes several, I was living twice as fast, speeding through life faster than the pace of my heartbeats and settings of suns.

On amphetamines, the brain tells the heart to beat faster and raise blood pressure through the overproduction of adrenaline. This affects the entire cardiovascular system, resulting in the hardening of arteries, a sign of aging.[2]

I can't blame it all on the drugs. Amphetamine was just interacting with my personality, despite its influence on my entire development.

I had a glass of pure human energy I could have carefully poured into a creation. My creative hand was shaky, and energy spilled all over the ground into some music here, a splash of painting there, a drop of film-making here, and so on. Furiously spreading my creative energy in no particular direction, landing nowhere near anything fertile. I was loose with intentions. I approached the creative process with too much chance. Something *may* have ended up created.

I needed to heal my heart. I'd never hurt like this. Throw in being a vegan, social isolation, seasonal depression, a brutal winter, the task of editing dozens of hours of footage into a cohesive documentary, and copious amounts of amphetamine use, and it stacked up.

I kept wanting to do everything myself. I wouldn't take any help or support, guidance, or mentorship because I had a grandiosity about myself that I could be my own guide, and the only person who understood me was myself.

The amphetamines have a way of creating euphoria despite external circumstances. Things were not okay at all, but having an artificial feeling of confidence made me settle into the mess and not seek to change what needed to be changed. Euphoria protected me from the reality of my situation.

I hesitate to say I worked hard up there in the cabin. It seems more accurate to say I did a lot. Staying busy, tinkering, and being productive on Adderall is compulsory.

I edited several parts of the film. I made lots of paintings. Some of them were good. I thought of myself as an artist. Sure, I was an artist. But being an artist doesn't mean you don't need to be responsible, reasonable, mature, and disciplined.

Many people bike across the country. Many actually raise money for causes; I crossed paths with them. I wasn't unique for doing this. I didn't even finish it. Maybe it had nothing to do with being on or off meds. It's possible my subconscious sabotaged my film because I was ashamed that I hadn't biked the entire distance. I was hard on myself.

Adderall kept me constantly hopping to new ideas, starting them, discarding them—escaping from one thing to another to keep the brain busy, high on the excitement of newness and beginning.

I began to look down on the use of paper and plastic plates. At gatherings with them, I would have the gall to ask for a plate from the host's collection and promise to wash it when I was done. Yes, it's silly to buy something that we know is destined for the trash. However, there's more value in the courtesy of not being a self-righteous asshole.

If I was one to talk of waste, there was an economy of time and personal energy that I completely trashed. It took a lot of energy to haul across almost the width of my country on a bicycle and film people, tuck myself away in the woods, take lots of Adderall, and invest in art that nobody ever saw.

It's a disservice to society to not finish things you start. Panels of art, dead in a landfill. Footage, vaulted on a hard drive. I didn't do a proper job of bottling all the creative energy I felt like I was channeling. I just spilled it all over the place and let it evaporate in moments rather than mementos.

I couldn't live there forever. No way. Leaving the cabin without a finished film didn't mean I was giving up on my art. I wasn't. I was going to return to Florida, rent a room in a house with friends, and complete the movie there while living and working.

ORLANDO'S MAGIC

I returned to Florida with my pills. This was the first time since before preschool I had no school to look forward to, no cross-country bike rides, no winter of solitude in a cabin.

After twenty-two and a half years, I could finally just be a person without a repetitive schedule, critical performance evaluations, or a giant project. The only jobs I'd had up to this point were retail, camp counselor, food-service, and some construction.

My amphetamine use was still a truth only I knew. Secretly, I took scientific brain candy regularly. I had a few months' supply left from probably a refill before moving down, but my doctor was in Maryland and I was in Florida, so it wasn't always easy to arrange a refill.

I got a job at a local health food grocery store chain. The store was at an out-of-the-box retail site, with high ceiling fluorescent bulbs, linoleum floors, bent steel gondola racks, and elevator music, and was next door to an electric transformer site.

I was blown away by how boring it actually was. Early on, I suspected the electric current was affecting the quality of produce. I was instructed to go around the entire store pushing an empty cart, empty every shelf, wipe down the shelf, and then restock it.

I could see how this activity was giving me a better sense of the store and where everything was, but my mind was racing faster than the things I was doing. I needed something to figure out.

I'd thought it would be easy to work an "easy" job. I developed a tic because I was bored, malnourished, and on speed. I would close my eyes and twitch my neck a few inches to the left. It felt like I was doing it on purpose or out of habit, and I don't know if this is how tics start or what, but it never happened again outside of this brief stint at the store.

I imagined it was the power plant down the street. Maybe Adderall put my mind at some sort of heightened adrenaline, epinephrine-fueled sensory attunement that had me operating on a frequency differing from that of someone who isn't on speed, and the electronic waves interacted with me because I could sense the waves...

This is an example of the thread of subtle paranoia that can develop on Adderall. I suppose you can get there without it as well. For me, it was like this.

My housemates and I hosted lots of parties and get-togethers. I remember at one loud gathering, I felt quietly alone. I froze in emotional overwhelm. I hid in the bushes outside for some peace and quiet and became paralyzed with a traffic jam of emotions. I had to reassimilate into social environments after time in solitude.

Bombarded with anger, regret, jealousy, self-hatred, with amphetamine mental execution, I experienced these emotions going both inward and outward, losing myself in a hyper-analytical experience of painful emotions. Highly stressful. All the while trying to melt them all down into compassion, forgiveness, and some absolution of emotions. But I was wide-eyed laying in the bushes–staring at the sky. I didn't want to be seen. I tried sitting in my room and working on my movie.

An "alone at last" feeling often accompanied my stimulant use. Maybe it was the tendency of the drug for me. Maybe it was that with the heightened cognitive effects, I thrived in a solitary environment. Also, perhaps I enjoyed being alone because I could freely express what I was feeling without masking myself as someone who doesn't take amphetamines. I never masked my ADD, but I masked my full-body amphetamine giddiness.

I WENT OUT and did graffiti at night in some kind of attempt to be heard, rebellious, artistic, and interactive with the world I lived in. I climbed up to a billboard to make a smiley face on the frame of the board. I saw police cars looking around from atop the building with their headlights off.

Someone had probably seen me do it. The billboard had lights. I ran into a school's baseball field and laid in the dugout for about half an hour, my heart beating out of my chest. I used a fat marker to write stream-of-consciousness rants on electrical boxes as I biked around town.

Listening to Michael Jackson's "Beat it," I packed a can of red spray paint into my backpack and biked to an abandoned building on a busy street. This building was two stories and already had lots of graffiti, but everyone else painted from the ground only six to seven feet up at the highest.

I wanted mine to stand out. I climbed up the air conditioning unit to the roof, standing on my bike to get up the first part. Once I had my arms up on the top unit, my bike fell. I knew I had to climb up this now or never, or I could take a nasty fall, and I was all alone. Dangling, I pulled my body up onto the dusty rooftop. I took a moment to soak in what I was doing. It was absolutely thrilling from an adrenaline standpoint. Stupid from others.

I crawled across the flat roof toward the edge of the building. A helicopter flew over. I was wearing a white shirt. I stayed still and acted fast. I crawled right up the edge of the building and hung my arm over the edge and wrote upside down from the top "Can we do this?" Then I quickly climbed down and biked toward home.

I wanted to look at the work before going home, so I turned around and biked back down the street.

A police car pulled me over. I didn't have my lights on. I said they didn't work. They hadn't been. And then they turned right on. He could obviously tell I was up to something. It was past one in the morning on a weekday.

I was out biking with a backpack that held only a can of spray paint. If I did a jumping jack, a middle schooler would have recognized the sound of a spray can. The roof I was just on was disgustingly dirty; my white shirt was tie-dyed in black soot. I looked like a late-night chimney sweep. The officer asked me why I was so dirty. I was trying not to look at the drying paint facing his back.

Thinking fast, I told him that me and my buddy were wrestling in the dirt in his yard cause we were just wild dudes. I also told him I had not been drinking or doing drugs. He asked if I was ever arrested and I told him yes, for weed. He asked how he could know I wasn't high on weed or carrying marijuana.

I explained that after I was arrested, I grew from my mistake, and the corrections I received as punishment were effective and I didn't smoke anymore. I did learn a lot from the experience of arrest. But I still smoked.

He asked for my life story and called for backup, and they stood around waiting for me to make an incriminating verbal mistake. I put my hands in my back pockets while we talked. They had red paint on them, and on top of not wanting to get in trouble for committing crimes, I couldn't let myself provide the satisfaction of letting one of these officers get to use the phrase "red handed."

Photo by Dave Plotkin.

AFTER MORE LEADING QUESTIONS, I finally remembered my rights, asked if I was being detained, turned my lights on, and rode off. Something in me looked past the destruction of property, the obnoxious inserting of my message being more valuable than the existing structures, paint, money, and effort functioning members of society were putting toward this town that were interrupted by my grandiose desire to say, "I was here."

Unsurprisingly, despite being someone who didn't value money, I wasn't making any. I was barely making progress with my movie. I prioritized my own idea of self-development over any kind of career. This is a kind of stagnation. I was having interesting adventures but feeling these had become routine. I felt lonely.

I was surrounded by loving friends but felt that I existed on another side of a wall of behavior because of the things I did alone—taking amphetamines, biking around town, staying up late, doing art projects, dumpster diving, showing up at parties where I knew nobody, and sitting at bars drinking one glass of wine over the course of three hours while sketching and journaling.

The stimulants interacted with my general state in an interesting way. They turned a lower emotion into more profound expressions of themselves. Interest became enthusiasm and then—excitement! While sadness became depression and then despair. It was a roller coaster.

If I was five days on meds and a day off, I would just feel down, slugged out, cynical, and depressed as I crashed into my dysregulated chemistry. Exhausted from going up and down in that whole thing, I was neurologically, cardiovascularly, emotionally, metabolically, and energetically inconsistent.

I got fired from the grocery store for taking pictures of the deli section because I liked the light that came in around late afternoon. I was told that if "corporate" saw that I had a camera in my apron in the back of the store, I'd be in big trouble.

I ran out of Adderall and felt quite depressed. An unexpected part of this depression was how inconvenient my needs felt to others. When I needed help the most, I was most afraid to ask. Not being able to take care of yourself leads you to lean on others for support. Asking for help meant I had to surrender the control I thought I had.

Gratefully, I came across a state change.

SUMMER CAMP

I left Florida again, uncertain if I would return after the summer. I spent a summer teaching photography in a darkroom shed at a summer camp in upstate New York.

Summer camp was a great environment in which to come off Adderall. It's a place you don't have to leave. They make all your meals for you. There is a clear routine laid out for you and a lot of fun young people to cheer you up.

Being chatty and even a little bit flirty came back without Adderall. On the meds, I was *talkative*, which isn't always as conducive to enjoyable dialogue. On the meds, I would often grab someone's attention, but, over time, lose my grip or squeeze too hard.

Off Adderall, I could connect. On the meds, I used other people's attention as a blank sheet of paper to verbally scribble all over. Clear and off Adderall, I listen to others without jutting in with my own stories, perspectives, and commentary. I could actually listen.

I took one Adderall at camp with a co-counselor. She threw it into a blender and made a smoothie. She and I spent hours from evening into the rosy dawn, over-making the props for our kids' play.

I wasn't reminded of the film, my failures, or the uncertain linear progression I was on. I was reading more, drawing, writing, playing guitar, doing pushups, and just being.

I liked myself. I felt good. I felt natural. I felt that fewer people related to my complexities than to my simplicities. I learned that letting go of the self can let others be known to you.

PRESCHOOL

When camp ended, I returned to my parents' house to—of course—finish my masterpiece film.

At the post office, I ran into a childhood friend who worked at a preschool. She thought I should apply to work there as well.

She arranged an interview for me for a teacher's assistant position.

The night before the interview, I went to a concert with a friend and ate a weed cookie. Its effects were mild. Sometimes in these homemade cannabis confections, the concentrations between cookies can vary immensely, depending on the degree to which things are measured and mixed.

The next day, I ate another one before going in to interview for the job. Was this susceptibility to self-sabotage? Did I subconsciously fear that another job would distract me from my "actual" purpose of making a film? I got lost on the drive there. This cookie hit much stronger. I was really late, lost, and accidentally stoned. I thought about turning around and forgetting about it.

I decided to call them up, and if nobody answered, I would just go home. I didn't have it in me to just say I didn't want to do it. But I remembered pre-school and remembered how magical of a time it was and did think it would be fun to draw pictures and sing songs with four year olds.

I thought maybe this would make it so I didn't get the job. They answered the phone and gave me specific directions. It was no issue. I didn't want to do it. I was high. I wanted someone else to cancel it, though. I had to follow through.

Sometimes, I had a way of being weird when I was sober, yet, when I was not, I was *almost* normal, casual, and calm. I figured I didn't really want the job and wasn't qualified, so I would just go in, be high, not get the job, have a weird day and go on living with my parents doing nothing but editing my movie a little bit every now and then.

During the interview, I was asked good questions and I expressed the importance of giving children an opportunity to represent a positive future for all of humanity, how impactful the work was, and so on. I was hired on the spot and in fact was sent into the classroom to meet my four-year-old coworkers.

I was hired on Halloween, and all the kids were dressed up. It was weird being thrown into the classroom in my state. I really hadn't thought I'd meet any kids that day. I was high enough to know it wasn't impossible that the kids were psychic, that with age, many of us degrade these powers and forget about them.

I adjusted my mind forever when I worked with small children, with the intention of making my mind a place where they would be safe to visit were they actually able to read minds. Even if they weren't telepathic, this was of benefit for my well being as well as someone who had to be there for kids. I never went to preschool while stoned again.

As a preschool teacher, I relearned a lot about how other people should be treated, how to share, how to be respectful, and how to play, going back to the basics of being a person in our society. I really enjoyed the job and was fulfilled. I developed a routine.

I was never high again at school, but I rolled a joint often in the morning, then smoked it on my commute home, where I would work every evening on my film. No, that's not true.

I spent several months making a five-foot-tall painting of some cats, a spaceship, Hukwe Zawose, and some other shapes and colors. I worked on the painting almost every night. I loved this painting. I had no discipline and was only willing to focus on whatever I was inspired to do and what aroused me at that exact moment.

I was displaying the ADD they said I had. The fundamental difference between this painting and the ones I'd made on medication was that I returned to it for dozens of sessions. On the meds, it was rare that I would work on something twice. If I didn't finish an idea immediately after its conception, often it was never worked on again.

EUROPE

I took leave from my job as a preschool teacher's assistant. I packed a backpack and got on a flight to Poland, returning to nomadic solitude. I traveled, I visited, I read books on the train.

I spent time in Poland with a young woman who'd worked in the kitchen at the summer camp. I then took a bus to Prague, a plane to Milan, a train to Bologna, had a thirty-minute stop in Florence, and visited Lucca. Then to a train to Rome, a plane to Athens, a plane to Tel Aviv, and a hitchhike to Jerusalem.

This was a foundational trip. I collected on the privilege of being able to travel like this. I slept on people's couches and spare beds and in hostels. I learned the importance of clean and extra socks. I learned how to bind a book.

In Prague, I stayed with two American girls I connected with through a website that facilitated "couch surfing." Whenever I stayed over with these generous sharers of homes, I tried to find some project to offer as courtesy to my hosts, typically housework, chores, or making a meal.

I can't recall their names. They were teaching English or something like that, and they were kind, welcoming, and liked to party. Their flat was not just messy; it was disgusting. Dirty dishes from days of being idle had morsels of food welded onto them through the process of sauce dehydration. Crispy rice from pots had been soaked well beyond necessary. It appeared they would clean and dry a dish as needed from on top of the pile of dishes filling the sink.

On my second evening there, while stretching on the living room floor, I saw a plate underneath the couch with some kind of food item adhered to it. I decided the token of my gratitude for hosting would be to do all the dishes and clean the stove.

I went into their rooms to ask where cleaning supplies were and if they were okay with me doing this. They were happy to have me do the job. They were each in their darkened bedrooms, their upper halves illuminated by the blue-white light of their laptops, just as I've done as I scribed these lines. One of them was binge-watching a popular series about an Italian-American mobster. The other was video-chatting with a friend back home.

I got started. As I took the first steps in what proved to be a lot of work, but gratifying, I realized that while the three of us were all in the same flat, all with our minds intact, doing different things, consuming our personal resource of time and energy—what we were doing dictated exactly nothing about our state. That it was the management of the state that determined how we felt.

I was able to encourage myself to be in a place of true contentment with the dishes. A contentment that would have served me well when I was pot-washer at the summer camp.

When I was at that job, I was juggling personal drama with a late night job and a time of self-medicating with gas station energy pills. Now here I was under no such spell. I was choosing to put myself in a state of complete presence and almost gratitude to be *able* to do dishes.

I realized that how I carried myself dictated how things happened. It didn't have to be the other way. I could be doing anything, whether walking around a foreign city, biking across the country, experiencing heartbreak, watching TV in bed, sitting at a computer writing, or doing the dishes. What I was doing didn't need to determine how I felt.

This wasn't always the easiest thing to embody, and it didn't last forever, but that evening at the sink, the idea remained, and doing hard work was a skill that needed some development. It wasn't pleasurable, but when finished, it was satisfying to reveal an empty sink and an inviting stovetop.

I WALKED around a lot and met people. Traveling alone is a different kind of traveling. I had done it before. I was med free and stable, yet totally ungrounded. I had no plans for my life beyond this trip at the moment I took it. I had nothing really to go back to anywhere. I had achieved this goal of nomadic existence within the paradigm that included airplanes, little money, and sleeping in hospitality.

I made friends and left behind nearly each one. This separation made me start to long to be in one place long enough to develop more meaningful relationships over time. I became adept at saying goodbye.

In Rome, I visited the Pantheon and other places, sometimes taking a guitar with me. I notebooked and listened to music. I was the first American a group of women from Iran had met, and they interviewed me about being American.

I flipped a coin to make the next move and ended up in Athens, Greece. I spent days taking drawing lessons with an eccentric painter, Kyriakos. I have a quote from our conversation in my journal:

"Don't take advice. Never worry about anything. Just act."

A woman my age saw me notebooking and struck up a conversation. Gabriela brought me into her home and showed me how to bind books. When I was in her room, she showed me all her tools, and we each bound a book. She gave me one she'd made. She continuously expressed visible love and affection for her tools, her materials, and her books about crafting.

I was bubbling with inspiration. I wanted to be like this. I wanted a well-arranged work space where I could make objects. I loved my notebooks so much; I was excited to make my own.

Gabriela invited me to come and eat with her family. I was delighted. When her grandmother offered me chicken soup, I ended years of vegetarianism. She had put love in that soup.

Gabriela ignited a creative spark in me to approach this creative destination. Things I wanted that didn't exist could be made by my hands.

In Israel I hung in the city. I picked up window frames and painted on the glass. I cleaned my friends' entire apartment without asking, insulting one of the residents by cleaning his kitchen without permission.

I hitchhiked into the Holy City, where I stayed in a hostel for all pilgrims to speak and interact. There were pilgrims from all over, and the theological discussions of the evenings were lively and seemingly unresolvable.

I was invited to a Rainbow Gathering by a woman I almost ran into while skateboarding down the sidewalk. I hitched to Nazareth and spent several days at the festival. I continued the aimless journeying several days later when I ran into two people I met at the gathering.

I am thirsty. I am awake. I am sitting on a large cube of concrete on the north beach of Israel, a few miles south of Lebanon.

At the Rainbow Gathering I met two American girls I thought I would never see again, Ina and Jana. I found myself sleeping in a triangle with them around a fire on a beach.

My dreams were deep. I don't remember because of the excitement of waking up on the beach. I don't know where we're going. I know where they're going.

There's an Ayahuasca ritual they're attending on the Jordan River in two days. They don't know if I can come as well.

Ina passes me half of her persimmon. I eat the rest. It reminds me of a pumpkin sweet potato orange...

I flew back to Poland and spent a few more days there. I took a final train to Berlin the evening before the day of my flight back to the States.

I arrived in Berlin and had no francs, and all the cash exchanges were closed. I walked around all night until everything opened, from about eleven at night until eight in the morning.

I sat in a train station, trying to meditate. A drunk woman was being forcibly placed on a stretcher. It seemed like a bad night both for the officers and her. I felt the helplessness of not being able to help.

This, and the rest of 3:00 a.m. Berlin at the train/bus station, was hard to tune out. Sitting on a bench, I pulled out a lined notebook I'd bought in Athens. I loved it. The cover was black. It was paperback, with a nice thick, bendable cover and printed lines. I started writing.

There was a boy who was an active child.

I was just having fun recollecting memories and experiences until I came upon second grade. I hadn't really examined the Adderall thing retrospectively. Not from a place of being off of it. It looked different from there. That became this book.

———

REUNITED with my bicycle in Orlando, I rode without haste to an art supplies store. I bought a few essential tools: an awl, a bone folder, and some thread and needles. Then to an office supply store to buy a multicolored stack of construction paper. I made a few sketchbooks with a Coptic binding, using the cardboard they were packaged with as covers. I cherished these books immediately.

I visited Miami to spend time with family members, then flew back to my parents' home. I ran into the same friend who'd provided me with the preschool job, this time at a pharmacy while I was there to develop film. The school needed someone for the summer camp, so I joined the team again. I planned to work on my film despite my dwindling interest as I settled into a more simple life.

I had my computer set up and sometimes poked around at my footage. I mostly spent free time binding books or attempting to blend the peaceful, human sound of a nylon-string guitar with the technological, penetrating pulse of a synthesizer.

My parents left town for a week or so. I had their house to myself, which inspired me to loosen up and get to work on the film for a weekend (really just spent bookbinding). Prior to their leaving, knowing it was coming, I called the doctor I'd approached in the past for Adderall.

I am going to switch to a transliterated journal entry (written on Adderall after successfully obtaining it) to tell this portion of the story. I am submitting it nearly verbatim (with some redactions for anonymity; some removals for the sake of brevity; grammatical corrections for readability; and fact checking for the sake of accuracy, though some factual errors may remain). Allow this part of the story to be told from the past, on Adderall.

ADDERALL RESEARCHES
ITSELF

C irca summer 2012:

Where to look for inspiration?

I guessed first to look up.
But I find I can look at anything and see what it inspires.

The music box.

This is the story of what happens when I take lots of Adderall.

I'm sorry, it's the horrible truth.

On Tuesday, after dropping my parents off at the airport, I'll be left to watch the house and dog, for some reason... reason. I thought I would be more productive and focused on projects if I took Adderall.

Today is Monday and I want to flush them down the toilet. But I don't want to put amphetamines in our gray water.

I left two voicemails at [Redacted] office because at first I left it in the wrong mailbox. I think they called me to let me know...

I got a call on Friday from an assistant at [Redacted], telling me to pick up Adderall prescriptions. I was excited about this and went to pick them up.

While waiting for the prescription at CVS from this really cool guy, Jonathan, at the DRUGSTORE, I walked around a shopping center in Silver Spring and went to Starbucks to get an iced coffee using the $10 gift card my new boss at preschool gave me.

While in line, I met this woman. I wrote about it, I think. I can't find the book these pages are glued in right now, but it's real important that I write this.

Found the pages:

I just took Adderall for the first time in a long time and I would like to talk about my day.

I woke up at 7:30 a.m. in my closet, went downstairs, turned on rubbish on TV, and I think I fell back asleep. I need to do yoga now.

Drove to Silver Spring.

Helped two sixteen year olds pay for fingernails and a sandwich by going to an extra bit of effort to get them this dollar. Hopefully generate generosity.

Tacos, lady in front of me ordered extra rice, both beans, fajita, extra sour cream x 3! Cheese, double chicken.

Starbucks gift card from [Redacted]. Iced black medium. Old lady talked to me about [Redacted] High School. How she worked at [Redacted].

She introduced herself as Ms. [Redacted] and forgot her bag, and a young Pakistani girl reminded her.

I said something like "straws" as the girl and I grabbed straws for our drinks. We sat down and talked together. Her supervisor came in strong with a tuna sub and joined us.

When Ms. [Redacted] came by, she thanked me and told me how nice it was that I talked to her.

I talked with the two women about how the more we are present online, the less present we are in our real lives. Lady left. I talked and talked with Fatima, and we traded phone numbers.

I got the mail, smoked a roach, stacked firewood, and gardened.

A lot of things in my life are floating. And I would like to gain the means to ground them.

Dr. Grossman is partially responsible. I am fully.

Banter. Part of being human.

Sleep now. I am cranky. Why am I awake writing on paper that's just gonna be a fire one day?

Back to to original text:

It really is great to be able to have a genuine, true conversation. Adderall makes me upset about paper and plastic plates and silverware and bottled water.

But also maybe I'm just seeing something I didn't know was there. The Adderall probably wore off. But it lingers. It's made me crave weed.

This isn't who I was meant to be. The chemical extracts the fire in my heart and blasts it into my brain.

I think it makes me kind of crazy, and if I want to focus more strongly, I only need to commit to my body.

Commit to yoga. Commit to meditation. Herbs and teas that may help direct my focus.

Like tea is a calm, natural, lasting, pleasant, satisfying breeze, and Adderall is a tornado. Intense, eye-opening, brain-zapping wilde-beest, ripping through its own time.

On Friday I took Adderall. Monday it should be worn off?

Friday: 20 mg amphetamine salt and 20 mg XR, taken between 3:00 p.m. and 5:00 p.m.

Came home Saturday morning at 7:30. Had trouble sleeping and tossed and turned—sort of eclipsed by my own thoughts.

When I really think about it. This white powder. This pink powder just gushing through my veins... changing my brain?

None of the teas drug you out like this and overpower your living sphere like Adderall does.

It affects 100% of my life.

Sometimes it feels for the best, but there is definitely a better way. No shortcuts. Accept who we are and the conditions pertaining to what we can do about it.

On Friday, I began organizing all my photos into this giant book. I didn't make my film. I didn't take the dog swimming. I looked at all my pictures. I cleaned my living space too.

I slept probably three hours Friday night and had lunch with my grandparents Saturday. I had slept, but I was still "rallin'," as I once called it. Lunch was great; I was all ears.

When I got home, I took a time-released Adderall and played the banjo and learned two songs and a few on guitar too.

These are the times that attract me to the medicine. Creativity just seems to flow.

I don't know how to explain it, but I'm suspecting it makes me a certain kind of crazy.

I had people over on Saturday, and I was really worried about having people over.

Here's what happened. I made plans to come home and stay with the dog. Awesome. I told [Redacted] about this while I was in Miami.

[Redacted] was quick to tell me about toning down on his Zoloft. [Redacted], his friend, and I all talked about prescription drugs.

His friend told me how if she didn't take her pills, she'd be cooped up in her place, locked in some sort of corrupt thinking rhythm that caused her to continuously roll over herself so many times until her brain drifted, and it made her have self-conscious thoughts, condescending her body into lethargy.

That's sort of how I felt Sunday morning after the party. I probably woke up at ten.

I had come out of the Adderall, and maybe I felt sort of hungover, or maybe I'd given myself a coffee headache 'cause I had coffee the day before, so I made coffee in that terrible resource-wasting, laziness-promoting Keurig machine.

I want to talk to Keurig users about why it is bad for all of us. Not like when I say it's a waste of plastic. You don't need to make a reason; it's okay that you have it.

We just might want to agree it's not the way coffee was meant to be prepared, but like Adderall, it's not my fault; it was the doctors, the pharmaceutical company, the Illuminati, the Annunaki, my second grade teacher, and my mom who made me do it.

But not this time.

This time it was all me. I reached out. Justified it as some sort of curiosity that is justified by the fact I hadn't done Adderall in a long time.

So until I put myself into overdrive, I had some food, drank water and that coffee, and lay on the sofa watching a movie.

Jennie came by to pick up her cellphone she'd left at the bonfire party, and I went to the skatepark on Sunday.

I think the Adderall makes my sweat sticky, my mouth dry, my teeth grit. My jaw protrudes out over my rolled upper lip as I look around, flooding my mind with the possibilities of everything around me.

Acting on one here and there, I do things around the house. Art. Music. Cleaning. Writing.

Even now, I feel jacked up. I didn't sleep last night. It was an all-nighter into preschool.

It was the weirdest day at preschool today. All I heard from the other two teachers was "no," and all the kids were saying "no" at the two ladies' rapid, aggressive orders to stop doing things.

Never asking the child why they did it and constantly threatening as well as occasionally isolating the child and humiliating a boy named Nathaniel while I read a story.

Ms. Sok said to be quiet and stay on the white line and sit crisscross applesauce on the rug, while I read over the painful wails of sadness coming across the room from Nathaniel.

The kids rolled on the floor and moved closer to see the pictures, and I took time to show them pictures in the book and let them make comments on the animals, since every page is about different animals.

Phillip lay next to me and was off on another planet while his body acted out what was happening over there on Planet Phillip on the blue rug in the classroom.

I thought to myself, "He's probably getting a more useful education on Planet Phillip than knowing what kind of bird eats what kind of snail here on earth."

But I, too, wish I hadn't forgotten something I'd thought.

There was a volunteer today, Lilly, the twelve-year-old daughter of Lauren, another teacher at school.

She was shy with the kids and Ms. Sok and I.

Ms. Sok was always working on cutting and pasting photos of the kids and giving the photos colored paper borders and taking photos and changing diapers, writing down the kids' favorite animals in a comp book.

She inquisitively went down the white line and asked children what their favorite animal was for masks we were making later. She rushed them to come up with an animal. She never plays.

They'll watch you monkey bad. Pick up the phone or eat some sand-box cake, I'm always the monster. Sometimes, Samantha is the monster too.

What if you can just take Adderall sometimes? Like Jana told me on the beach in Acco, Israel, while we camped on the beach.

She liked doing heroin from time to time to endure the pain of recovery, as some sort of rebirth into life perhaps, or maybe that was just how I saw it.

But I can see that in the abandonment of yourself to a drug, sometimes you leave your body.

But what leaves your body leaves your consciousness with a body, and the energy of the substance replaces you who have left.

I'd like to be more aware of my outer body experiences, but these drugs keep me in my mind and body.

In the warmth and beauty of natural, true honesty there is heart and soul. Mind. Heart. Body. Soul. Angels. Gods. Demons. Urges. Impulses. Reactions.

I believe teaching preschool needs to be about talking to kids. Asking questions.

Never telling them, this is this; this is that, but asking, What is this? Why? Would it? What is that? How come? Why not? Is that something you think is a good idea? How would that make you feel?

I'm in the house alone, and I keep hearing something. I feel tense and scared. I'm gonna check on the dog. He's okay. We're okay.

Today at school, I noticed I was telling kids to sit, like I tell a dog to sit. There's a vibe in here.

I feel like my heart is pumped. He, too, is chasing his tail.

Tonight, driving home from poker night, I thought about Adderall and my social life.

It's immediately affected, and personal conversations can go so awry, and I feel like I'm just... braining out.

Tonight, driving home from poker...

Maybe the sound was the alarm radio that sounded off about ten minutes ago.

I can't stop writing. It's such a release.

Tonight, driving home from poker, I felt the force advising me to flush them. Immediately. Keep the 10 mg salt and XR in your little pants pocket, and flush them all.

When I got home, I greeted the dog and started up the stairs to get the little orange plastic bottles with the plastic white lid that requires the strength to break peanuts to open and see pills.

Today at preschool, I took 10 mg before driving to work, had black tea and apples, and had the other .5 of the tablet and an XR in my little pocket in case I felt like I needed a jet pack to boost me away from the natural gravity of the lack of a good night's sleep.

Food and sleep seem like trivial things while on Adderall. It gives you so much energy that you just don't need food, and sleep feels like a waste of good time.

Sleep is an investment in wellbeing and a preservation of our system. We just seem to need it.

I didn't take Adderall again all day. Just 10 mg at 8:00 a.m. Prob-

ably the dosage and time I take the drug may be not gearing towards the abuse of the substance I have committed. And I do get things done on it.

But like we say in the classroom when we hand out placemats to put on the white line of the blue rug, "You get what you get, and you don't get upset."

Earlier today I said, it's not always about what you do to change, but the thing you stop doing as well.

And then back to the thing you start doing: Stop eating crap. Start eating food. Stop taking Adderall. Start doing yoga. Meditate. Learn how to harness that energy.

From Monday to Friday, I thought about how it was stupid that I asked for Adderall. They called me Tuesday and told me that I could get the script if I came in for a checkup because I hadn't been in a year. When she tried to schedule a checkup, I said I'd call her back.

Saying it was all I did. I figured it was for the best, and it would be better not to take amphetamines in order to edit videos or paint pictures.

But on it, I feel so happy with my drawing, my singing, my dancing, my drumming, my jokes: "Jim was always napping, and he really cherished sleeping; he is very into-resting."

I enjoy the sunrise and the bonfire with friends. I am all over the place socially. Probably talking more than listening.

Having a blast.

It's hard to let go. It makes you feel so good. It connects you to your thought ideas and seems like it makes you achieve very well.

I understand why [Redacted] *doesn't want to stop taking Zoloft. I'm depressed when I come off Adderall, and I combat that with weed.*

Then when the weed literally retards me even more, I could end up taking Adderall and becoming the steam engine worker bee, ignoring phone calls and moving the things on my windowsill or skateboarding.

I have a better understanding of the relationship between a skateboard and a man and the ground on Adderall. Completely evident correlation.

On Adderall, it's a discovery, not a challenge. Yet, I feel like I may not have credit for landing the jumps.

Sure, I landed them; my body performed the motion; but Adderall helped my marionette strings and saw the physics I can't see.

Really, the credit goes to whatever scientist invented Adderall.

When you see monkeys who seem educated and skillful, it is sometimes credited to the trainer.

In the same way, the works I produce on Adderall are using my mind as the brush and amphetamines as paint, the world as my canvas, and the one holding the brush (me and my body and brain system) is [Redacted] *pharmaceuticals.*

Back to Adderall. We can do politics later.

What does he have to do with the salt that makes me Mr. Hyde... a scientist or whatever, and what is happening in the body when I take Adderall?

Let's ask the internet: how did the modern-day archangel of intensive focus, Archangel Adderall, come to appear in the form of salt?

[Redacted] pharmaceuticals created Adderall in 1996. I was eight.

I'm forty-five minutes northeast of my elementary school. It's an hour drive. I can go there; they must pump amphetamines into the gray water at their plant.

I can show them all the art I did on Adderall and say, "Look what you made with my brain!"

They claim to "enable people with life-altering conditions to lead better lives." Now I don't know what's worse, having ADD (which we will talk about later) or being fixated on your product.

Adderall was adapted by [Redacted] pharmaceuticals based on a pill called Obetrol. Obetrol is a stimulant amphetamine that was used as an anorexiant to treat obesity[1] with racemic amphetamine, methamphetamine salts, amphetamine, and a combination of dextroamphetamine saccharate, amphetamine aspartate, dextroamphetamine sulfate, and amphetamine sulfate.

The inactive ingredients are compressible sugar, magnesium stearate, maltodextrin, microcrystalline cellulose, sodium saccharin, and pregelatinized starch.

Clinical Data: Pregnancy category C^2—animal studies show adverse effects on babies.[3] No studies on humans.

We'll get back to what these chemicals do. First, how did Adderall get here?

Come the eighties, the medical community disapproved of the use of amphetamines to treat people who have gotten in a situation where they're too fat. And mind you, it works. I'm practically anorexic on Adderall.

In 1995 they reformulated Obetrol to a combination of dextroam-phetamine sulfate, dextroamphetamine saccharate, amphetamine sulfate, and amphetamine aspartate.

The United States DEA says Adderall is a substance with a high potential for abuse with legitimate and accepted medical uses.

It also has euphoric and stimulating properties and the potential to cause psychological withdrawal symptoms.

It's used for narcolepsy and ADHD. Only legal in USA, Canada, and the UK.[4]

It is a psychostimulant, so it stimulates your psyche. It is in the family with caffeine, nicotine, MDMA, cocaine, yohimbe, to name a few...

So Adderall is a racemic amphetamine aspartate monohydrate.[5] *Racemic is a process of bonding chemicals.*

Amphetamine—phenethylamine—a natural monoamine alkaloid functioning as a neuromodulator or neurotransmitter in the nervous systems of animals.

Normally it passes through us when ingested because MAO (monoamine oxidase) turns it into phenylacetic acid (reduced ammonia in blood).

If paired with an MAO inhibitor, significant concentrations of phenethylamine can reach the brain. The reason phenethylamine is in pills is for stimulation of the brain. This can be found in psyche-delics such as MDMA.

Phenethylamines release norepinephrine, which makes your heart contract at an increased rate. It is a neurotransmitter that causes a synapse allowing neurons to connect and send signals.

Norepinephrine affects the sympathetic neuron system, the fight or flight response. It makes your heart beat faster.

As a hormone, it affects the amygdala, where response and attention is controlled. It increases oxygen to the brain. (Which can also probably be well induced through yoga and breathing.)

As a drug, norepinephrine increases blood pressure and affects quite a few components of the neuron system and nervous system.

It helps in learning by increasing alteration detection rate, seeing possibilities and releasing moments of "unexpected uncertainty."

It is quite miraculous. It affects decision making. A lot. ADD meds seem to share qualities with antidepressants.

The recipe for Adderall is racemic amphetamine aspartate monohydrate, racemic amphetamine sulfate, dextroamphetamine saccharide, and dextroamphetamine sulfate.

Amphetamine is an abbreviation of alpha-methylphenethylamine.

It is also known as "speed."

<u>Known effects:</u>
Hyperactivity, big pupils, decreased blood flow, bloodshot eyes, flushing, restlessness, dry mouth, bruxism (teeth grinding, jaw clenching), headache, tachycardia (faster heart rhythms), bradycardia[6] (slow heart), tachypnea (fast breathing), hypertension (it really fucks with the heart; interesting, because it smothers compassion with thinking), hypotension (faster or slower, it just fucks with your heart), fever, diaphoresis, diarrhea, constipation, blurriness, dizziness, twitching,

insomnia, numbness, palpitations, irregular heartbeats, tremors, tapping of fingers, etc., dry, itchy skin, acne, pallor, convulsions.

In high doses:
Seizure, stroke, coma, heart attack, or the inability to live.

Psychological effects:
Euphoria, anxiety, increased libido, alertness, concentration, energy, self-esteem, self-confidence, sociability, aggression, psychosomatic disorders[7] (which deal with mind over matter—positive thinking areas of thought), psychomotor agitation (which makes you pace around, creating mental tension and anxiety, caused by too much stimulants), said to cause ripping off clothes (which I did... last night), grandiosity—an unrealistic sense of superiority (today I thought it makes me feel "bigger than myself"), a sustained view of oneself as better than others (like not using paper plates), also a sense of uniqueness that those who are in common are few and esoteric. It is narcissism—repetitive and obsessive behaviors, paranoia. In high doses, amphetamine-psychosis.

This is all true. This shit for real makes you crazy. I have felt all of this. All of it.

Lying to myself about myself and now experiencing a relapse in the lie.

Back to the grandiose-idea man, furiously creating obtusely unique pieces of art and media. Scribbling away in a countless barrage of notebooks, researching his own disorder and addiction, and describing it with grandiose metaphors.

Withdrawals:
Mental fatigue, depression, and increased appetite for a few days following occasional use and which can last weeks or months with chronic use.

It's hard every time.

It puts you up on that big cloud and makes you feel like you have such a good grip on things, like you are so connected to all tasks at hand.

Then when it wears off you feel like an idiot.

You can also experience anxiety, agitation, excessive sleep, vivid, lucid dreams (cool), deep REM sleep, and suicidal ideation (thinking about suicide without the intention of fulfilling it).

Which, I must admit, is also true. It's like brain invaders.

FUCK THIS DRUG!

It makes you feel too good! Then, too bad! It makes you think about dying when you stop taking it.

WHAT THE FUCK?

<u>*Side effects:*</u>
Weight loss, addiction... I think I lost five pounds this weekend.

Tolerance is developed rapidly, causing addiction to be accompanied by more and more. Clinical studies show it just makes you crazy.[8] *Psychoamphetamines release dopamine.*

Dopamine is a reward for you. You feel good and accomplished. Good job, you took a pill.

Serotonin too, which brings euphoria and a heightened sense of wellbeing.

It is a fantasy world of the brain. Not only is dopamine released, it causes one to feel hedonistic. Just enjoying life, etc.

They gave amphetamines to soldiers in WWII, during which the British consumed 72,000,000 pills.[9]

It is known to be anti-social.

Jack Kerouac took them. Hunter Thompson took them. Musicians take them too. Professional ones.

Storytime:
Paul Erdős, a well-known mathematician, took amphetamines from ages fifty-eight to eighty-three; he'd previously been a notorious coffee-head.

His friend bet him $500 that he could not go a month without amphetamines, which he did, then gave this remark:

"Before, when I looked at a piece of paper, my mind was filled with ideas. Now all I see is a blank piece of paper."

On Adderall, paper and pen together are a doorway into a universe of discovery.

Racemic amphetamine aspartate monohydrate: Amino acid transmitter that opens an extra channel of physiological processes and affects pathological processes.

Aspartate, or aspartic acid, can also be found in: sprouting seeds, oat flakes, avocado, asparagus, sugar, beets, aspartame.

Racemic amphetamine aspartate monohydrate: indicates water.

Dextroamphetamine is 75% of Adderall. It's given to HIV+ patients experiencing fatigue and depression.[10] *It has mostly the same effects as amphetamines, with added psychological excessive feelings of power and invincibility (why it's given to soldiers).*

How to wean off Adderall:
_20 mg, 20 mg, 15 mg, 15 mg, 10 mg, 10 mg, 7.5 mg, 7.5 mg, 5 mg,_
_5 mg, 2.5 mg, 2.5 mg 1.25 mg, 1.25 mg, 0 mg._

Herbs for focus:

- _Ginkgo biloba—memory retention, concentration and cognition_
- _Hyoscyamus—relieves restlessness_
- _Valerian tea—helps you sleep_
- _St. John's wort—keeps you from being depressed_
- _Eucalyptus_
- _Rosemary_
- _Omega 3s_
- _Probiotics_

Eliminate dairy, wheat, corn, yeast, soy, citrus, eggs, chocolate,
peanuts, and artificial colors and preservatives

———

offer healing
healing is togetherness
healing you is healing me
understand and see
feel it
go through
don't take your time, share it
this is it
no more waiting
the noise heals
the light heals
the earth heals
the sky heals
screaming loudly heals
crying and laughing
sitting and walking

Hocus Focus

lying and being
speaking and saying
it's all the same
we're little parts of something
the wind is glass
and it gently refracts
bits and particles
giving us a slide show
of a moment's pass
we are allowed freestyle with interaction
all is possible
choices are responsible
for our situations
and everything matters
and you'll always be okay
we rip off plants' branches sometimes
to guide their growth.

FULLY IN

I was now familiar with the risk I was taking. Even after the Adderall-fueled excavation of the rabbit hole I had dug myself into, my desire for taking Adderall scaffolded a habit that would be the substrate of my addiction. I did all this privately without supervision, and I leaned in a little too hard. It felt like a reunion with an old friend with lots of catching up to do.

I talked myself out of flushing them. A deep part of me knew that was what I should have done. I had put it in ink on paper, but I wasn't strong enough.

I just kept taking them. I obsessively organized my photo collection into categories and put the photos into a folder for a photo book for years to come.

I always found time to *start* new projects on Adderall, but if they couldn't be finished on that first dose, completion was a figment of my imagination; as more ideas flowed, their conception was a higher priority than that of visiting old ideas. That's where bookbinding really worked. A book can take anywhere from fifteen minutes to two hours to make. That's a project that can be finished with this all-in-one-go approach to craft.

With the meds in the system, time felt abundant. Like there is an eternity at your disposal with enough time to spend on any one thing. No such thing as a waste of time. You can go deeper, you can let go, you can follow your whim into the sunrise.

You join a lacrosse team, go for a bike trip, start a YouTube channel, organize your room, learn a new song, do all your homework—whatever the impulse or new idea, I was committed to it completely. I executed with vigor and excitement, but follow-through was not a guarantee. The interruptions of hunger, boredom, sleep, or other distractions dissolved when amphetamines were in my life.

I went on that date with Fatima, the young lady I'd met at the coffee shop. When I met her at the cafe, it was while the pharmacist was preparing my pills, the last ten minutes I was amphetamine-free. She was interested in spending time with me and offered up an opportunity to meet up, insisting I take her number.

I was on Adderall during our date, and my ego was tripping and falling. I couldn't stop talking. On Adderall, words just felt so good coming out of the brain and through the mouth. It was intellectual self-pleasure. I ignored her while I told her all about me and what I thought was interesting.

We went for a stroll after dinner and I boldly reached out and held her hand. She put my hand back on my body and told me not to make this any more awkward than it already was. Up until then, I'd thought it was going great.

I avoided being on Adderall whenever I went back to work at preschool. Besides weakening my ability to connect with the children, that day, I drove to preschool after three hours of sleep. I'd taken a small dose of Adderall before going in and thought I put a half of a tablet in my small jeans pocket, the little one that's there to hide drugs in.

While I was sitting in the car's bucket seat that morning, the pill must have rolled out of my little pocket into the canyon between the seat adjustment rails and the center console.

While I was with the kids, playing on the floor, I checked on it by putting two fingers in the pocket and felt its absence. I went to the bathroom and examined my pocket a little more closely and, without hesitation, left the building and power walked to my car to look in the spot I knew gravity would have had it fall to. Thank goodness I found it right away.

My immediate thought upon realizing it was lost was that my recklessness, my fixation on these pills, could have led to a child inadvertently taking amphetamines. I tried to relax, but I was so disappointed with myself that I created stricter rules and protections about how I showed up in a building full of kids. I left the pill in the console. I took a serious exhale. I recognized the danger I presented and felt gratitude, shame, and relief.

When someone is taking drugs, the habit can, and will, in ways big and small, touch every element of the user's life.

I knew from my research that what I was doing to myself was dangerous. It didn't stop me. Maybe I saw it as some sort of sacrifice for my work. I didn't want to bring anyone else on the ride with me. I didn't even want anyone to know.

I was willing to burn myself out for art, exploration, curiosity, and fun. I didn't think about the problem, even though I was aware of it. Hoping somehow things would just work themselves out, I continued taking them.

I felt activated. Mentally attuned, efficient, and effective. I felt great working all day and often all night. I kept myself busy.

When I came home from work, I'd take my medicine, then bind books, make art, play music, organize my room, make a mess, clean my room again, watch movies in the background, smoke joints, and think about editing my movie.

I was still on my normal dosing, a 20 mg XR in the morning and occasionally 5–10 mg of amphetamine salt later in the day if I didn't work at the school. This was the most common way I would take it. Occasionally, I'd find myself awake beyond twenty-four hours.

I recalled my tendencies from the cabin and took them "as needed," sometimes having several days between doses. I wasn't strict or regimented. They were just at my disposal.

Everything seemed possible and achievable, with a renewed sense of heightened productivity. I committed to bookbinding with the same conviction I had devoted to my other creative endeavors.

In my mind, I impressed everyone with my work ethic, electric candor, and interesting lifestyle. I got enough positive feedback to believe this was a good thing. Doubts and fears about being on Adderall were subdued by my enthusiasm toward this new craft.

When it came to my film, I tended to make the process more chaotic and complicated. I just needed to draft an outline, follow a schedule, and tell a story. But I obsessed over small details—the soundtrack, the color correction, making it weird and keeping myself out of it to let the footage tell a story without being involved in my own story. I wanted so badly for it to be mysterious.

I sent my film to the Sundance Film Festival. It wasn't ready, but I thought there was an infinitesimal chance it could speak to someone as avant-garde. I had title slates at parts, excusing some of the unfinished film, saying, "This part still needs some editing," or "Soundtrack being composed." I couldn't burn a DVD properly until right up to the deadline. I hired a courier service that showed up at my parents' house, took the DVD, and delivered it to Utah.

Someone had to have watched it. I had an unbalanced idea of the self-help kind of "leap and the net will appear" perspective. I believed I could get into the Sundance Film Festival with my self-absorbed "make the world better," naïve, middle-class-altruistic, bike-trip, useless-film-degree, mid-20s-deadbeat entitlement.

They're not just dreams if you're making them happen.

The world is your world.

Sometimes you go off in your own world and it gets caught up in
itself
and I can't find home in a brick box and there's no love in the
refrigerator.

The Hail Mary to Sundance fell out of bounds, and I think having sent it somewhere made me feel like it was done. I had tried. Now, I could forget about finishing it.

I was bothered occasionally by it not being done and would pull it up a few more times but with lessening enthusiasm—till now, where I have no clue where a DVD of it is. It's on a hard drive in the attic. The digital file that at one time held the fate of my future is now an untouched collection of zeros and ones.

BOOKBINDING

Patterns repeat themselves. Supplied with Adderall, I moved back to Orlando, Florida, ambitious to bind books professionally. I arrived with a bicycle, a footlocker filled with art supplies, musical instruments, the burdensome computer that held my film, some clothes, cameras, special rocks, and so on.

I took residence in a house full of complete friendship, love, laughter, support, gardening, food, music, dancing, togetherness, and growth. A light that still and forever shines.

I stood at my desk in the corner of my room. Two windows on each wall looked out at the intersection of two streets. We lived on a busy corner that had a traffic light. Bypassing folks on foot and bicycle could hear my music if the window was open, maybe even catch a glimpse of me working in my room. A combination of dancing and crafting as I stood at my desk, spinning a bone folder in my hand, creasing archival paper into stacks of folded pages.

I could be seen putting down the bone folder and grabbing an awl, using a paper template to place perfectly spaced holes into folded pages (folios) grouped into stacks (signatures), then tying them together with each other and two covers made of hardboard with fabrics and papers glued onto them in a distinct pattern.

Bound in the fashion of the Coptic Bible, the oldest book in human possession, this was the perfect bind for a book to lay completely flat—great for journals, as they can be used on both left and right sides with ease.

I wore colorful Hawaiian shirts, Ghanaian fabric shorts, and cotton shoes from the import store; the cotton soles helped me slide my feet on the hardwood floors. I dressed like I had a prescription for color. I moved like hot steam, my entire being a fluid wave of the body, expressing the mind for the sake of artistic creation. At the final edge of my movements, my fingers crafted empty journals.

I slept on a twin-sized piece of foam, with a single pillow, a sheet, and a blanket my grandma had crocheted. During the day, when making books and doing art, I leaned my bed against the wall and turned my bedroom into a studio. I built an organization system for my tools and surrounded myself with thousands of various paper items.

It was a control room connected to a portal of creative works, where I stood at the gate and ushered in notebooks out of the mixed paper recycling environment I'd created. It wasn't uncommon that when I finally crashed into bed, I would prick myself with an errant needle or scissor that had found its way into my unkempt mattress on the floor.

Music or movies would play all day on a laptop in the background while I manipulated the materials around me into one-of-a-kind journals with mechanistic, Adderall-fueled precision.

Small bits of chaos surrounded my hands. Little polygons of paper on the waste end of the scissors fell into mounds around my feet. My business was called "Hand Bounds Books." I cut my business cards from large sheets of home-marbled paper stamped with my logo.

The books were beautiful. Scattered into them, I hid beautiful paper, magazine clippings, flyers, cutouts from optical illusion books, and Hubble space photos. I obsessively created collages, using watercolors, pen and inks, homemade paper, origami, and other paper crafts.

The designs went beyond utility. I valued the exploration of creative expression I experienced in bookmaking more than the books themselves. I priced them negligently and sold nearly every last one throughout my bookmaking career. I charged $20 for something that could have been part of a really nice art exhibit had I kept every single one.

I was so desperate for validation and admiration that the fact someone liked the books made me fulfilled. They sit on Florida shelves in the homes of many special folks who crossed my path. I rarely made the same one twice.

I spent hours going out, buying materials, developing skills, making designs, secretly taking Adderall, and standing at my desk cutting, folding, gluing, and stitching empty books together. Locked into an amphetamine-driven craft wave. I was able to seamlessly execute tasks one after the other in a sequence to produce a binary outcome. Results-oriented working by way of process. Taking what was already there in the world and changing it simply by interacting with it.

Previously, I'd approached these creative endeavors subjectively. My film, for example. I just *went*. Films could and probably should be produced in a process similar to the way I made my books:

- Know what you're making before you begin
- Clean and organize the workspace
- Gather and sort the materials (raw footage, paper)
- Organize the materials and tools
- Trim material into manageable pieces
- Arrange in a congruent order
- Fasten them together consistently
- Embellish when function is achieved
- Only do one step at a time, and foresee and prepare for coming steps

When creating music, film, writing, or drawing, my approach was rooted in free association. I could proficiently operate an instrument. I created tunes but didn't have anything structured that I could play for you.

Even when I recorded music on the computer, I lacked plans or vision. I just perpetually saw what happened as I tinkered. I didn't have a song; I just played. Same with film and art. I had a unique way of noodling through all these skills. I was always a jammer, never in on a session.

Until the book binding. Rather than allowing my creativity to determine my process, the process created a structured place for my creative choices to be organized. It differed from art for its own sake—it was artisanal.

The covers were often wild collages or sometimes very special geometric fabric collages. Sometimes, I'd find antique books with beautiful covers, rip out the pages, fill the book with empty pages, add a back-pocket and sometimes an elastic closure or a bookmark, and sell it for the price of a hotdog and a beer. I also made paperback covers for the discarded text to retain the integrity of the original book I had dismantled.

Paper marbling is a mesmerizing, visually kinetic technique that creates interweaving, non-objective interactions of colors and shapes. I marbled paper to keep as a resource for the inside page of books, covers, postcards, letters, etc.

Marbling paper is a technique where ink is floated on top of a liquid, swirled around to make an image, and then transferred to a sheet. When I mixed the bath to make the viscous liquid that the ink sat on, I tried to use it all up in one sitting, since used "size," as it is called, is just a mess.

I had marbling days, spending eight to ten hours transferring liquid swirls onto paper. I'd take the paper outside and spray it with an alum and water mixture that provided adhesion between the swirled ink and the paper. I then took inks and squirted them on top of this thick water.

I used needles to drag colors into one another, using drips and a needle to make images, and when I saw something I liked, I'd lay a sheet of paper down, transfer the image, walk to the bathroom on a towel-laid path to collect the drippings, wash the page in the sink, then return to my bedroom studio and clothespin it on lines of twine tied to window lock handles. Laid out towels and drop cloths on the floor would collect the inky water drips.

I marbled hundreds of sheets of paper. Swirls of color in psychedelic mesmerization. I loved the process of standing over an ever-changing tray of color. I loved colors—all of them at the same time. I had dozens of little ink bottles I'd choose from to drop ink onto the methylcellulose bath.

I got to interact with it by using a small needle tool, a comb, and a straw. I pushed and swirled blobs of color in a gelatinous, manipulative state, communicating through the portal to reach an agreement from this higher place as to when to put the paper on the size.

Once I saw something in the tray I liked to look at, I laid a sheet of paper carefully on the size and reveled in the magic when I washed off the inky goop to see how it looked.

I sold the papers. I helped people at my booth at the markets to marble with me and take home their own piece for a few dollars. For one custom order, I made a huge book with a 16-inch spine, every page marbled on both sides. The buyer had it made custom so he could fill it with letters and drawings for his child who lived away from him with the mother. I was so excited to deliver it that I didn't even take a picture of it.

———

I DIDN'T WANT to be alone all the time, but Adderall made me really prioritize alone time because I operated at a different life pace. The idea of dating was nice, but the feeling of "alone at last" was entrapping. The medicine made me seek solitude. The amphetamine habit put me so much in my head that I didn't pick up on social cues.

There was a noticeable difference in the way people reacted to me socially on Adderall as well. My "vibe" was unpredictable and, at times, off. Yet sometimes, I was like a creative zenith, inspiring others and giving them some of my energy to feed off of. I was into dancing. I'd dance, and others would join in. In a way, I was an antisocial life of the party.

Even when a particular young woman was interested in spending time with me and I in her, the disruption of the Adderall in me made me blunder. She wanted to come over for a private marbling session; I experienced reality in such a different way than her. Things just couldn't work out.

Maybe she needed me to just be, and all I wanted to do was instruct her how to marble and in the nuances of marbling and show her that not only could you marble with ink but I'd found that ammonia, isopropyl alcohol, and hydrogen peroxide all influenced the movement of ink on the size bath, and you could use it to control the image.

She sent all kinds of hints. In my mind, if I could do the job well, she'd be impressed and then maybe she would like me. In reality, she just needed to be seen.

I couldn't spend casual time with others without analyzing everything or becoming the life of the party by parodying the behaviors expected at parties. I very well understood how *things* work on Adderall, but people aren't things.

Failing desperately at life, it seemed, in the cracks of time between this and that, there was a sadness. I was full of ideas. I believed I was peaking, physically. My beautiful hair was having its last expression before amphetamine, malnourishment, sleep deprivation, extreme stress, and, of course, genetics all conspired to extend my forehead backwards.

I also believed I had a superb physique because I was skinny. I was significantly underweight. My ribs were visible. I probably ate a small bowl of food every day, lots of fruit, and sometimes binged at night when the drugs wore off if I didn't just go to sleep. Sometimes, I biked to eat any fast food that was available, despite my dietary virtues.

JOURNALS

On Adderall, journaling was a release, one of my favorite things to do. An empty page is a place for ideas and the mind to see themselves. It wasn't just "writing what was on my mind." It was casting a net into the great ocean of ideas. There was great joy in bringing them in.

Notebook transcriptions from Summer 2012:

I like how at restaurants they give you a light piece of paper to rub on your grubby face.

What is. How does it feel to think so many people are crazy?

The blinking, seat-changing, strange-mannerismed mad woman is crazy? No. You don't know them at all. You've been far crazier than blinking. Is she crazy too? Maybe we could exchange recipes.

I'm in a cafe with three women all eating at once. 64, 32, 36.[1]

It's do this thing to that thing.
Verb, verb, verbing, always verbs. Be a noun that verbs. Be a verb

173

that nouns. Send signals made of a reflection of the signals you receive.

Choose mindfully.

Signals you allow into your system TV screen.

People biking

Lactic
Elastic
Carbon
Bread
Weet weet sugar
Water water sun
The godly hand of man
Giving it the name of love
Elegant wires
Smooth travel across
Pieces
Heart heat
Beat feel
Electric snowbird catcher
Elfish airborne spirit particles
Reflexive diffusion separate
Adhesion. Radical cohesion.

Supplementary exhibition
Elevated ideas personal description.

So what, and what are you bringing?
Is it vegan?

Children mining for lithium. Small hands. Big eyes.

Dark tunnels. White sands. Scatter spread the liquid light into.

In two.

Unearth wish a waterfall pen. Enable laughter with a swing of the hip.

Agree with your camera. Believe in the hype. Believe because you can drink water to stay cool. Make money so you can release it. Enable plants. Plant heirloom watermelons. Sweep the floor. Take it easy with bookbinding. Do all the chores. Get a job. Let the world spin. Sleep is the cure for darkness.

Completeness is a division.
Division is a separation. To be separate is to observe and be observed. Making a to-do list is a lot easier than doing a to-do list.

Blind dates with eyes wide open.
She's been nudging her husband all day.

DISHED OUT

Journal entry from 2012:

In radios make something of this blue light face culture anonymous.

Street people and urban creatures and the concrete aura system, belligerent expressions, dotted lines, connecting our dots with your dots.

Elevators. Bicycles, robots, birth control, popcorn ceilings, backpacks, the virgin Mary, double exposure, water, colors, mayhem, beautiful, puffy clouds, board games, swords, iPods, dildos, yo-yos, knickknacks, doodads and chachkas, jazz, Facebook, fingerprint protected diaries, elevator music, pyramids made of apples, high heel echoes, helicopters, 2-party systems, 12-step programs, church and state, eggs, grits, waffles, peanut butter, bread, honey, and sesame seeds.

I interviewed for a back-of-house position at a freshly opened fine dining establishment. I took a shower, shaved my stubble, put on a brown flannel print shirt with a collar and buttons, and biked to the cafe. I got along with the woman who was the head chef and owner.

I was given a meal. The cucumber mint water was refreshing. The interior was beautifully designed with pallet wood, reclaimed beam wine racks, and a wall of air-plants. I was reunited with my previous station. Washing dishes. I'd previously failed; now I had an opportunity to redeem myself.

The first night, I rode my bike there at around dusk. It was a beautiful ride to a promenade of high-end boutiques and restaurants. I loved the roll of the gaps in the bricks against my bike tires, the fun of the unexpected bumps and humps in the brick road, and the special treat of riding around a large lake in a wealthy neighborhood on my way there.

It was a slow night. The owner and I shared our life stories with one another, just the two of us in the kitchen, drinking and eating together. We bonded. My friends came in to support me. What great friends, showing support for me getting a job as a dishwasher. I loved them for that. I waved through the porthole window. I was soaking wet. I hadn't yet learned to carry myself dry in the dish space.

There was no dishwashing machine, just me and three sinks. When a dish was bussed in, it was emptied into a trashcan, either by me or a server, then either placed in the wash sink or an adjacent bin on a stainless steel table to my left. Washed by hand, placed into the rinse sink to remove soap, then placed into the sanitize sink to kill all the living things on the plate.

My scent was a curious combination of food scraps, soap, and bleach. I smoked a joint on the ride home, passing through a chorus of frogs and crickets.

Next shift was a hectic Saturday lunch. It was rough. A sous chef, Hillary, who was also new, immediately began to show me disrespect. She was fresh out of the CIA (Culinary Institute of America).

I endured a day of abuse while also being overwhelmed by a flow of dishes that came in faster than I could clean them. Hillary made food for everyone—some off-menu thing she'd learned in school. When I went for some, she told me the dishwashers didn't get any. She wasn't kidding. I didn't fight. I just did the dishes.

I ate bussed food that looked good when it came back. I looked out the porthole and saw where it came from. They seemed like fine people to share a meal with. Especially fries. Who wouldn't share some fries? Yucca fries with garlic aioli.

Not only was I splashing in mucky water, trying to wash myself out of a swamp of used plates, cutlery, and cookware, I was suddenly dumped on with emotions about my entire life placement, situation, and decisions (or lack thereof) that had put me where I was in space and time.

Over the course of fifteen years, this drug that was intended to help me keep up at school, be less disruptive, and ultimately be the stilts upon which I would stand to be at eye level with success had turned me into a dishwasher.

I needed a moment, but the entire staff was sharing a collective panic consciousness. I was also feeling the fear that the restaurant was going to crumble under pressure. Every human element in the building was going at full capacity. I was too, but it was all new and I was colliding with this emotional weight distributing itself all over my body.

Dishes kept stacking up. I wasn't even in the infant stage of my priority systems to sort between beverage, dish, cutlery, and cookware. It was a mess. I burned my hand on a hot pan handle that melted through a plastic bin. Servers needed cups, runners needed plates, cooks needed pans and tongs. My burnt hand was chemically re-burnt every time I reached into the sanitized compartment to get a clean dish.

I was down on myself some for being a dishwasher, but what made it even worse was how hard it was for me to do a good job.

A positive outlook was not accessible by asking for one. I couldn't conjure the peace I'd felt doing dishes in the Prague flat. People were yelling at me; things were piling up. The dishes all got clean as the lunch rush calmed down.

I walked out, unlocked my bike, and pushed off out of there. I flew home in the highest gear, my thighs pumping—pushing air, salt water leaving my eyes. For a moment, I fought to keep the tears in, but I lowered my shoulders and let go, just let the pain be part of my existing physical expression of being.

I biked by kids playing outside, watching the wet, fully grown man who smelled like industrial detergent and garlic release emotions at full speed. Like an asteroid burning itself out in the atmosphere, tears peeling into his ears.

I saddled my bike at the traffic light at my house, waiting for my signal unashamedly in my emotion, until the owner of the restaurant, who'd left in her car at the same time as me, pulled up and yelled, "Hey, you're fast!"

I pulled the tears back up my ducts and scrambled to say, "Yeah! Uh, I am! See you later," and crossed the street in front of her, opened the gate to my backyard, parked my bike, and sat in a chair and just sat.

My friend asked if I'd been crying. "Yes," I said, then helped prepare for a party at our house. I watched in envy as people performed music. I was slated to play as well but was bumped off at the last second because I had nothing to perform; I was just going to play.

My thoughtful friends offered to give me time after the performances to lead a jam session. They knew this about me. They were aware of my strengths, and they wanted to protect me from failure by encouraging me to do what I was best at. That was kind. I probably would have been a mess with the delicate privilege of an audience's undivided attention that evening.

My ex was there. Everyone was. I wanted to be alone. Friends heard I was now washing dishes. A girl I knew came across, drink in hand, moved my hair over, and studied evidence of receding. I was aware and ashamed of this sign of aging. Research has shown Adderall accelerates the aging process.[1]

She put my hair down and walked away without saying anything. My friend played some music he'd been working on. It was incredible. I sat right in front of his amp and it shook my whole body. I remember at some point the music touched me so hard in my heart that a friend came over and put her hand over it.

After the show and the jam session, as the party de-escalated to pockets of conversations, I retreated to my room to smoke green plants and make notebooks. I felt good alone. I felt safe. I could control this.

Solitude is solace. I was a full-grown cry-it-out man-baby who'd been conditioned to handle stress alone. I was somehow conditioned to not know how to ask or even receive support from anyone but myself in my own space. Alone, with compulsory tasks, I could focus on paper crafts to avoid deeper self-reflections.

HILLARY WAS FIRED. I executed protocols in order to most efficiently clean and sort the main plates, small plates, alternative main plates, bowls, ramekins, cutlery, wine glasses for whites and reds, flutes, pint glasses, mugs and their saucers, tongs, pans, pots, knives, cutting boards, and at the end of the day, all the containers from the line.

I was in charge of taking out the trash and was given the privilege of music selection in the kitchen. I believed if the dishes were cleaned, I could sit out back and smoke a joint or something while the restaurant's dirty dish production caught up to my speed until the next lot of dishes were in.

Little did I know about "Time to lean, time to clean." I discovered that if I worked too fast, I was punished for my efficiency with toilet scrubbing.

For a time, I was happily habituated to dish work, bookbinding, a joint after work on the bike ride home, yerba mate, and regular Adderall. At times, crushing the Adderall into my homemade teas.

Adderall not only made being a professional dishwasher manageable, but satisfying and easy. I continued to survive on profits from bookbinding, ten dollars an hour, free leftovers from the restaurant, and a shift meal.

Substances were common in this work environment. There was cocaine. A line chef was slowly becoming a junkie, the head server was on Vyvanse, I was on Adderall, and everyone was drinking.

I took my role as kitchen DJ seriously and made small fun talk with everyone as I ritually cleansed every vessel of the establishment by hand. I developed systems of dirty water study and sink refill timing.

I optimized the timing and layout of the drying process. Staring at the wall, wondering how it was I got here. Only for a moment before a plate came in and I practiced the angle and spin of how I tossed it in the sink to allow it to slide through the surface of the water, do a little gesture, and fall gracefully to the bottom on the sink, making a pleasing little sound that reverberated through the water.

The dish water was disgusting, yet dirty plates emerged from it clean. I pondered this often at this station.

I was offered training and promotion to line chef. I turned it down. I didn't want to get committed to the food industry and waste anyone's time. I didn't want more responsibility. I wasn't making much money, and I seemed to resist the idea.

I was okay. I was dusty and adaptable, with low standards and few expenses. I was on speed most of the time. If things hit a critical point, I had the privilege of reaching out for help at the price of dignity and shame.

ADDERALL POEMS

I visited Seattle, where I fell in love with myself. I repeatedly wore a monochromatic turquoise outfit. I spent much time alone, riding the bus, going to cafes, talking to flowers, and writing poems.

———

like brushes we touch
streaks, dabbles, splatter drip
found a pen on the bus
cafe people archetypical paradoxical regressions
the spirit of the sound in the
frequent sometimes wave but
still water. swell and bellow
drum brake ribcage bubble
just a fork. for this food. this prayer.
this 3 ten book and the pen from the clubs.
all the foods are blessings
thank you refrigerator

———

leave death for the dying
leave words for the lying
bring touch to the truth
and life to the living

———

why I love you
feel see truth us
electric eyes light up
nerves move shines down
dreams come revealed now
sleep waits hidden past
awake patience
within passing
open virtue beyond acceptance
crack ribs expanded heart
rocks bones reaching soul
earth man hand foot
home lives digital ground
let us there. come here
just right with this
listen together every ear
fire inside lights us
burns heals true understanding
feel this love all ways

Clots and Castor Oil

Walking through a parking lot with a friend, either he or I challenged myself to jump up onto a cinder block retaining wall. Running toward it, I leapt up to get my hands on the edge and pulled my upper body up onto the top of the wall.

I kicked out my left leg to get leverage, like I was climbing out of a swimming pool, landing with such force that I bruised the back of my lower leg. Several weeks later, after the bruise had healed, I had a lumpy hardness remaining in my calf. I went to get an ultrasound and learned it was a superficial venous thrombosis. They told me it was okay but I should observe it.

The day before Christmas Eve, the blockage in my leg went deeper under my skin and traveled up from my calf to my thigh, inching closer to my heart and lungs. The next day, a doctor friend advised me to go to the ER. My roommates with their cars were all visiting families, so I biked four miles to the hospital. I was diagnosed with a deep vein thrombosis.

The doctors went ahead and scared the shit out of me—they rushed into the room as a flock, pinned me down, and jabbed me in the stomach with a needle without explanation. I started freaking out. They said I had a blood clot that could transform into a pulmonary embolism, like a bomb of blood into the lungs. They used the phrase "unexpected death" to explain what we were dealing with.

Alone in the hospital, I read *American Shaolin* by Matthew Polly, a story of an American who trains in the Shaolin Temple in Zhengzhou, China. The doctors and nurses kept me there overnight, wearing a sterile cotton open-backed smock.

The staff lobbied to keep me there longer. I had to sign a contract promising that because I left early, I could not hold them liable for any medical situation I experienced upon leaving the building.

They instructed me to inject a blood thinner into my abdomen twice a day for thirty days. Hundreds of dollars of my family's insurance deductible injected into my belly. Being under twenty-six, I'd had the opportunity to remain on my family's health insurance, which also answers the question of how I could, without employment or much income, receive my Adderall prescription without copay.

For thirty days I'd lie down, lift up my shirt, remove the plastic cover on the needle, hoist the syringe eight to ten inches above my belly, stay still, commit to it, and with no pause, drop it into my tummy, thumb down the plunger, deposit the cold fluid into my body, and lie there while the chemical gushed into my bloodstream.

My abdomen became a cartography of bruises and veins from all the amateur inoculations against accumulative thinning of the blood.

When I got a scan after thirty days, in continuous contention and psychic friction with the staff at the clinic, I was dissatisfied to learn via ultrasound that the clot remained. The doctors shrugged and reminded me it hadn't grown larger and that wasn't a bad thing.

———

I STARTED to pick up serving shifts at the restaurant. One day, a woman came in right as we were closing. We decided to stay open to serve her. I spoke with her about the situation in my leg and my blood thinners and may have even shown her my bruised belly. She told me she was a medium, a conduit, a healer, a seer.

She told me to take a wool flannel, soak it in castor oil, put it on the afflicted region, and wrap it in saran wrap to keep it on me. Buy a heating pad, put it on my thigh, and go to sleep. I did this for a week and it went away. Poof.

She didn't have to check my blood pressure, make an appointment with a radiologist, have another person look at it, then call in for me to go to the pharmacy and get these needles. Twenty dollars at a drugstore was all I needed to follow her prescription. It worked.

————

ADDERALL CAN INCREASE heart rate and blood pressure, potentially triggering spasms in the heart arteries and producing blood clotting. In people who already have plaque in the heart, the pressure can cause a rupture and heart attack.[1]

Long term, Adderall can cause hypertension and tachycardia. Cardiomyopathy can be caused by long-term Adderall use.[2] Cardiomyopathy is a debilitating heart disease. With it, the heart's ability to pump blood to the whole body is diminished. I was potentially playing with fire here. The use of stimulants makes the heart work hard.

There may be consequences like this in the physical body in the future for myself and the millions like me who took these medications regularly as children and adults.

A 2018 meta-analysis published in the journal *Neurology* found that of the more than 90,000 subjects analyzed, amphetamine use was significantly associated with later development of Parkinson's disease. They concluded that more studies should be done to "understand relevant environmental factors as well as other drugs of abuse which affect the disease pathology.[3]

Not to say the medication caused the blockage in my calf. That was from flying full speed into a cinder block wall. However, the movement of the clot from my calf to my thigh could have been triggered by the increase in blood pressure from amphetamine use.

More Preschool;
More Art

A gain, I was requested to take on a job at a preschool. A noble woman was running a pilot program of her own pedagogy, and she sought a male to be present.

I loved the director of the school, Lizzie, a smiling, open heart with legs and arms. I was refreshed by lessons of sharing, caring, being nice, being honest, and not withholding honest feelings and desires, however hurtful they may be for others to hear.

Every day, outside in the sandbox, the playground, and the garden, I relearned lessons in sharing, communication, working together, and living alongside others.

We facilitated play without any direct lessons. I read *Education and Peace* by Maria Montessori, which implored teachers to approach children as our saviors because they might as well be.

The lessons I gave to kids were sometimes reflections of what I was experiencing. Regular conversation with a herd of four- and five-year-olds gets really interesting. At this age, kids are coming into their personalities and their bodies. Through teaching, a lot can be learned by revisiting the learning moment.

A child was telling me about all the things she could make. Maybe something like, "I can make a picture, a bracelet, a rocket ship, and so on." I asked her if she could *make* the decision of which to make.

I was crafting arts and crafts just as an exercise, letting the waves of what was happening around me choose my direction. There was no rudder or sail on the vessel of my life. I was adrift. I'd learned to be resilient and even joyful in this lifestyle—perhaps because I was taking drugs that made me so—but I was adrift.

Another child was once going on about all the things they *almost* did. I responded that anything you *almost* do is *almost* meaningless. Cynical, for a kid, and perhaps I projected my own lessons into my talks with them, but it felt like the reflection I needed at the time. I *almost* made a documentary about biking across the country. I *almost* biked the entire way. I needed to stop *almost*-ing.

I operated my station of cutlery and flatwares a handful of times a week and sold journals the first Monday of every month. I was never on Adderall at preschool, but I took it a lot in the afternoons and adapted my creative, amphetamine-fueled crafting sessions into the evenings and on into early mornings, listening to music while marbling, painting, and creating with great gusto, creativity, and follow-through.

Book art, collages, paintings, mixed media, watercolors, acrylics, colored pencil, drawings... I creatively manipulated whatever I had lying around.

I wrote poems on the computer and printed them on homemade marbling paper, cutting the poem onto more paper with borders and layers. I packed it in with some cool collage materials and sent them through the mail to an online collage material mail-swap organization I participated in. Our mailbox was flooded with interesting paper scraps as I mailed out wild paper assortments in handmade envelopes.

I fell in love with making things—objects.

I had a plastic skull and adorned pieces of mulch and stones onto it with hot glue. It sat on my desk.

On amphetamine, a line drawn from a pen in hand was *felt* by my nervous system up to my skin sometimes. It felt so good. If I was drawing, it was like the lines were working me—they were in control, and I was in the passenger seat watching.

An ever-living well of exploration, discovery, freedom, and confidence gave me the power to let go and draw, unattached from any outcomes besides the mental exercise of creating images. The art was good, and many times, I was truly pleased that what I felt or thought had been clearly expressed on the paper.

Inevitably, content was illustrated, and many of my drawings had a 'crooked' element. I believed it was somewhat due to the effect Adderall had on my personality. Adderall changed how I thought, and thoughts are pretty foundational to a person at large.

Usually I would end my nights alone in bed at around three or four in the morning, reading or watching videos. Even if I was lying there completely still, sometimes I'd focus on my breathing and the internal arrival and directions of the inner monologue. Meditation was possible on Adderall, and it was like I could *focus* my energy. I could vibrate.

In the name of my amphetamine-induced paper obsession, I'd bike to the Big Box Bookstore and take fifteen minutes to browse the paper recycling dumpster out back. They put all of the previous month's magazines in it. After a few months they locked it.

I was so committed to my access to this material that, on one occasion, I pulled the pin from the hinge in the dumpster and entered it through the back. I sat in the mixed recycling dumpster with a flashlight in my mouth, sorting through box after box of magazines, choosing my favorite ones to read, cherish, or collage with.

Once while sifting media in that dumpster, two guys got out of a van to drop off the next day's newspapers ten feet or so from the dumpster. I stayed still and quiet.

"That's a nice bike."

I peeked out and saw he was holding the handlebars and sizing it up.

"Don't touch my bike." My voice echoed from inside the dumpster.

He put my bike down and finished delivering the newspapers. I continued my collection. I had magazines everywhere. The first time I found this dumpster, I was with a friend and so excited about it that we filled a car with boxes and ended up with hundreds of magazines, many of them multiples of the same one.

This was the reason I had to sit in the dumpster and pick out what I wanted. Multiple copies of magazines have real power for making collages because you can find multiples of the same image. I did not think of this as dumpster diving. I was dumpster *thriving*.

I kept all the best marbled pages, collages, drawings, paintings in a handmade portfolio that was later interpreted as trash and thrown away. An appropriate representation of this time. Creation for creation's sake. It wasn't meaningless; the process is always of value. Truth be told, anything you almost do is *not* almost meaningless; it's a meaningful step toward doing more.

I once stepped out of the house and started painting the pickets on our rental's fence. Friends joined in. Strangers driving by joined in. They put it on the cover of the art section of the local paper.

I made a backpack out of towels, using a borrowed sewing machine. I continued making dozens and dozens of books. I marbled shirts and underwear and socks and towels. I mixed up amateur perfumes. I was constantly shooting and developing film, cluttering my space with negatives, papers, and art all the time, all over. Sometimes I'd even peek at my documentary.

I made my own soap. I took a big empty jug of detergent from a recycling bin and sliced off the bottom two inches. Next I mixed a lot of cocoa butter with castor oil and some fragrance oils in a pot and warmed them up to 120°F. Then on the porch, I made lye with water and watched it shoot up to 400°F. I had to wait for it to cool back down to 120°F before I could mix them.

So I waited. Then when it came to mixing time, it had to be mixed by hand. I laid there on the concrete slab, nodding off to sleep on a school night, holding a whisk and mixing my soap until it reached the right consistency. I used that soap for many, many years. It felt great on the skin.

With found scraps of lumber, trashed doors, and a box of 16d nails, I intuitively built a bed. I built a workbench for the garden area and another for the shed. I biked to a bagel place at 6:00 a.m. after a sleepless night of bookbinding and doing paperwork for a nonprofit I never submitted. I had to park my bike outside in view of the window, as they had no bike rack.

So naturally, I spent the morning building one for them out of a futon piece from the trash and some 2x4s. They accepted it, then weeks later, threw it away. I did projects like this all the time. I just liked doing things. I had a compulsion to move my hands, and then, when the project was done, I couldn't care less. Nonstop movement for movement's sake.

I found no greater satisfaction than, on an average dose of amphetamines, staying in and spending about three hours cleaning my room. Put on the entertainment, scan the space square foot by square foot, decipher, sort, and act. Then bask in the brief calm I'd created and start the next opening of the creative craft portal.

I attended kirtan chanting sessions, yoga events, group jams, dinners, dance parties, and foot washings, and hosted comedy night/variety show potlucks at my home. I made a sculpture of a man out of trash—using mostly baling wire and plastic bags.

For a week or so, I spent all my free time on this trash-man. I built him sitting in a school chair I'd acquired from the side of the road and based his body on my body. His arms went to the ground, and he had long, spider-like fingers that held up his body when the chair was removed. From the trash he came, and to the trash he returned.

———

I MET a guy who rented a garage unit just outside of the downtown region of Orlando. I went there to work with him. He rented out mountain bikes with trailers that attached to their seat column. There were lawn chairs, tools, tubes, tires, a refrigerator, and always people hanging out.

The bike trailers were used to move people around the block of bars downtown and sometimes at other events.The trailers were all custom welded by a fabricator who lived about a fifteen-minute bike ride away.

They were made of square stock, plywood, two bike wheels, and bearings, etc., welded to the framework of a restaurant booth without the table, and were seated with plywood-based plastic and upholstered cushions. They could seat six.

Drunken escapades were debriefed by those who paid me. Laughter and selfies happened behind me, while I, in ripped jean shorts, a Hawaiian shirt, and a handmade pouch attached to my waist with safety pins for all the cash, pushed pedals with Converse chucks I'd painted phthalo green and gold, pumping my legs down on this crank, uphill on brick roads.

On a rare occasion that I had six passengers, they had to be towed using a 1:1 granny gear. Standing up, using my arms above the bars to press my legs down for each rotation on each side. Focusing on my breathing and balance as three large men who could be described as "corporate" cheered me on while their wives (I assume) clavered and laughed.

As I made it to their hotel and stopped, the bike, no longer having forward momentum, succumbed to the pressure. Over a thousand pounds on its saddle stem just pushed the bike straight into the ground like a pancake. I gingerly lifted off in the nick of time. Their chariot dropped eight inches, and they paid me and howled their way further into their own evening and out of mine.

Rides were typically two to four people, and were supposed to come to around $20 a person, but drivers could name their price or bargain however they pleased. In fact, to skirt liability, riders did not ride for the man in the storage unit. Riders obtained a specific license from the city to collect payment for pedicab rides, and the man in the storage unit only rented out the trailer for the evening.

I rode bikes all night and made decent money, typically orbiting around $100 a night. It could be as low as nothing or as high as $300. It was a good workout. A peasant's job. I was a peasant in many ways; I certainly dressed like it. I honed crafts at home. I was charming, skinny, friendly, grateful. I washed dishes. My labor was the leisure of another. I carried people around during their sabbath of drinking and dancing. I cleaned their plates.

It was fun working on Adderall. The best ride was the ride home on my road bike. It was like wearing ankle weights all day and then going on a trampoline. I flew home, always in highest gear, pushing through space at a clip. Sometimes I'd bind books for a bit after. As long as the Adderall was in me, I could burn the candle at three ends.

I was always on Adderall for this job. I hadn't worked a nine to five since working construction when I was eighteen. I was professionally undecided. A full-time part-timer. I repaired a moped and once tried to photograph dozens of raccoons around a dumpster. They chased me away; I feared for my life.

Even though I was taking meds, I was still distracted, just better at it. I was on the quest for self that lots of successful business people go on in their forties when they've made enough money but feel they lack substance in life. I was on that path but hadn't done the work to be able to embrace the path fully.

Every distraction was a distraction from another distraction. Some lasted for months, even years. I had more thoughts about things than actions toward them. Whatever I was doing was so captivating to me because—let's be honest for a second here—I wasn't just "medicated"; these drugs got me *high*.

I was high most of the time. I wasn't following up with a psychiatrist. I took these meds "as needed." It may have looked like "There's no social event this evening; I think I'll take an Adderall and see what I can get into."

I was selling books and paper crafts at the market, spending five afternoons a week at preschool, doing two to three shifts of dishes at the restaurant a week, and pedicabbing one to three nights a week.

I also maintained an active social life with a revolving door of fantastic roommates. I had monstrous energy. Time moved slowly enough for me to do it all because I was operating on an imbalanced consumption of time. Time slowed down when I sped up.

SOCIALITE ISOLATION

Journal entry – August 24, 2012:

Everyone here is beautiful. The fire breathers, the dancers, the chemistry sets, the laptoppers, the no-bottoms, the evil eyes, the ink spots, the angry vegans, the look-aways, the bellies, the waiters, the bailouts, the lunars, the followed, the yogis, the truth.

Sometimes I became hyperfocused on one of life's biggest distractions —myself. I found myself in a pursuit of feeling good, until that pursuit became the pursuit of feeling okay, then deescalated into the pursuit of not feeling bad.

This is the case with addictions. The longer we are in these hotwired states of feeling good, the farther down the resting state goes when whatever wears off.

There are some very nuanced social side effects of taking Adderall that slowly creep in unnoticed over time. Grandiosity, narcissism, self-importance, and so on. It was changing my personality but in a way that I felt like I liked, so it seemed like a benefit. Also, on Adderall, sometimes, there is a lapse in bladder control and it's hard to stop peeing.

I was a fixture at my local coffee shop where I journaled, drank coffee, sat around with the other usuals, and supplemented my diet with food left on plates that hadn't been bussed. Feeling empowered by saving food from the trash, I ate half sandwiches before they got taken to the dishwasher, slicing off the part someone else had bitten off. I would eat the guacamole out of chipotle dumpsters as well as bagels from the bagel shop.

Even when as a whole I felt depressed, I felt great during the small moments that made up this whole. I truly enjoyed myself. Some kind of sad life built out of happy moments. I was often chipper and outgoing during the day, but lonely as the evening struck my mood into self reflection. Riding a daily rollercoaster of serotonin, dopamine, and norepinephrine waves. Surfing.

Restless after taking Adderall late in the day, I would ride around and see what I could get into, youthful wonder being carried into the half moon of my twenties. Pedaling through warm nights, sneaking into swimming pools, having dance parties, showing up.

After a day of bookbinding, I still had a lot of steam in me to release. I rode to a new bar that gave people a beer for every karaoke song they sang to keep the party moving. I sang like it mattered. I got on my knees. I wanted to get over the fear of microphones. I put my entire soul into it for an audience of two people.

Afterwards, in the alley, I struck up a conversation with a radiant woman who was stunning to witness, friendly, approachable, and interesting to talk to. We talked through the night and I went home, still buzzing from the Adderall. I liked her.

I remembered we'd talked about my books, so I stayed awake beyond sunrise, making her one. I made one of the coolest books I'd ever made: purple, black, and turquoise, with a marbled paper cover and fabric spine. The flyleaves were photos of the cosmos; there was a pocket in the back, and maybe an elastic closure or a ribbon bookmark.

Lonely, over the top, and boiling over for some deeper human connection, I put all my desperation to be intimate, loved, seen, and appreciated in this gesture.

The next day, devoid of sleep, I rode my bike to her place of work, a cafe, and delivered the book to her, having met her only twelve hours earlier at karaoke. She was politely taken aback. She served my meal and made small talk.

I was at times performative in social situations—portraying myself rather than being myself. I overthought social cues, or I just talked and talked. Super brain.

Confidence, arrogance, bravery, recklessness. It wasn't all the meds; I was also on a big dose of being myself. Sometimes the medication ignited a glowing spring of self-confidence. My friend and I were once at a bar, watching some band play a show.

When they were done, I had the gall to ask to play their drum set. They obliged, and I began to play like a hyperactive spatial calamity. I kept a rhythm that expressed the way amphetamine made me feel. My friend ended up playing guitar with me. It was fun.

The Fall

Our landlady passed away and her daughter inherited the house. The daughter collected our rent in cash and never paid the mortgage. She pocketed our cash while the house foreclosed and was sold at auction. The buyer wanted us out. We had to find a new place within a few weeks.

What were once full, rattling bottles of orange stimulants were becoming barren orange plastic cylinders. Usually, I called the doctor's office back in Maryland and got a prescription mailed or picked one up on Thanksgiving or something.

They said that as I hadn't had a visit in a while, I'd need to come in to get the script. Probably a good call. Check in, talk about how it was going. But I had no trips planned up there, and they wouldn't mail it.

I'd been doing Adderall regularly for a long time. Rarely did I miss more than three days. I had a few doses left and thought of ways to get more out of them. I cut them up into pieces and tried to ration them, but the low doses seemed meaningless if they couldn't make happen what I wanted to happen, the "giddy glow, get up and go, this and that, let's do that, why not? let's try it, sun's coming up, that's okay, that's fine, I'll sleep next time" kind of day.

But no. I looked everywhere. I got the knife and dragged it through the floor cracks and probably consumed literal who-knows-what trying to get a speck of amphetamine. The lights in my mind were dimming. The mirror was clearing. I was about to be very tired for a very long time.

Withdrawal began. Gravity seemed to be turned up. I gained weight. I always had an appetite. Hunger that was never satiated and an exhaustion that sleep never seemed to satisfy. I was so lazy. Everything was a burden except lying around, watching cartoons.

Nobody around me knew what I was going through; I wouldn't tell them. I'm grateful for my friends who stayed with me without knowing that what I was really going through was a strong chemical withdrawal. I was going through life as well. The withdrawal, much like the drug, changed the way I experienced reality.

I suffered emotional exhaustion from a chemical deficiency in the body. My external circumstance and daily life was falling apart due to my expectations being set by me on Adderall and needing to be fulfilled by me in an Adderall withdrawal.

The pilot program at preschool ended. I'd quit the restaurant when the work environment got tense. Doing a shift of dishes off Adderall was like doing needlepoint while riding on a rollercoaster and wearing winter gloves.

The clatter of plates annoyed me. I complained about how the servers dropped plates on the table beside the sink. Not *that* they did it, but *how* they did it. I wanted them to be gentle. The water seemed wetter. I was keenly aware of how disgusting everything was.

There was no more boom boom, finished. I could do it, but I was thinking about other things. My mind was speaking to itself about the half-eaten lunches in my bare hands. There was a voice in my head:

YOU NEED ME. YOU'RE USELESS WITHOUT ME.

My roommates and I luckily found a new place. Moving from one house to the other during amphetamine withdrawal was like getting a marionette puppet to eat living mosquitos with chopsticks. All I wanted to do, other than take Adderall, was lie down for twenty hours, eat a warm meal, smoke cannabis to ease the stress, and watch a movie. I was cranky and unkind.

I had a gig at a DIY music festival one evening. I ran the door, checking tickets and IDs for about four hours in exchange for admission for the whole weekend. I'd arranged this months in advance. I had to watch the door until one in the morning. I was tired. I wasn't even in the mood to enjoy music. I didn't want to be there in the first place.

Being a happy figure at a concert, dancing with every cell of my body, was the last thing I felt like doing. Watching musicians play, I imagined they had to have been on Adderall. How else could they function so efficiently? I certainly could only imagine playing like that on Adderall.

I wanted to back out of the doorman job, but I'd said I would do it, so I did. Someone brought me some food truck empanadas as a kindness. I dove right in. The woman who I'd served who had led me to using castor oil on my leg showed up to enjoy the show. She openly criticized me for eating that greasy food.

I wasn't in the mood for her intuitive healing right then. She had no clue that, in this state, these were medicinal empanadas. I was dopamine deficient and needed to not feel bad more than I needed to feel good. I probably told her, "I know." Eating well would have helped. She was right, but the truth at that moment was irritating.

I kept making books, but I changed my approach and made copies of the same book using simpler, easier designs. I did runs of four to ten books, making the same pages, the same text block, several of the same covers, and assembling a more boring but simpler inventory.

I did pedicabbing sometimes, but it really was challenging to bike around hundreds of pounds of steel and flesh till four in the morning without amphetamines after doing it for months on them. I still did it, but it was more tedious peasantry than it had been before. I drank whatever liquid at the convenience store had lots of caffeine and even found myself eating during a shift.

Adderall used my brain to construct temples of logic to defend its own use within me. This kept going, these threaded inner monologues that were presented in my head about how it made sense to take them. This voice, like an advocate of amphetamine. A pharma rep living inside me.

I made long, desperate explanations from and to myself about why I needed them and why they weren't a bad thing after all. And maybe they weren't, but I accepted that this was how I was going to have to live. I tried to accept that I needed to do some growing, but I didn't know how.

I got books about ADD and medications, behaviors, how to raise children with ADD, and how to manage ADD. I accepted that I would have to research and learn my way out of this.

I read *The ADD Myth* by Martha Burge. The book was more about having kids with ADD, so I parented myself through this transition. It helped to identify what was happening to me rather than just blindly fall into the spiral of chemically induced emotional malfunction.

I learned about amphetamine withdrawal. I continued my research. I got back into writing this book as part of my withdrawal treatment.

When dark thoughts showed up into my inner monologue, I knew they weren't me.

YOU NEED ME.

It was a guest. Outstaying its welcome. Making demands in my mind and not willing to be quiet unless I gave it what it wanted. It wanted amphetamines. I sometimes had conversations with the advocate. Other times I practiced ignoring it. I told myself that as a parasite is starved, it cries out for help as it withers away. This parasite was addiction. This sort of imaginative visualization helped me heal.

A known side effect of Adderall withdrawal is suicidal ideation. I experienced these kinds of thoughts. They would intrude out of thin air. I had no plans to hurt myself or act on these thoughts. Ideation meant I just thought about it.

In some sense, there was a part of my mind that couldn't see a way out of the pickle I was in, and my brain's problem-solving equipment knew the problems wouldn't exist if I didn't exist.

One of my most precious tools at this time was simply remembering that these intrusive thoughts were not me, they were the withdrawal. However, these thoughts would just arrive, bursting through the door of my inner dialogue.

I knew it wasn't the truth. It was incredibly annoying. But it was something I needed to get through.

PSYCH

The industry of psychiatry was contested during its rise in acceptance as a legitimate approach to mental difficulties. The theory that ailments of the mind, emotional or cognitive, could be treated with medical interventions has become commonplace.

If a psychiatrist doesn't prescribe any medication, they probably won't have many patients and they lose access to the money they receive in exchange for an incredibly challenging academic commitment. The distribution of these medicines accounts for upwards of tens of billions of dollars in sales.[1]

―――――

I WAS tired of the lethargy, saddened by the depression, muddled by my lack of focus, constantly sleeping, always hungry, irritable, and not a huge fan of the thoughts of dying. I had to take action.

The jets cut out, and I began my descent to earth. I pulled a chute and was safe. However, I moved slowly now and had less control over how I felt. I went from being like a joyous sprite of creative inspiration into a cynical, touchy whiner.

I spent more time staring at my desk than I did using it. Sleeping in, taking naps. I had a true appetite for rest.

I'd built a bigger gas tank in my life and lifestyle and now, without my secret ingredient, I couldn't seem to afford more than a half tank. The long-haul, anorexic behavior of the medication was reversed. Even after meals, I still sought sizable snacks, my body seeking to rebuild a fat layer. I enjoyed bread with peanut butter, banana coins, and honey—a nice filling snack.

My patience was tested, and outbursts of frustration were self-directed. It was as if my higher self was frustrated with all the work it had to do to pick up the lower self, who was detoxing from years of amphetamines.

I desperately wanted to be back on stimulants. This quitting was a matter of circumstance, not of will. I hadn't decided to stop. I bought an old, beat-up pickup truck for a few hundred dollars. It didn't have a reverse gear.

I found an office in our insurance network who offered a consultation with a psychiatrist and a talk therapy session with a counselor. It had a $90 copay, and I asked my mom to help me with it.

I told her that ever since I'd stopped working at the school, I'd been depressed and wanted to talk with a therapist about it. This was not a lie, but it was just scratch marks on the surface of what was going on. An addict telling stories to his mom about what he needs for this or that, when the focus was truly getting back on drugs.

These drugs designed a lifestyle that could only be maintained while on them. There was an Adderall-shaped hole in me somewhere. I loved Adderall, and I wasn't ready to say goodbye. Here I was inviting Addy back into my heart. Asking to be taken back.

———

I WAS in my standard attire, wearing cotton kung fu slippers, jeans I'd turned into shorts using scissors, and an inside out thrift store T-shirt. I didn't like having logos or words on my body, but I liked solid colors, so I had a handful of shirts I always wore inside out with the tags cut off. I was never formal.

I passed the waiting room's home improvement shows, magazines, clipboards of medical history, and waiting patients, then I was in her office.

Her office was in a medical center. It was dimly lit and cozy. She was only an upper half of a person behind a robust wooden desk. A large window on her right cast light through the blinds. There was a young student on a couch in the corner, shadowing her, taking notes as she and I spoke.

I did not find her friendly. I didn't feel like a liar or that I was doing anything wrong. On the books, I had ADD, and there was a treatment for my disorder that she was well equipped to treat me with by using a notepad and pen.

I wasn't sure if what I was doing was right or not. I felt dirty going in there. I figured I would get through with it and be on my way. It felt like something was being betrayed—asking again for them. She probably sensed I was a man in conflict with himself.

I told her I had a hard time focusing, that I'd taken Adderall in the past for ADD and had stopped, and that I wanted to learn more about Vyvanse. This was my mistake, and a mistake I'm grateful to have made.

I asked her for a specific *brand* of drug, not for help. I didn't ask her to lead the treatment. I asked for a specific medicine that there was no documented record I'd ever taken under medical supervision. She didn't trust me.

And I didn't trust her. A few weeks prior, I'd rescued a little kitten that needed a home. It scratched me up. The doctor thought she was clever when she abruptly asked, "How long have you been cutting yourself?" I thought she was messing with me; I never had. I looked over at the student, feeling embarrassed and defensive now that I was suddenly alone and outnumbered.

I didn't even connect it to the kitten. It took a stoner's moment for me to realize which cuts she was talking about. Here I was, walking into a psychiatrist's office with scratches on my wrists. She didn't seem to believe my explanation.

I went on my phone to show her pictures of my new kitten. She said not to worry. She asked me why my shirt was inside out. Asked me if I did that often. It felt like she was more focused on her student watching how she talked to me than she was on talking to me.

She asked if I took any other drugs. I told her that I had done LSD and mushrooms to help develop as a person with friends, seeking deeper truth in the reality of life.

She didn't seem to care or to believe that this was anything other than degenerate behavior. All of a sudden I was opened to judgements I usually dismissed. I felt totally embarrassed and self-conscious about this honest sharing of something that, to me, felt like an enormous boon of self-growth and personal development. It made me feel unsure of my own habits.

Perhaps I was in too deep and was delusional about psychedelics being as helpful as I thought they were. Maybe I was always just getting high and telling myself it was for my benefit to excuse my impulses. Her response made me doubt myself.

Maybe since I'd always been taking drugs to be better, I thought all drugs were taken for purpose and not recreation, and it was hard for me to distinguish what was therapeutic, what was reckless, and what was other-wise beneficial or degenerative.

To her, the only healthy drugs for the mind were the ones she prescribed, and the ones I mentioned were illegal. I felt like a criminal.

She and I were not hitting it off.

She correctly identified that I was drug seeking. At the end of our talk, she sighed and opened a desk drawer, slapped a pad of paper on the desk, armed her pen, looked up at me, and told me she was writing me two prescriptions. One for a urinalysis and the other for Wellbutrin (an SSRI antidepressant).

I verbalized my frustration, offended that she would write me a script for treating depression. I explained I was not seeking aid with any depression.

She advised me to take it anyway and see if I felt better in two weeks. Two weeks is a long time to let a drug kick in and a fair amount of time to build a dependance. Maybe she thought I was using drugs to feel good, yet she prescribed drugs to help me escape my feelings?

I did not feel heard or supported. I did not tell her the whole truth about my relationship with Adderall, but I shared about my other drug use, my new cat, and my preference for inside out logo T-shirts.

I wanted to reach across her desk, grab her pad, and scrawl "Adderall

XR 20 mg," make a doctor's scribble, tear it off, and be on my way. I was mad about everything. Why was I in this situation? What had I done?

Adderall was the cause and the only solution I had to this damaged state I was in, and I could not get that solution on this day. I couldn't regain my desired state, and all of this medicine was in the way of what I thought was my true self that I'd drifted away from.

The included therapy session was also wiggidy-wack. The therapist recommended I go out, get drunk, and have sex with someone. With a condom, she added. She thought I was tightly wound. I was just reeling from the psychiatry session.

I tossed the prescriptions in the trash and never called the office again. I bought some Vyvanse from a server at the restaurant. All I wanted was to get them, drive home, take them, and bind books. For days, I'd tried to bind books and ended up smoking weed and watching background cartoons in the foreground.

I got the Vyvanse, went home, and started to bind books. I was finally back in it. Driving home with that Vyvanse in my pocket had been like finishing three days walking in the desert, being met with a chilled glass of cold water, and letting the condensation roll over your thumb knuckle.

I got home and took a sip. I was the familiar "me" again. I put on loud music, danced at my desk, ripped papers to the same size, folded them in half, put them into groups of four, poked holes in them, stitched them together, glued paper to board to make an interesting cover, glued paper into the cover, and put the book in a pile ready for the market. And it felt good.

At around 9:30 p.m., hyped and ready to go, I went outside and grabbed my bike, put my headphones in, and listened to music while I biked downtown to rent my favorite bike and trailer. I picked up rides all night, feeling pretty good. I made a decent amount of money.

I got home and crafted a little more. I took the other few pills over the next few days, rinsed and repeated. Then I found myself a few steps back in the withdrawal again.

GUINEA

Flipping through the city paper, I noticed an image of an average adult male resting head in hands over a cluttered desk. Just like me. It was an ad for a clinical trial for treating ADD in adults. I dialed the number, made an appointment for an interview later that week, and rode my bike across town.

I recall falling on the train tracks on the way when my bike's front tire became aligned with the rail and dado in the pylon at the railroad crossing.

The office was on the other side of the tracks, an area that I never spent time in. Notoriously unsafe. The building had stained linoleum, an elevator that had been used as a urinal, and everything else one finds in a low-rent office building: flickering lights, brown stains on drop ceilings....

Regardless, this was the location where this unnamed pharmaceutical research study planned to build their treatment arm.

Just as I'd looked past the discomfort in the psychiatrist's office and the awkwardness of buying amphetamines from acquaintances, I just wanted to get through with it and leave with a bottle of stimulants.

I was willing to overlook whatever kind of danger this trial involved. I'd already risked plenty. Now I was willing to take the stimulant behind door number two just to have the potential of escaping the shadowland of withdrawal. When you're wearing rose-colored glasses, red flags are nearly white.

I hoped the drugs they gave me would be stimulant-based and that I wouldn't be in the placebo group. For the sake of being scientific, they couldn't tell me what was in them. The nurse told me I was a perfect candidate and would be included in the trial.

My eyes widened and I hid a smile. Alright, give me a bottle of swallowables and I'll be on my way, I thought.

I was disappointed to learn the drugs weren't distributed on this day. They were just setting things up for the trial. I had no clue how this kind of coordinated effort operated, when we are offering living bodies to science. She may very well have seen the same drug-seeking tendencies on my sleeves that the psychiatrist saw and capitalized on them for the sake of their study.

I was honest and told her I'd taken drugs for ADD since I was a child. I didn't admit I was currently fiending. I told her I was experiencing difficulty focusing and wanted to give something a try. She checked my blood pressure and assured me they'd be in touch.

I was grappling not just with the truth that I was an addict but that I had to heal like one if I wanted to shake this thing. I seemed to have closed my eyes one day only to open them as someone in recovery. I guarded this secret with the same vigilance I did my previous drug use.

Since Adderall came from the pharmacy and my parents and teachers supported its use, it had taken me some time to become aware I was an addict. These were not just drugs; they were "medications" given to me by intelligent medical professionals.

It had started at that cabin, the addictive behavior—amphetamine and me taking our relationship to the next level.

In shameless desperation, I reached out to the server again. This would be the last time he sold me drugs. It wouldn't be the last time I asked. He never again answered my texts of varying pleas. This day, however, he shared some Vyvanse in exchange for paper money, and we smoked a blunt together by his pool.

He showed me all his DJ equipment and performed for me alone— like I was an audience of thousands. I felt embarrassed to just sit there and wait for him to finish. I saw much of myself in this performance.

I also had a gregarious, uninhibited performance style. I also puttered around with DJ equipment—arpeggiators, sequencers, samplers, oscillators, etc. Behind musical instruments, I felt safe to let my behavior show the amphetamine within. Any odd behavior or displays like that of some kind of "possession" could be excused by viewers as "feeling it."

The server showed me a CD he'd made for his mom. He'd even designed its cover. I, too, made obsessive gifts for people when on Adderall. I wrote incredible letters on handmade paper and sent loved ones books I'd made especially for them. I sent them to people just for the sake of it, even to those who didn't have any appreciation of my paper craft.

I didn't like this reflection. I was in a place where I was only accessing meds through few-and-far-between chances to obtain them and, for the first time, was starting to know myself off as well as on them. I felt stupid that I wanted to feel the way he felt.

I was also high on the weed we smoked together. The mixture of this and the setting unleashed a twisted spiral of destructive introspection that bled into my inner dialogue. I took the four Vyvanse home, bound some books until 9:30 p.m., and then biked downtown to work an evening of pedicabbing.

Vyvanse is amphetamine-based like Adderall but contains lisdexamfetamine, which has a longer-lasting onset and duration, so the effects are less intense than on Adderall.[1]

Those four Vyvanse probably lasted me a week. I ended up buying some Adderall from a cashier at a grocery store. Taking these got me through a film project for a private citizen I'd found through online classifieds, and the client was impressed.

But without the synthetic boost, the flame went out on my books. It felt like work, and I was no longer on the same blazing trail of creative exploration. I had operated this business for over a year and made no economic growth.

It seemed anytime I tried to do anything, I heard a voice in my mind explaining how it would be easier if I took Adderall. The advocate. The idea of supplementation to avoid distractions became my primary distraction. Trying to bind books, I couldn't focus on the process because thoughts would interrupt my inner dialogue with,

Maybe you really have a problem. Maybe Adderall is what you need to get this done. Maybe all the doctors were right. Stop fighting it

and understand that your brain is wired differently. You aren't like the rest. You need pills to function. You aren't strong enough. You need help. You need me.

I had to trust this was just the advocate lobbying for its own survival. I didn't need the pills. I had to believe there was a shore beyond the doldrums. It felt like unknown territory to get off them. I had to get to know myself again. I wasn't prepared.

CLAIR DE LUNE

As we were settling into our new home, I cruised to a nearby skatepark one morning after a late night of carrying happy people on a bicycle trailer.

When I arrived, it was all BMX riders zipping around the ramps endlessly on their bicycles. Dang. I did my best to dodge their circular runs and waited patiently for an opening. I dropped in, floated over the table-top, came up for a frontside tail-stall on quarter pipe, then my back foot missed the tail of my board. My front foot remained on deck and slid away from my right foot, which was planted on the ramp. My fibula snapped —again.

I fell to the ground, moaning in pain. The BMX kids asked me to get out of the way as I lay on the ground, eating my hat and catching my breath. This felt just like the previous fibula break. I climbed on my board and scooted out of their way. I convinced them to give me a ride home in their minivan.

My career as a bicycle taxi driver took a pause. I went to my parents' house for about two months to heal my broken leg. I thought about ordering Adderall and arranging a visit with the doctor, but I'd broken my right leg and couldn't drive myself around discreetly. Ball and chain.

Like a typical addict, I had a hidden hit squirreled away in a little wooden box in my childhood bedroom, a single 20 mg Adderall XR in a wooden box that had an eagle wood-burned and painted on it. My dad gave it to me when I was a kid, and I'd always kept my little treasures in it.

I hobbled up the stairs and into the closet, reached onto the shelf and pulled it down, opened up the capsule, and divided the little beads within into three piles. Three doses.

I put each pile into a piece of paper and folded the doses up. Over the course of a few days, they vanished into my metabolism. I'd lick my finger and stick all the tiny beads to my salivated fingertip and into my mouth; they all swirled off in a spiral of saliva down my throat, and somehow, with scientific magic, made me see the line before I drew it and hear the note before I plucked it.

I played guitar and drew fun little pictures, some of my favorite things to do on Adderall. Under different circumstances, I may have driven myself to visit the doctor and had the chance to re-up. But I couldn't drive. I broke that leg.

On these rations I drew pictures and played guitar. Watching lines unfold was pleasurably entertaining, and the opportunity to plan and execute a thought was so expeditious that it was hugely satisfying to me, no matter how twisted and strange the final image appeared.

Likewise, with music, it was like the notes never needed to be thought of. Whatever I felt just transmitted through the instrument. I was there to listen to what the instrument would express as it played me; the pen was in control as I effortlessly allowed it to create images through me.

On my last reserved dose, I went into the basement, sat at my piano, and began to watch a tutorial on how to play *Clair de Lune* by Claude Debussey. I learned the intro note by note.

I came back the next evening without Adderall, repeated the process I'd developed, and learned to play the next part. I did this almost every evening and practiced at several opportunities, day and night. I treated learning this song like it was my job, and I showed up to work, inspired or not.

On Adderall, the process (of anything) was electric and interesting. It felt like there were no limitations. All I had to do was decide what to do, reach my hand out, and everything made sense somehow.

It was still possible, but it was a struggle; I was beginning to embrace it and felt pride in enduring the slog for once. It didn't come naturally. I had to force myself, slow-mo the YouTube video, and back it up over and over until I could play it without thinking.

Once I'd hammered the sequence of keys into my muscle memory, the magic was that the music was coming through my body. I felt that by playing it, Debussey was able to tell me his story intimately through time, from his heart, to his mind, to his hands, into the pages of history, to the guy on YouTube, to my eyes, to my fingers, into my ears, and into my heart.

Having a heart to heart through time, using pianos. The process was now beginning to be boring for long periods and rewarding for short ones. The reward was not just to play it and hear it but to experience the song in a deep, profound way each time I played it.

I was developing a discipline muscle. Having that magnificent song play through my body and mind activated my soul, and the tedious task of memorizing finger movements was worth it for those moments where the music completed a circuit through my own fingers into my ears.

I couldn't read music. I just mimicked the hands on YouTube move for move. I ended up playing it at a wedding. This was the first time I had really learned something difficult the slow way. It was physical therapy for my brain's ability to focus and work hard without amphetamines. It was possible.

My parents' home was an easy environment to be in withdrawal. I was injured, so nothing was expected of me. I didn't need to work or provide. For this, I was grateful.

VIDEO

After my leg healed, I returned to Florida and resumed my job with the video client I'd worked with before. There'd been a gap in our schedule that breaking my leg fit into.

I bought a few Adderall from the cashier at the grocery store again. My last illegal purchase.

On Adderall one evening, while editing a video for my client, a friend texted me to ask if I could make something for him for free. I told him sure and spent the next four hours building his organization's acronym out of chicken-wire.

We'd never spent time together like this before, but I had a reputation for being helpful for this kind of thing. The purpose of the letters was to be filled with trash to make a statement about trash. I clipped and twisted wires, cutting my fingers until it was done. He stood around chatting, smoking cigarettes, and sharing life stories all night. I took pride in my work building the "S."

Then I went back inside and didn't sleep. I edited and finished the video and sent it off. On Adderall, it was common for me to see that it was 12:28 a.m., get to work, and seem to notice the sunrise through the window after what felt like twenty minutes.

I relished the immersion into the computer screen and the building of these little timelines with little rectangles; cutting and arranging them;

changing the colors; adding music; sliding things around; sorting keyframes, overlay, titles, and transitions; and color correcting timing action to the music. Watching the same video over and over, looking for what stood out, whatever music it was being set to ringing in my head for weeks or months after the project was sent off.

I emailed the final product to my client and they were pleased with my work. I couldn't find any more Adderall, Vyvanse, or whatever for the next one. That was it. The grocery store cashier mysteriously died. I'd known her through a friend of a friend of a friend. I didn't know her well enough to feel comfortable asking how or why she died.

I told myself I didn't need the medications. I did my best to make a video that matched the standard the amphetamine version of myself had set. I obtained whatever herbs I could find for focus and energy, in the form of loose teas, capsules, and tincture. Ginseng, gotu kola, Bacopa, Ginkgo biloba, Rhodiola, and more.

Swallowing a pill and then entering a new state of mind—one of productive nature—was a conditioned response I had developed. I tried to take advantage of that Pavlovian response the best I could, but was ultimately frustrated that nothing I took compared to what amphetamines did. Not even close. It was gone.

I'm sure it was beneficial for me to work with these herbs to manage the withdrawal, but I wasn't trying to manage the withdrawal. I wanted the power back. I needed it. I missed it.

I couldn't access my video editing skills. It frustrated me. It was boring. I started to think of reasons the client didn't understand what they wanted. I knew it was bad. The ability was in me, but somehow the fluency to navigate the space effortlessly and perform as a human was significantly affected by Adderall withdrawal.

I knew that what I'd made this time was below the standard I'd set for myself. I was waiting for them to ask for a re-do. After hitting send on the video, I was promptly fired from the project. My client emailed me that the work I had done lacked "umph."

Sleeping in the Garden

I started to see the way out. I did some odd jobs, being a helping hand here and there to various folks and acquaintances. I helped my landlord with plumbing jobs. I was offered a truck driving job. I couldn't even consider it; my driver's license was suspended.

Back when I got hit by that car, on acid, I actually got a visit in the hospital from a state trooper who wrote me a ticket for the reckless operation of my bike. I gave the money and the ticket to a friend to pay the fine when I left for my cross-country trip and they forgot. So that all had to get sorted.

I had a brief job as an aftercare teacher at a daycare for elementary-age kids but quit due to the director treating the children like dogs that needed to be trained.

In an effort to maximize book production, I threw the floor mattress in my bedroom into the trash. I pitched my tent in the garden and used my former bedroom as a creative studio. In the beginning, like all things I seem to do, I loved it and was thrilled about this uncommon and inconvenient change I'd made on a whim that would be life-changing, idealistic, and inconvenient.

I slept to the sounds of crickets and woke with the morning sun. My day began with unzipping my tent and checking in with the plants. I had so much space to work on bookbinding. It seemed like a good balance.

Rain, cold (occasional chilliness), extreme heat, and other elements came into play from time to time, and I worked with them as best I could. I loved camping every night. I continued working on this book and researching ADD, amphetamines, and education.

Taken from early drafts:

> *I call upon a prescription meditation*
> *but it is so hard to take.*

> *I am engulfed in my distraction*
> *of tamping out words*
> *about personal freedom*
> *from those pill-making heathens.*

> *Stricken from youth*
> *with an inflicted affliction*
> *that turned to disease*
> *and disease was*
> *addiction.*

> *If I think too much on the future, I feel physiological reactions in my body to that anxiety. I tense up my muscles and breathe rapidly, and thoughts fire off a lot, playing out scenarios fueled by worry and fear.*

> *I dismiss all logic and go into fits of imaginative, destructive scenarios, and I emote the responses and feel devastated. This is anxiety.*

> *Depression is a slouchy lunge into the past, a dwelling on mistakes made and the difficulty of putting them behind. Embarrassment, shame, and guilt live here.*

> *Depression is a hopeless attitude, painful to the user, keeping one stuck in an avoidance of the future, taking excess time to mourn personal loss.*

How is it that mental afflictions became known as illnesses? How did we end up thinking it was a good idea to medicate the mind with substance—as if it was that simple?

There is something dreadfully wrong with the current state of public education. I could go on and on and on.

My reaction to being an attendant in this is that it was a big job training. I was seldom given the opportunity to solve problems, was usually given opportunities to follow directions at the scrutiny of a teacher, who was more like a boss than a guide.

Often I felt misunderstood, and this led to my being medicated.

They modified my behavior to suit their needs.

If I was working on a farm or doing some art or other work more aligned to my mental composition, there would not have been this struggle.

But because there was a requirement for all people to go to school, and my path led me to this part of school, I complied with the struggle.

This is so hard. I get so distracted. I know Adderall will help. But it won't really help. It just tricks me into thinking it is helping.

I am not the sum of substances I have consumed.
I am not my distractions.
I am not my thoughts.
I am not my past.

These things take control of my movement as a being.

Never addicted to the cigarette; addicted to the break.

SECOND STAGE

After accepting I'd become an addict, I was angry and grew a resentment that took time to heal. I had never been truly aware of the progression into addiction while it was happening. Ever since I'd done all that research at my parent's house, I knew it was wrong.

Still, I longed for a version of myself that I no longer had access to. I had developed a personality, work ethic, creative approach, social tendency, interests, and way of life that lived in a bottle. Now the bottles were all empty. I was left with no choice other than to rebuild myself from scratch.

Adderall gave me unrealistic expectations of my own personal productivity. Dig a hole, bury it, mourn, and move on.

My constant energy morphed into constant lethargy. With Adderall's power, I did not need food or sleep as much because I was some kind of high-functioning amphibious creature.

In reality, I was being operated by a third-party energy source that likely created deficiencies from lack of sleep and nutritional depletion while reshaping neural pathways and modifying my brain.

Some Adderall users create an entire system to combat this: meal plans, rigorously tracked dosing, regular blood work, etc. They know they're playing with fire, and therefore they are careful. Fire can warm your food, keep you from the cold, and provide light. It can also burn you and your home to the ground.

Myself, I just went; I thought of myself as fireproof. I liked the heat. Blasting dopamine and norepinephrine on all cylinders. Firing synapse firecracker-focus-laser-burn-out. Zoom, kerrpow... poof.

I experienced resentment toward my parents. I resented the doctors. I resented the businesses that had sold them to me. I resented the chemists. I resented the entire system that had graded me as a child and sent me bills as an adult.

I resented the entire system I failed to participate in. I resented the fact that this was all done to make me productive—and I still failed. I resented myself for becoming a secret amphetamine addict and a hypocrite.

My research and knowledge of the condition of amphetamine withdrawals kept me mentally equipped for the brooding condensation of chemical depression happening in the walls of my skull.

I knew that the voice in my head selling me on my own worthlessness was an unruly guest that would leave in due time and did my best not to feed it.

I was keenly aware that I'd invited it in some time ago when I brought Adderall in. This voice, this advocate waited for the amphetamines to stop coming before it sang its little song, pretending to be me, telling me I was no good.

You *really* have ADD. You need those drugs to be regulated.

Unnatural substance for an unnatural world. You are a natural person and you are unable to adapt to this wretched world. Everything is fucked as it is. You may as well ride this sucker to the ground anyway.

You suck, you're worthless without Adderall, you've gone too far, you need them now for the rest of your life. You can't even wash a dish without them.

———

I VISITED California to be with friends to support another friend's healing. Being without Adderall wasn't much of a problem here. It was always easier when I didn't have to worry about work and other necessary obligations.

However, it is notable that when quitting a drug, leaving the routine surrounding the habit makes the process seem to have less resistance. I started to consume excess food and cannabis.

I exhibited this with the bike trip, working at summer camp, going to my parents', and taking this trip. Perhaps it is easier to change your insides if your outsides change too. Or perhaps life is easier when you are having fun and not working.

When I returned home to Florida, I again found myself struggling to make moves, find work, and be effective and productive. Back at home, on the linear path of life, I was stagnant. I had roots in Orlando that Adderall had planted, and I just could not maintain the routine Adderall had set up for my life.

I fell out with some friends and became less gregarious in social situations. I connected on a deeper level with fewer people instead of connecting with everyone superficially. I no longer used other people as verbal scribbling pads for whatever nonsense I felt like talking about. I could listen.

My appetite returned. I could finish a meal and it felt like I had room for another. The anorexic appetite from regular Adderall use was reversed. Each time I'd taken an Adderall part way through my initial loss of prescriptions, I had set the clock back on all of this progress.

Once lying around and being a pile of a person gets old, it's time to get a footing out of the hole. I ran almost daily. I'd run as far as I could and then run home. The physical exhaustion allowed my mind to calm down. And it was a free dose of the sweet dopamine I'd become so accustomed to. I could focus after a run. It felt good.

Despite the chemical depression, intrusive suicidal ideation, and general scatterbrainedness I was feeling, I started to crawl out.

VINE JUICE

Ayahuasca is a natural substance from the natural world. It came to pass that I was invited to drink Ayahuasca ceremoniously, under the guidance of a traveling facilitator of shamanic work. I knew this was unique from when I was with mushrooms or LSD or even DMT.

Having someone there to facilitate and hold the space was different in a big way. There was an intention for healing and growth. I had been waiting years for this opportunity.

Ayahuasca is a psychoactive plant-based brew that comes from the indigenous people in the Amazon basin. It's commonly known for its ability to deposit significant loads of DMT in the brain. It induces personal mystical experiences as well as an exposure to a spiritual, or alternate, realm.

Seekers may confront themselves, their past, their trauma, their habits, and their nature and receive profound guidance on how to improve themselves. In clinical terms, it has been proven to treat psychiatric disorders as well as addictions.[1]

In preparation for the ceremony, it was recommended I prepare with two weeks of dietary guidelines that included avoidance of dairy, pork, alcohol, sex/masturbation, news, and medications that could interact with the brew. I took this seriously and prepared myself physically and mentally for what was to come. Another opportunity to be disciplined.

During this preparatory time, I was biking down the road with some groceries in my backpack. My phone rang. It was the woman from the clinical trial. My number was up! It was time for me to bike downtown and get my bottle of experimental drugs. Not only were these drugs free but they offered me cash in exchange for whatever risk I was putting myself into.

Months ago, I was scrounging for this opportunity. In my deep hole, stimulants were a rope and fill dirt. At this point, however, I had started to carve footings into the wall of this symbolic hole and figure out a better way out that had structure and longevity.

The idea was still tempting to me, however, so I told her I would call her back in a few weeks. I had in my mind that I could call up the trial office after the ceremony and see if I could jump into another queue. Although I was making progress in my withdrawal, I hadn't made a conscious choice to truly quit. I was just dealing with the situation of being unable to obtain the medication.

I went home and researched Ayahuasca's interaction with amphetamine and discovered it was potentially deadly but certainly an unpleasant interaction. Of course, there were varying opinions about it relating to half-life and timing, but I didn't want anything to get in the way of a clear experience. I was at a crossroads between medicine of the earth and medicine of humankind.

Ayahuasca is a whole being of its own—existing out of its own will to live and grow independently from us in tandem with thousands of years of tradition surrounding its worship and consumption. It is as perfect as every plant that grows.

The other medicine, likely an iteration of amphetamine that has existed for ninety years or so, was made in a lab, is unable to exist on its own without people synthesizing it in a lab, and having been made by people, potentially reflects the flaws of mankind.

———

I WAS WELCOMED into the ceremony space. I was unprepared. I had no mat. I hadn't understood how critical it was to be comfortable. I lay on the floor, something I always seemed to end up doing. I had no bed at home either. My room was still messy. A pole had broken in my tent, so I was sleeping on a sculpted pile of laundry on the floor. I was used to being on the floor. I accepted discomfort in the name of some unnecessary display of resilience.

I stated my intention to "let the medicine do what it needs to do and be open to receive it." I drank the brew and sat down. The songs began to interact with the medicine and create images, encouraging my eyes to close.

The visuals were powerful, colorful, vibrant, and mostly indescribable. Shapes, colors, and light all interacting with divine precision and compassion toward me, both viewing and participating. It was heavy on my shoulders.

I wasn't weeping, but tears were rolling out. I lay down to receive what was coming to me. The visual lines made themselves clearer; little men in technicolor outfits were climbing and creating scaffolding, higher and higher, climbing on one another up and up, and I realized as I looked down on them that they were setting up to work in my body. They were a cleaning crew. The cleaning crew got to work and told the medicine to put the visions on in my mind while they did their work elsewhere.

Daniel, the man who held this space, sang beautifully for several hours. His voice gave motion to the medicine's work within my body, mind, and spirit. In so many other times, substances had made it into my body, but there was never this sense of being held and guided toward healing.

Being sung to is different than listening to songs, and being with someone was different than being present with someone devoted to holding space.

The geometric tapestry that served as a membrane between reality and whatever substrate is beneath it faded away as I began to dig through memories and myself.

The first person I saw was my parents' cleaning lady, Elsa. How at times, when I was a teenager, I'd scramble out of bed when she came into my room. Remembering how I was so embarrassed to have a disorganized, messy little room and how judged I felt for her to clean it for me. How hard she worked, how I hid and did anything to avoid her. She was a reflection of my slovenliness.

I shed tears as I felt a deep sense of respect for her—not only for her work but for how she carried herself. Hard work. Years and years of cleaning the same homes over and over, bringing her daughter to teach her the way, and on and on. I thought about how she was like most people, while I had such a hard time being like most people. How I resisted conformity to a fault and sought to be someone else.

I thought about all those people I thought of as rude for not saying "hi" back when passing by. Seeing that they were not rude, they were focused and centered on their goals for the day, while I was there to see what happened, see what passed. Soft work. I worked soft.

I had many passing visions and reflections, many so rapid my memory was unable to grasp them as they flew in to be embedded in my subconscious. I saw myself being handed pills. I saw people taking pills. I saw pills creating geometry that interrupted nature's patterns. I saw pills take people. I saw myself awake at a kitchen table under a lamp, staring at a glass of water while the whole world was asleep, resting.

My consciousness was reduced and placed into my own stomach, where I was in a mucky swamp. I placed my hand into the liquid and pulled up a frail, damaged little bird. It spoke and asked me to help it, to save it. The bird had been in me for some time and was a close ally. I cared about it. I wanted to help, but I had no idea how to. It hurt to look at.

Here, in my stomach, I started to feel a lot of pressure. A moment of panic and overwhelmed confusion set in. I told the bird I could not. I was sorry. It felt like the ground beneath us was shaking. I sat up in the room, grabbed a bucket, and purged.

I walked to the bathroom and saw others lying on the floor, experiencing their own experiences. The room smelled of sacred herbs and humanity. There was a haze. I likened the room to dishwater. We all emerged clean.

After vomiting, the experience was much clearer. I saw myself creating a pergola, climbing up a post, hammering. Working hard, sweating, making things happen. In this vision, working, moving, like the cleaning crew, like Elsa.

I was myself hammered with an insight over and over. "Hard work, hard work—hard work is supposed to be hard, that's why it is hard. You need to work hard." I referred back to the technicolor ninjas and their clear practice of hard work.

I concluded that I had worked a lot, I had worked strenuously, I had worked for hours on end, I had worked constantly. But it wasn't hard. Work on Adderall was compulsory and almost effortless. Now I needed to work hard.

I quit Adderall in my heart. I wanted to learn to work hard on my own. I was ready to move forward and learn to work hard. The rest of the evening was a beautiful display of what could be rather than what had been.

Daniel's devotion to this divine work was truly admirable, and I noted the way his work was clear, simple, and at the same time, profound. Not only did the medicine send me the message of hard work but his hard work served to inspire. I saw him manifest this devotion to one's own purpose in his devotion to his role as facilitator, creating space for healing and growth with clarity and intention.

———

THE FOLLOWING MORNING, I was introduced to breathwork. The style we did was a holotropic technique. I was electrified by the breath. I was totally present in my body. I was in constant motion. It compelled me to move with the breath. I wasn't concerned with others looking at me as I moved, shook, and cried. I was in communication with my body and how it wanted me to move.

I knew there was some blocked chi, and I was pushing through it. I felt chi. Stirring the blood, moving the energy of myself. I felt supported, encouraged, and inspired.

I was wide open to my sensitivities and examined the fabric of my character and my life. How I lived my life. How I approached this beautiful opportunity to be alive. I felt gratitude, love, peace, and understanding. I wept at remembering everyone will die, and it felt good to release those tears.

This helped me process the medicine's lessons and integrate the wisdom and guidance into my life. Everything that needed to come up came up, and solutions were obvious and clear.

With everything we do as humans, the first thing we learn to do when we get here and the last thing we do before we leave is breathe. I have found it to be worthwhile to pay attention to it and develop it as a skill.

———

THE NEXT DAY, when I got home, I bought a bed, a mattress, and a box-frame. I stopped sleeping on the floor. I realized I had a lot of work to make myself closer to the person I needed to be, and it was better to take small steps than to waste time lamenting the colossal amount of work in front of me.

It may seem easy to read this and think ayahuasca changed my life. It did. However, I would feel more in line with the truth by saying drinking ayahuasca inspired me to change my own life. A small distinction, but it speaks to how this medicine works. Providing a space for some instruction.

Ayahuasca didn't *make* me commit to quitting Adderall. During the ceremony, in that space of healing and reflection, it was simply clear to me why I should. During the ceremony, a powerful force used parts of my thoughts and memories to deliver divine wisdom.

An internal dialogue was initiated that would have been harder to come by without the guidance of this sacred medicine. I'm certain these moments of clarity can arise through other therapies, events, and paths of self-discovery and healing, but this is how it happened for me.

The medicine is truly that, and using it is not to be taken lightly. I had been available to many powerful healing plants and medicines before but I was not held then. Maybe I wasn't prepared to be.

It's not just the medicine. Intention setting and being held in a cere-monious space makes a difference. It isn't like acid was when you were nineteen and you wore a funny hat and engaged in goofy shenanigans.

Perhaps instead you will examine why you behaved that way. You may end up examining why you wear funny hats. You may come face to face with a certain truth that is—you wear funny hats because you are worried you are not interesting enough to others on your own, that ever since some kid called you boring in sixth grade, you've made an effort to be unique because you felt ignored by your parents and brother and wanted someone to notice you. You found that when you wore a silly hat, people came up to you and said, "That's a funny hat," and then you had a conversation and felt seen.

You have a fear of dissolving into the static of the masses. You don't confront this fear, and rather than coming up with a new solution or action to make yourself feel special, you ask some questions.

You assess your attitude and maybe consider that it is okay to blend in with the mass of humanity and that to try to make yourself interesting, you're actually insulting everyone by assuming they are not as interesting as they are.

You realize that most people are interesting and have so much going on inside that they're too busy with their lives to broadcast it with a hat or something. You do this because you are insecure.

You realize you would be more secure maybe if you stopped all that regressive, self-destructive behavior where it starts, with your thoughts. And for Pete's sake, stop wearing hats to gain attention. You do still remember that it's fine to wear funny hats if you like them and they make you happy. It's not the action; it's the intention.

The term "healing" is broad. When healing takes place, it spreads from within into the outer spaces of your life. The healing turns to growth and the growth into a better life. The pills I took were "treatment."

Treatment is not the same as healing and neither are "cures." Adderall pulled up the drawbridge to the castle instead of fighting or training the dragon waiting beyond its walls.

Taken from a journal following this event:

Dearest Mother,

As this medicine slipped into my being, I was completely overwhelmed with an exquisite amount of love for you.

Endless amounts of tears escaped my eyes as that love was brought home to me.

All that you do.

I love every decision you made—made me.

Thank you for making me into the person I am. For birthing this spirit into this body.

Kung Fu

Ever since I started film school, I drove and biked past an ornate red and yellow kung fu temple. It was just a few miles away from my house, where I slept on my new bed in a windowless room discreetly constructed by our landlord behind the garage.

Standing alone on a grassy stretch of road approaching a local intersection stood the temple's walls. It was no shopping-center dojo. It was beautifully ornate, inside and out. Grand Master had many plants, a koi pond with fountains, and ever-calming, precise ghuzeng music. In the lobby area where you checked in and bought shoes and pants were pictures of kung fu legends and photos chronicling the Grand Master's life and achievements.

Inside, in the main space, floors were worn through thousands of feet placed during disciplined forms, movements, and other repeated maneuvers of the body. In the front of the main room were statues of deities and jars of sand holding bouquets of spent incense sticks.

Talking to whoever was at the front desk, amidst the distant sound of a call and response between a sifu and his students, I asked about joining and was told to sit in and watch a class.

I watched them warm up, running in circles in unison, doing stretches while counting in Cantonese. Then they held the main poses of praying mantis kung fu style. The warm up finished with five uninterrupted minutes of "Buddha breath."

Standing in horse stance, feet forward, knees bent over the feet, legs beyond shoulder as though riding a horse, students held an imaginary ball of energy about 5–7 inches in front of their chest on the inhale, then on the exhale, they pushed the hands forward and let the ball go, catching it again on the inhale.

Then the class split up for drills or practicing forms. Forms are sequences of moves that incorporate martial maneuvers into a practiced routine. The shoes and pants were super cool-looking and comfortable. I was sold.

My father's encouragement for me to study a martial art had previously fallen on deaf ears in the name of nonviolence, laziness, and who-knows-what-else. He agreed to support my interest financially, and I signed up for two kung fu classes a week and one tai chi course every Saturday morning. I never missed one.

I was now committed to living without Adderall. It was my project. I thought about who I was before this entire saga of being on and off amphetamines began. I'd been a seven-year-old boy who could have used some discipline—not in the distorted sense of punishment, but *self*-discipline.

What caused my ADD, anyway? I wondered if I had it, if it had me, if it was real, if I was misdiagnosed. I resolved that no matter the answer to this question, my actions were unchanged: Work hard. Improve.

In my early life and development, I had experienced consequence, punishment, reward, and persistence. I was persistent but only on the whim of inspiration—different from discipline. The lesson in discipline I needed was more centered on hard work without instant reward. Building faith in long-term positive outcomes from consistent investment, despite any lack of motivation or inspiration.

Kung fu changed my posture, the way I walked, and how I carried myself. I learned that "kung fu" means "hard work" (actual translation "acquired skill"). It was explained to me that you can see a man cutting vegetables, sweeping the floor, or going about any business, and he could be employing his kung fu all the while.

Wushu was the martial form we were applying our kung fu towards. I loved kung fu and tai chi as an introduction to discipline, and although it was late in life to begin, it still helped me crawl out of my withdrawal and into a renewed self. It felt important because I made it a priority.

By using pills to be productive, I'd conditioned myself to believe that there were quick and easy solutions to problems that were deep-seated, personal, and challenging. I had glided through what should have been hard work, but I was having too much fun to call it that.

I needed to be an actual adult, which meant the things from child-hood I was leaving behind were not just interests and activities. Mindsets, attitudes, and strategies of living.

When I bound books on Adderall, I was dancing and excitedly watching my hands create. It was as if my hands were possessed, putting on a show for my enjoyment. I was highly energetic and motivated by the pills.

On the pills, I would be overwhelmed by the potential of ideas the end user was going to unleash into the space I'd carved out for them in these books. I thought about visitors from Cape Canaveral visiting Orlando, buying my book, and designing rockets in the pages.

Take the pills away, and the big picture of the books holding brilliant ideas was reduced to a smaller room where there was a desk and a stack of papers I was stitching together with a needle and thread.

I believed I was making the world better by giving my customers space to have their ideas. I was—but I was internally grandiose about it. I saw myself as a gear in a great clock. I felt it. I felt that being in my room, gluing paper to boards was a critical act. In amphetamine withdrawal, I felt rushed to get books done so I could hope to make enough for rent and wouldn't have to ask for help.

Ayahuasca collaborated with me to give these instructions but did not hold my hand as I followed them. I had to do that work all on my own—and I still am. It was hard. Studying kung fu was hard. I no longer slept in the tent or on a pile of laundry. I meditated regularly—actual meditation. I retained my energy, whereas on Adderall, I'd spilled it all over the place. I went for runs. I struggled to find work.

But I had kung fu. I went to the temple three times a week. I still sold books. I was making maybe $400 a month, if I was lucky. I helped my landlord with some plumbing, and he gave me some money from that. I still did bicycle taxi work, but it was hard.

On Adderall, biking patrons around felt like a workout and a social experiment. Off it, it started to feel like the same weekend over and over of witnessing drunk people having trouble walking and hiring me to carry them. On the meds, a lot of times it was an enlivening evening of physical and financial rewards, but I couldn't get tired, hungry, or uncomfortable. In this withdrawal, I could.

But I could rebuild. I had visions of a brighter future. I was still withdrawing but remained conscious I was doing so and committed to getting through it. Every day got better. I was waking up, departing from the delusions of grandeur that I was endowed with a big mission. I thought I was destined for greatness, but I was learning that goodness is just as good. Maybe even better. Finally, I was just a guy.

I thought I had trouble interacting with others because I was operating on a different frequency, and that since there was nobody around like me, not many people understood me. I was also on drugs all the time. High-quality amphetamines. All the damn time.

I was in a delusion. All the substances we take are like filters over a light. The light is the same, but whatever diffusion you put over it changes how it shines on its surroundings.

Now, I could start to be happy just living my own life as it was. If I wanted to save or improve one person's life, it was the guy in the bathroom mirror. If I couldn't even take care of myself, how could I help anyone else?

I am forever grateful for my time at the temple. I learned to just go. Stop thinking my way out of it. Show up. Take a backseat to what I'm going through and pay attention to what is happening now. Things take time. The most gratifying gratification is delayed. Learning something bit by bit and watching it accumulate.

The tai chi form was just another *Clair de Lune*. Learn a bit, then once it's understood, introduce the next part, and over time, build one thing you can return to.

Something is always happening, and you are part of it. You *are* it.

Stand up straight. Observe your form. Be flexible enough to modify. Eat better for your kung fu. Meditate for your kung fu. If you slip at other parts of life, your kung fu will reflect that. Slip all you need to, just don't slide.

Northern Regression

Despite my improved posture and an ability to kick above my head, I remained in professional stagnation. Regardless of the rich spirit I was developing, on paper, I was poor. For a long time, I neglected some crucial aspects of life as they related to career. I prioritized the development of my state.

I conceded my pride, packed my things, and hitched a ride home on a road trip with friends. We had a delightful trip northward. It was a bittersweet departure from the life I'd lived before I again placed myself in my parents' suburban dwelling and regressed into past behaviors the house held to re-experience, learn from, and move on from.

I was on the home stretch of my recovery and healing the resentment I felt toward my parents. It was good to be there with them. Still angry with the pharmaceutical companies and society at large for allowing this to happen, creating a civilization so committed to productivity that we chemically modify ourselves to increase the value of our productivity output over our well being.

This intention is not new throughout history, but the application is contemporary to the 20th century. Looking back at the whole experience reveals a big misunderstanding between who we thought I was going to be and who I became. It can't all be blamed on the meds. I made my choices, I got the rewards and the consequences.

As I recovered, I felt a sense that I'd been tricked. All my usage served to channel insurance money through commerce while also adjusting my brain chemistry to be better equipped for control, obedience, and productivity.

But again, I was a dishwasher/bookmaker/preschool assistant teacher/pedicab driver/co-op volunteer/bicycle documentarian/mad artist/all around professional weirdo. The meds never made me into a career maverick while I was on them. I seemed to just follow my distractions into the woods, like the pinging pile driver that led me into a hornets nest.

The meds are just a treatment. Treatment quells symptoms. Healing gets to the source of them. How long would I have taken amphetamines if I'd had continued access? It wasn't until I engaged myself into healing practices that I was able to feel any kind of lifelong developmental growth in this area when it came to things like focus and work.

I resented that who I had been for a long time was contingent on a manufactured product. It's a hangup. I stigmatized myself and was pretty hard on myself. I had a yearning for independence, and the threat of withdrawals was in conflict with this value.

I felt embarrassed and ashamed of this past of addiction and dependency, and I naturally looked to shift the blame away from myself and onto my parents, public schools, psychiatrists, the government, and industry. I had to let go of it and take accountability for my own situation in a proactive way.

I loafed around at my parents' house and got a job at a used bookstore making minimum wage sorting romance novels. It was challenging living with mom and dad at twenty-five. We operated within different systems of life. Returning to this environment, I found myself seamlessly regressing into adolescent behaviors.

After a trip to the all-you-can-forgive buffet of compassion, I was able to let it go—most of the time. Once I get to places where I am content, I feel a warmth of gratitude for the trouble I had to endure to get there. After all of this, I was ready to just be a normal person. No more grandiose plans.

My mom found a job opening for me to teach ukulele at a private school. When I interviewed, they had me play guitar and ukulele and hired me to teach guitar. Looking at my resume of childcare, they offered me the position of running the aftercare.

There was a really nice, lovely young lady running the aftercare for the kindergarten. I took the job and worked with her taking care of kids on a playground every afternoon.

I was empowered by my decision to exist with ADD without medication. Still, when my cognition paused and I stared off into space, the advocate would whisper in my ear from inside my mind,

This would be easier with Adderall.

Eyes widen, head tilts, vision blurs.

You could get more done, you could write cool music. Maybe even finish that documentary you shot four years ago. Bind books again.

Snap out of it.

If you had Adderall, it would be a lot easier to focus right now. You could get things done with ease. You would be spry and upbeat. Ready to take on everything. You wouldn't feel so weighed down by responsibilities. You would be proactive rather than reactive.

I would dialogue with the advocate rather than outright dismissing. "Yeah, but I also get weird. I don't get good sleep, I barely eat, I age faster. Who can really know what I'm doing to our neurochemistry and our cardiovascular system? I'm delaying important lessons. I become socially robotic. I make other people uncomfortable. I have a weird, ego-driven perspective of myself, and it's not natural. It's not good for me. It's abusive."

The advocate would respond,

It's not me or you. It's that the world isn't a natural place, right? Remember? The world is out of balance. There is so much expectation of productivity to make it in this place, and you can't keep up without the assistance.

Maybe it's too late, maybe you are broken beyond repair. It's too late at this point. You just have chemical problems that require persistent chemical intervention.

"Sorry," I'd tell the advocate, "A deep part of myself refuses to believe that excuse anymore. Let's get our shit together and try to get this done. Let's try. We'll figure it out. Even if it takes a lifetime. We can't know what full commitment will yield unless we commit."

The advocate spoke to me softer and softer as its voice, over a period of days, months, and years, became a memory. Adderall was an old friend I let out of my car as I moved through life. I watched it grow smaller in my rearview mirror as time drove me forward.

––––––

WITH MY JOB at the school, I was able to move out from my parents' and rent a room downtown with a cousin and her friends. I occupied a cozy attic, and I had a routine that I didn't mind operating.

Being a normal person is not always exhilarating, epic, or intense. I spent my days waking up, drinking coffee, reading books, driving to work, coming home, having dinner, running, doing pushups, watching something, playing guitar, staring at the phone, going to sleep, and waking up.

I needed that. I found beauty in the simplistic things I'd previously neglected and introduced myself to feeling consistent and secure.

DR. LEE

I found someone, fifteen minutes away from my parents' house, who was practicing holistic psychiatry. I'd heard before of holistic psychology, but Dr. Lee is a psy*chia*trist. I was inching close to a year without amphetamines, but I was ready to carry some tools and skills to develop this ADD without meds project I was working on. I was out of the hole and on my feet; I wanted to move now.

Alice Lee had a history in child, adolescent, and adult psychiatry and practiced traditionally for eight years. When I was visiting her, she had a practice to help individuals depart from psycho-pharmaceutical drug use. She truly loves her patients and is notably courageous for walking this path. Dr. Lee gave me the privilege to interview her in addition to being her patient for five or so sessions.

She herself had experienced taking SSRI medications, and in her own process of withdrawals, gained an understanding of what her patients were being set up to experience. She shifted her practice into one with holistic intent to help individuals release themselves from the medication's dependence. She seemed to be the right person for the job.

Dr. Lee described taking psychiatric meds as putting your hands over your eyes to handle being in a dark room. You don't *know* it's dark; you are a little less scared, less prone to freak out. Her mission is to not just help people remove their hands, but to find the lights and turn them on.

She told me about a process she endured in medical school called "pimping," where students were humiliated for not memorizing rote info, and a traumatic stress response was developed in relation to saying, "I don't know."

Whether or not they know something, doctors are trained to behave and speak as if they know everything. Dr. Lee believes that medicine does not own all the information on healing. Healers should be humble and teachable.

The business of giving pills to people with conditions like ADD is big business. It's a rare individual who retains their license to practice psychiatry and is helping people by reducing prescription use.

She fought hard to keep her license to practice medicine and retain the ability to write prescriptions, which allowed her to write step-down doses for patients who needed to soft land their way out of pharmaceutical dependency.

She explained that ADD is the attention span of a soldier rather than a scholar. A warrior in combat would be in trouble if he were focused narrowly while screening out external stimuli. The warrior's attention is a 360° span with fast reflexes, intentionally available for distractions. Their attention works in a way that their mind is connected to the muscles of the body.

In contrast, the scholar's attention allows the scholar to sit at a desk for extended periods, handling whatever data, reading, etc. that needs to be processed. They can sustain boredom. The scholar can screen out stimuli and hone in on whatever is in front of them.

In our current societal paradigm's educational system, both kinds of thinkers are placed into the scholarly environment, where they are asked to sit in a chair at a desk for most of the day, processing information.

Dr. Lee pointed out she believes the reason more and more children have this warrior attention span is due to the stress of an internal battle in their body or life that is creating the stress response of being in battle. Because in one way or another, they *are* fighting a battle.

I noticed this in my own life, which was often a bit chaotic and without structure, keeping me on edge. Although I liked it at the time and convinced myself I could thrive in chaos, it weighed a lot.

If a child is experiencing abuse—verbally or physically—it makes sense that the child exists within a state of sympathetic nervous response and may react to many stimuli with fighting, fleeing, or freezing.

A person can experience an internal battle of toxic nutrition, causing inflammation and a battle between their body's adrenal system and invaders. Inflammation can lead to stress, and stress can lead to distractibility, restlessness, and impulsivity—ADD. The more I look, the more responsible the duo of stress and inflammation are for so many problems.

When Dr. Lee received a patient, she asked them questions to find out what was causing their internal stress. It could be diet, genetic snips, or something else. She educated me about the body's ability to methylate and accumulate toxins and heavy metals. High stress in pregnancy can cause certain chain reactions leading to ADD in children. She reiterated what I was already learning and assuming:

> When you integrate all the tools to help you figure out what's going on, you can decrease stress. The more you decrease stress, the more the attention span shifts to more of a relaxed attention span, where a person can focus.

I wanted to know about my old friend, amphetamine. She explained that when a person takes amphetamine, it initiates a process where the recycling of dopamine is inhibited in the neurons that release the dopamine. Amphetamine causes the presynaptic neuron to release more dopamine and ultimately, decreases the storage levels of dopamine in the presynaptic neuron.

> You're causing the body to shift and change its natural neurotransmitter mechanisms, rather than increasing the levels of this helpful neurotransmitter naturally. Amphetamines will impose its actions on the body.

The body can tell the difference between innate (natural) and exogenous (fake/synthetic) dopamine. Given the additional dopamine effects from amphetamines, the body will lower its innate production of dopamine because an external source is available.

Amphetamines create tolerance, which means that over time you need more of it in order to have the same effects. When you take more of a medication for its effects, there may be more side effects too.

Pharmaceutical medications consist of (currently or previously) patented molecules. This means it is not found in nature and is created by humans in a lab. Dr. Lee explained that amphetamine increases inflammation and can damage brain structures, and lead to stress dysregulation and more ADD when the meds leave.

It seemed clear to me that to manage ADD, I had to manage stress. Stress management is a key for a better life all around.

She explained that withdrawing is the experience of you, without your drugs, but also the remembrance of whatever untreated condition you have experienced from childhood. I needed some emotional regulation, self-control, and to know myself well enough to be useful.

The longer I took Adderall, the longer these lessons laid in wait. My ADD may have easily gotten worse, as my time on the medications delayed these processes while blazing alternative paths in my mind.

———

I HAD NEVER HAD a valuable therapy session where I could be heard and understood and been asked questions that were helpful. I had a handful of sessions with Dr. Lee. I always left her office feeling empowered. She recommended supplements to help my body and mind reclaim its ability to focus, have consistent energy, and be happy. She charged me with good intentions. This helped me immensely.

The path out is a healing process of the person as a whole. These practices reflected the difference between *treating* ADD with medications and doing what it takes to *heal* the ADD. It is never completely gone. As I could heal some, I could grow a little, and with the growth, these ADD behaviors are not eliminated, they're managed.

I continued a more ordinary lifestyle. I found that I was not in the fantastical, electric, hyperkinetic state of mind I used to identify with. I was more relaxed. Easygoing, maybe even lazy—something I was previously frightened of being in a zealous effort to be paranormal, extraordinary, and unique.

LOST & FOUND

I didn't really drink or party with my housemates. I enjoyed chatting with them but stuck to my routine of work, come home, and typically play guitar and enjoy my own company.

I once saw where my roommate put her bottle of Adderall and went in there when she wasn't home. I opened several of the XR capsules, took a small amount of the little sprinkles, licked them, and recorded some music.

It wasn't right, this subtle addict behavior and trespassing into her things. Total violation of her space. I knew exactly where it was because I'd seen her put it there. I didn't rummage and look around. The advocate broke through the mind/body barrier. It waited.

Hey, why not?

I'd lapsed in my conviction to avoid this substance based on a chance encounter. I recorded some music and had a decent time. I wasn't opposed to doing it again, despite actively writing this book.

Then one morning, months later, as I looked down at my key entering the lock as I left for work, I saw a small, blue diamond on the porch. Embossed into its face was "b972." My amphetamine salts were orange. This was blue. I had to look up the code online.

I sat in my car, reveling in the fact that I'd found a generic amphetamine. I thought that despite my recovery and commitment, this was a sign, this was meant to be. I should take this. Not right then.

If it was a sign, I suppose I saw it. If it was a test, I failed. I had to go to school and work with kids. I didn't want to waste the power of amphetamine teaching barre chords to teenagers. Nor did I want to introduce that version of myself to the peace and tranquility of the school.

I began to plan on making art and music and cleaning my room and tinkering until noticing the warm glow of the sunrise. I decided to take some of it when I got home, after dinner.

Over the course of the day, I rationalized that I would take the pill and work on this very book.

Taken from a document written that evening:

Just hours ago, I took a half of a half of a half of a half of the pill. I believe it was a 10 mg dose divided into approximate milligrams.

I feel it.

It makes me feel uncomfortable. It is tightening my neck and making me feel a little jagged.

Today I told a fifth-grade boy he shouldn't be doing amphetamines at night because he won't get sleep. He said he had been awake all night. He didn't sleep at all. He is a great kid. He is unique, interesting, and fun, but he is annoying.

When he told me he didn't sleep the night before, I asked him if he took any medications. He said yes.

I asked him if it was ADD medicine, and he said yes and asked me how I knew. I told him that I took them as a kid and they make it difficult to sleep.

I feel it. It makes me uncomfortable. I feel my skin crawling and I feel anxiety for no reason.

My shoulders—tight. It's harder to focus. My mind is jumping all over the place instead of gliding.

I should throw it away right now. In writing this, it is confirmed. This chemical force must exit my life and exit my body completely, and I must never return to it.

I feel the conviction ever so strongly. This substance is poison. The perilous venom that crawls from toxic warehouse buildings where matter is chemically converted into beta-phenyl-isopropylamine.

A pill I found? And I mindlessly took it. I recklessly let myself fall into it. I kept it. I found it on the porch and now took a little bit of it. A little rock. A chip of a rock and a bite of a pebble.

I took it and it is causing me to type in a whole new crazy way, fast and ridiculous. This is exhausting.

OH MY GOD. Why did I take an amphetamine at 6:20? It is now 6:50 and I am just so bad on this. It feels so weird.

I've got a lot in my life to hold onto. I've got a lot of things I want to preserve.

It is scary to be here again, in this place where I am taken over. It's a drug that can access your nervous system.

So it's like getting into your core mainframe computer and overriding specific parts of your brain to mimic the reaction of actual experience.

It releases dopamine. Similar dopamine antagonist drugs are also some of the most effective antinausea agents.

Restless legs syndrome and attention deficit hyperactivity disorder are associated with decreased dopamine activity.

Dopaminergic stimulants can be addictive in high doses, but some are used at lower doses to treat ADHD.

Dopamine itself is available as a manufactured medication for intravenous injection; although it cannot reach the brain from the bloodstream, its peripheral effects make it useful in the treatment of heart failure or shock, especially in newborn babies.

Is this to say that people with ADHD have an innate, decreased amount of dopamine, as in saying they are dopamine deficient?

So for people who are born with or acquire, for some reason or somehow, less dopamine in their general constitution, it is suggested by a number of American child psychologists that to counteract a decreased level of dopamine in a child, they give the child amphetamines to increase their dopamine levels?

I am so jittery right now.
This is not what it means to focus.
This is mental restlessness.

Why have I taken the ground pill outside?

I scraped some dust off with a knife into my being tonight. But as a choice of betterment for myself, I threw away the remainder, most of the Adderall pill.

I wrapped it in paper and put it in the trash can, along with the modafinil (strange anti-narcoleptic pills I ordered from India and tried two or three times). I wrapped it in paper because I have a mesh trash can.

I felt a little baby tiny little part of me, a little thing inside me that said, "Let's keep going."

Once I wanted Adderall so badly, I turned a toiletry bag inside out and licked the inverted seam edge of the bag to pick up these little pebbles, maybe time-release capsule beads or dust from broken tablet pieces.

I was so addicted to this medicine, then I suddenly ran out of it. It affected me so much that I was that desperate to have it give me my energy back.

Because I'd let Adderall borrow the controls of my focus and my mind for so long, it took some time to take it back. It was a weird obstacle for personal development as a child.

I thought of talking more about it to the kid at school. It seemed like he didn't want to talk about it.

"You need to get him off those meds very soon." I imagined myself telling the parents this.

But his uncle came. And I feel like maybe I shouldn't approach his parents and say, "Excuse me, your son told me he didn't sleep, and I had a hunch he was on ADD medicine, so I asked and it turns out he is, and I think he shouldn't take them anymore!"

Do I explain to them at length how I started taking them in second grade? Do I go on about licking up orange dust from a crack in a hardwood floor?

Do I tell him that in 1887, amphetamine was first synthesized on earth by Romanian chemist, Lazar Edeleanu? He did not find it of much use or interest and created an extraction method for taking an aromatic compound like Benzene from a pool of kerosene using sulfur dioxide...

THIS EXPERIENCE LET me take one last look at what I was leaving behind. I would seriously not recommend an addict take their drug again to make sure they don't like it. It was stupid and reckless, and I was lucky to not spiral.

It took willpower to not ease back in. My intention was to do like I used to do. To have that connection with a blank piece of paper and let my creative mind run rabid for an evening, but the part of myself that had moved on was upset about it. The weight of this book likely saved me.

I took my trash can and emptied it into a trash bag, tied it up, and put it in the trash can on the curb.

As of this writing, I have not taken Adderall or any amphetamine since. The advocate got quieter and quieter until it became silent.

I have resolved that the only time I would ever take an amphetamine is if I am aboard a plane and the pilots cannot fly the plane and I am suddenly tasked with landing via instruction from air traffic control. If that ever happens, I hope someone on the flight can pass me an addie.

As long as that never happens, I don't see it making a return into my body for the rest of my life. But then again, looking at that passage, I probably have better chances without them.

SELF WORK

Taken from a notebook after work with plant medicine:

The message that comes, comes forth in hard work. Hard work and ability.

This is always there, but it is the habit forming of constant consumption of the beautiful hard work of others that stops me from doing that work I have to do.

I should welcome boredom. Not everything has to be a thrill to be beautiful. Not all things have to be impressive to be important. Not all things need to be intelligent to be wise.

This is all the same. Go forth and continue to be the self without conflict and struggle. To be annoyed is to be annoying. It no longer serves you.

Servitude and devotion to God can be a kite in the sky. It's not what puts it in the sky, but it must be assembled in order to float through the sky.

Canvas and dowels stay on the ground. Thoughts of things you cannot attain create longing.

Remember what you have and what you are. Remember, you are a tomato off the vine. All these people were plucked and born. And they are beautiful for existing.

Things come up in the details that derail us and confuse us, and sometimes the solution to confusion is more of that or diving deep into distractions.

Remembering to just come back to what you're focusing on without attaching to distraction is key.

That is focus. Focus. Choose what to focus on, and focus on it for as long as you must.

Expect distraction. Distractions will certainly present themselves. To be surprised by them is to give them power over you.

Do not be surprised. Be focused. If you're concentrating, let yourself be seen by the world and don't peek until you're ready. Take your time to become ready.

And then follow through with the hard work and move on.

Obsession is not necessary when immersion is properly attained. Obsession is bouncy and energetic.

Immersion is collected—calm. Truth is beauty. Find truth and speak it. Immerse in your own truth and listen to the guides when they speak.

Live in greatness and humility. Be there for those around you. Get help and be helpful. Teach and learn. Eat and cook. Work and rest.

Dream and build. Listen and speak. Go beyond hearing and talking.

In maturation, the lessons are solemn and gentle. Taking them in is more of a breeze than a storm.

That's what being mature deals with. Being calm. Loving, kind, and balanced. Telling jokes is one thing. Telling stories is another. Imparting wisdom is next.

So take these lessons of devotion, grace, will, and strength, and apply them to your life carefully and with time.

Don't try to do little bits of everything at once all the time. Take time to sit and breathe often. Be ever so mindful of what you bring inside. How you build and adorn the temple.

Be perceptive, awake, and aware of what you are doing. Don't live in words that have been said all the time. Don't obsess over the world outside of yours.

There's plenty going on at home to pay close attention to. Forces of power. But be aware, be ready.

Be well. Be kind. Loving and peaceful. Love your family and build a home for them. Take care of animals and plants.

Cook delicious, nourishing food; make music that is divinely inspired; tell stories that uplift; do work that is meaningful; be secure in your identity; identify yourself to your higher self.

Have a plan.

———

A SHORT TIME after I took that last Adderall, I mustered up the courage to ask the woman I worked with at the school if she wanted to spend an afternoon with me. I married her and have never stopped loving her since that day.

I can't imagine our love thriving with me on Adderall.

Healing is a unified experience between the body, the mind, and the spirit. Unifying. Prayer and meditation, plant medicines, daily practices and rituals enrich these things.

Sauna, ice bath, breathwork, and deep sleep to recover and maintain the body. Reading books, doing yoga, keeping a journal, finding higher power, changing careers, moving, doing whatever is possible. Attention goes *into* where it is put.

A crucial element of moving on from my Adderall addiction is a life-long commitment to self work. I'm always doing it, and it's never completed. There's no point where I smack the dust off my hands and call it a day.

"Self work" in this context is the investment of effort into the self to improve by way of better understanding of patterns, the deep self, better diet, optimization, fulfillment, what have you. These investments can't be withdrawn, but they generate returns.

It's constant, challenging, and rewarding. Pleasure comes in moments. Satisfaction builds over time.

ADD and Adderall

ADD is a part of who I am, and I have chosen to learn to live with it, even if doing so is a lifelong pursuit. ADD cannot be my "strength" if that strength is access to medication.

When someone says they are struggling with their ADD, I do not doubt that they are. I also struggle with ADD. I don't believe I have cracked the code into some permanent state of perpetual focus. I do believe it gets better with conscious attention. My ADD is inexorably linked to my life. Therefore, to manage my ADD is to manage my life.

The boring part of a tale of sobriety is that the ending is anticlimactic. There isn't a day or a moment or a single act that represents the finishing of a drug habit. It just gets a little better every day until it doesn't bother you anymore.

Some believe ADD is not an actual disorder. I don't know. Perhaps it's a true ailment of the brain. Maybe an evolutionary aspect of the mind, affected by a response in our biological environment. Or maybe even a social-neuro response to the budding field of technology, the biofeedback of television, processed food, and the internet, leading to an easily distracted, hyperkinetic individual based on a feedback loop. Or maybe it's just a different kind of brain, like there's brown hair and blonde hair.

I climb peaks and tumble into valleys but stay on the path through them. It seems as soon as I get a hold on things, they get harder. More challenges, more opportunities. Just because I write that I don't need to take Adderall for ADD does not mean I've mastered life.

Taking Adderall out of the equation has revealed where I was hiding the work I needed to do from myself. I do not think taking Adderall solved these deep personal challenges; they covered for them. The more Adderall I took, the more these deep issues were encrypted.

Perhaps ADD is a particular stress response. Some people, when stressed, may freeze up with anxiety; some may break down in sadness; others may look for distractions to avoid focusing on what is causing stress.

Taking Adderall out of my system was taking the bumpers off at the bowling alley, riding without training wheels, climbing without a harness. I get metaphorical gutter balls, scrape my knees, and plummet down cliffs, hitting rocks all the way down.

Through the trouble and pain of this metaphor, I become better the hard way. I am continually learning how to focus and what spirals of distraction to avoid while building habits and strategies to resist them in perpetuity. How to bowl straight, how to balance the bike, and to dust off and climb after a fall.

I still, on occasion, wonder if I really have it (or ever did). Granted, I check several boxes for an individual with ADD, but from the same place of insecurity I have always struggled with, I want to call that my personality, not a disorder. I can be scrappy.

Ultimately, whether ADD is real or whether I have it doesn't matter. I'm not taking any psychotropic pharmaceuticals. I choose not to focus on "my ADD" and instead look at myself as a whole. This choice is as personal as a choice can be.

That second letter—D. Deficit said I wasn't enough, I don't give enough, I'm not paying attention. As if attention is payment owed to any person or thing. I've tried to prove I am enough after being told I wasn't. I have had to learn to trust myself.

I wonder if I started out without ADD, and through years of the neurological chemical mental therapy, foundational neural pathways were blazed on amphetamine. It had to have had an effect. Did it leave an impression neurologically that would lead me to develop ADD character-istics in the medication's absence?

At this point, the forensics are irrelevant. I'm not conducting studies or applying for grants to do them. I'm just trying to live a pleasant life without amphetamines. But occasionally, as I stare at the defects in the drywall compound in the ceiling, I wonder if I had ADD, if it had me, or if I was just a kid who got wrapped up in humanity's effort to turn humans into machines, and the whole thing took me for a spin cycle. Then I snap out of it and do the dishes.

I gave a fraction of my attention to everything. A global attention span. This may be a useful asset in a time with different expectations of people and what they are meant to provide society with through their efforts, but in my situation, I wasn't properly adaptable.

Public school is a government institution. It is rigorously scheduled and regimented. It is simultaneously comedic and tragic that two of the main complaints in the document justifying my diagnosis were "standing up" and "asking questions."

In the classroom, I may not have paid attention because the lectures felt less valuable than the stories I was telling myself. That bird on that branch outside was fleeting and beautiful, and I didn't want to miss out on taking it in.

I struggled to see the beauty in the transparent sheet of notes squeaking out on the overhead projector. I was unable to prioritize. I was looking for beauty, interest, and stimulation. I wanted to reach out and interact with things.

I had dreams that didn't involve their assignments, and I was already imagining I had achieved them. I was already proud of myself for just imagining success. Emotionally high on the idea.

I know this is a symptom of ADD. Being unable to differentiate between tasks completed and tasks thought to have been completed. In my experience, Adderall didn't make this go away.

I've learned to appreciate the raw experience of being ADD without meds, or a former amphetamines addict seeking balance off them.

On Adderall, I thought my ideas were great. And a lot of them *were*. I was optimistic about everything and confident without accomplishment. I thought people couldn't "keep up" with me. Really, I couldn't be available to them. I thought I was on another level. What I was really on... was speed.

My drug habit contained within itself more habits, and within those habits, hobbies, opinions, and perspectives divergent from the off-med ones. There were books I'd buy on Adderall, be uninterested in off Adderall, and then back on, would find interest in them again. An alternative personality.

I had little interest in making movies off the meds, despite my degree. I occasionally took film gigs as a PA or gaffer. I got lost in the thought spiral that what I was doing was replicating life around me when I felt compelled to be *in* life.

I felt bored of obsessing over moments with editing. I got impatient with it. I would rather *do* things with my body and mind instead of pretending. Embracing the part of me that was my ADD inspired me to want to do things that generate tangible outcomes.

I needed to interact with my environment itself outside of the digital representation of it. Sitting at the computer piecing this book together was incredibly difficult without the aid of the constant visualization of it as a printed book, imagining myself flipping the pages from first to last and smelling that first book after carefully cutting the tape off a cardboard box. I had to focus on the tangible outcome of the digital effort for me to keep at it.

The cure for my mental ailment wasn't a substance. Sure, some substances helped me get off Adderall, and some come around to help me do this and that. Occasional visitors. However, what needed to happen was a change in the environment and my cohabitation within it.

Habits create situations. I had to be placed in a situation where the resistances I encountered matched my strengths and challenged me in ways to grow where my weaknesses needed it.

Who among us has not forgotten their keys, left cabinet doors open, dropped everything to master carpentry, or stood up at their desk in second grade?

Some chemical habits are hard to quit, and quitting can alter a person for life. Healing from amphetamine addiction allowed me to build off of weakness, taught me how to get through tough times that seemed impossible.

Within limitations, we can do what we want. Even if what you want to do is whatever a doctor tells you to do, or to love yourself, forgive yourself for your follies, radically accept yourself as you are, and instead of reshaping yourself to fit into a place you're being forced into, see where you fit.

ALTERNATIVES

There are natural substances for the natural world.

Being aware of my mindset helps. Sometimes when a distraction comes up, I try to identify it and ask myself if I really need to be distracted right now. Does it serve me? Knowing a distraction is a distraction as it's happening presents the option to not blindly fall into it.

These days, you can't accidentally not look at your phone. It takes a conscious choice to decide not to. Staying focused is a skill attained much like distance running. The first mile is hard and you want to quit. You do it anyway, and do it again a few days later, and it's bad but not as bad. Eventually, on a good day, you just go.

Choosing habits. Waking up early and doing breathwork and having some quiet time really can build a pleasant, eventful, and prosperous day. Life is built out of a series of days, and each day is a chance to improve, develop, sustain, and appreciate.

ADD being worked in the mind, it seems, is a problem for the mind, but taking care of the body is tantamount. The body is the foundation of the mind, thoughts lead to actions, and actions lead to what happens in your life. This is a balance to strive for.

When my ADD flares up and I find myself distractible—in a chariot without reins in my hand, horses of impulse and distraction pulling me along—I stop and do breathwork for ten minutes, and the mental clutter just clears up. It really can be that simple.

I see no reason to ever stop practicing breathwork. I hope to always build off of it, a regular morning ritual that engages the body, mind, and soul. The morning sets the tone for the day. I use an alarm clock. I aim to not hold my phone at all for the first two hours awake.

I have found practices that help me manage the affliction of distraction, impulsivity, and an errant mind—none of which are panaceas. These are lifelong pursuits of consistent habits to interface with an ever-changing world.

———

I AIM to consistently practice breathwork. I call on an assortment of techniques, routines, and online videos to follow. This has become the foundation of my morning routine.

The mental practice and full body focus on breathing primes my mind for the rest of the day. Focusing on one thing that I can control and focusing my attention in my body. Doing something uncomfortable that turns out to be rewarding.

A year ago, I had a herniated disk in my spine that caused immense, demanding pain. My ship was taking on water. I could barely walk to the bathroom without audibly expressing the nerve pain shooting down my leg and through my toes. It was like lightning struck from my spine, through my leg and out my big toe. I couldn't sit in a chair. All I could do was lie down.

Immediately I began to do the breathwork throughout the day. I would focus my attention on the pain and seek to commune with it because it was not separate from me; the pain was me and I could listen to it. Each intake of rich oxygen was sent to the pain; each exhale, I imagined the pain leaving with the CO_2.

During long breath retentions, I felt like I was inside myself, repairing the tissue, taking closer looks, having compassion for the inflammation of my nervous system, listening for what it might be trying to tell me.

I took regular ice baths as well during this episode, finding that the cold immersion calmed inflammation and taught me how to breathe through stress and discomfort. Reducing stress and inflammation improves just about everything else.

The benefits creep into every aspect of my life. I couldn't sit up or stand for more than a few minutes, and I couldn't live like this. I did the breathwork that I usually did for just eleven minutes and spent two hours breathing and moving until I felt done and found out immediately that I could walk and sit. I was still in pain, but I was so much better.

I was reminded during this experience that to heal, I had to be an active participant in that healing. I could take Adderall and perhaps find huge career success very quickly. But it just makes me go and doesn't seem to repair anything in a sustainable way.

Taking myself to kung fu, I was an active force in my desire to develop discipline. Someone told me once that the way you do anything is the way you do everything.

I think the ADD brain in me is somewhat passive, and overriding that impulse and all but forcing myself to run and go to kung fu changed the way I approach everything. Knowing things would be hard, but being willing to endure hard work, which means failure, which means burnout, which means stress, and stumbling upon unknowns that lead to opportunity.

There were situations where getting into a recycling bin full of cold water and breathing was the difference between a good day and bad day.

I notice that when I don't do my breathing in the morning, my day is thrown off. When I do it, I feel aligned, focused, and activated.

I confess, I don't take absolutely nothing. Although at the time of this final edit, I don't smoke or drink alcohol, I do drink coffee and tea and occasionally microdose mushrooms. I take some minerals and supplements and herbs here and there. Nothing daily. Not advice—just transparency.

———

MUSHROOM MICRODOSE. This is a tiny fraction of a recreational or ceremonial dose. Sometimes once every two months. Sometimes a few times a week. It helps with ADD and a whole lot of other things.

If the medicine stirs up something, it can be worked on, considered, and acted on. The fungi bring presence, clarity, tempo, and gratitude into my momentum, without dependance. There are emerging studies praising the magic in these fungal supplements for brain wellness.

Microdosing has become popular as a productivity hack in some way, and I get it.

I don't consume psilocybin microdoses on any sort of schedule or regimen. I am not advocating anyone to take them. Sometimes they help me to work. Sometimes they bring up emotions. Sometimes they guide errant thoughts to a more perfect inner union.

They enhance my senses, feelings, emotions, visual and auditory stimuli, and open my eyes a little more to let in some more light through the windows.

I could very well be conditioned to see substances as helpers instead of playmates. I struggle with the idea of completely giving away my ability to function in one way or the other to a swallowable capsule. The idea scares me. It could be a hangup. I have been traumatized by medicine.

I still seek altered states. By removing the substances that do it for me, I've found altered states through these practices. Breathing, being cold, getting hot in the sauna, vigorous exercise, meditation, working hard, natural supplementation, and occasional fasting are my chosen methods of seeking altered states.

Fasting is great for a brief current of mental clarity. It is not for everyone. I'll do forty-eight to seventy-two hours of only water and some minerals once a month.

A really valuable reward from quitting Adderall was the part where I tried so many different things to fill the void to see what stuck. Routines, teas, productivity hacks, advice, postures, kung fu, magic rocks. Anything. When I tried fasting, I noticed clarity of thought.

I see lots of people talk about similar benefits with intermittent fasting, but I have yet to explore that. It takes a lot of discipline.

Managing stress is massive. Anything someone does to manage stress will help their life. Things cannot get worse from reducing stress. There is a difference between avoiding stress and managing it.

I have tried many herbs and, at times, work with them through tea or tincture. I have mentioned them several times but here are some again that I have worked with that have shown some clarity in my cognition and mood: Rhodiola, Ginkgo biloba, St. John's wort, Ashwagandha, Gotu Kola, Bacopa, and Ginseng.

I would advise seeking a knowledgeable naturopath, herbalist or specialist to work with if you can. Find plants to work with to improve cognition, regulation, and homeostasis.

Caffeine was eager to replace amphetamine as my stimulant of choice during withdrawal. It is much less intense but perhaps scratches the itch. I have come and gone with the habit and honestly feel really good off of it, but I am at a coffee in the morning and a tea in the afternoon.

I have found some foods make things worse and some make them better. Diet is a consideration, and any food that causes inflammation will lead to stress and emotional and mental unwellness.

It's not only expensive to get the best, richest foods and supplements and herbs, but to avoid all the man-made chemicals mixed into food that can create the physiological atmosphere for ADD-like behavior takes tenacious dedication and massive restriction.

What you eat and what you choose to do with your body has a substantial effect on your mind, and mindset feeds your body into action, enacting a feedback loop that ends up positive or negative based on what you do.

———

LIMITATION of smartphone usage is something I have also dabbled in that profoundly improves my attention and focus. When it comes to priming the attention span, the phone really sets me up for distraction by having my brain stimulated rapidly with a passive stroke of the thumb.

I thought cartoons in the morning were a lot for my attention span; this is the evolution of that. With a smartphone, I can look at a hundred things, ranging from deep intellectual considerations of consciousness to someone falling down off a roof, people making food, geopolitical happenings, or urgent messages related to work, all before I set foot outside my bed.

I believe that habits are not removed, they are replaced.

If hard work wasn't hard, it would be called something else.

After the healing comes the growth.

PUER AETERNUS

I don't think I grew out of my ADD. I like to think I grew into it.

Recently, I was considering how to end this book. Do I just say, "So, yeah. I don't take meds anymore. I guess I still have ADD, but like, um, sometimes I do breathwork and microdose mushrooms and I am okay"?

I'll probably not work in a maniacal fervor on craft projects as I once did, but I am at least authentically myself, and the struggles I have encountered and learned from would have been bypassed had I been on meds"?

Throughout my life and the writing of this book, I have tended to lean into archetypes. An archetype is a primordial structural element of the psyche. As a child, I remember feeling misunderstood. A wounded child. Later, as a young man, I desired to be a goofy stoner, a clown, a trickster, an artist.

When I was biking across the country, I imagined myself as a brave and resourceful Odysseus, a true hero, making his way across a vengeful sea to rescue my family from a stubborn group of freeloaders.

Looking back, I see how much more I resembled Don Quixote. Nobody had asked me to do these things. I just felt like doing it. Odysseus' journey was one of necessity. He was going home after a successful, dangerous battle in Troy; I left home to wander the expanse of my country on a bicycle.

The bike trip was a desire for this edge, this forced hero's quest. I was tilting at windmills—technology, machines, and industry. I believed I was a noble hero, and the intention in my heart was pure, but I ended up staring at tumbleweeds in the desert and writing poems in a tent. Which was fine, but not heroic. I sought adventure. I was tired of adventure being limited to its representations.

The windmill I tilted at has been this medicine—this whole thing of paying attention, working, taking amphetamines, and not taking amphetamines. The state of mind achieved through stimulant use was an enchantment that misled me on errant quests, deceived me regarding my identity, and retrospectively became the scapegoat for my follies.

I was wounded and healed. I survived the sickness of addiction and withdrawal. Perhaps I can help others endure this process. A wounded healer.

A withdrawal is a great flood that temporarily demolishes the self, thus calling for some divine retribution in the rebuilding of the self. The prodigal son, Jonah and the whale, Sisyphus, a black sheep. All of them in varying constitutions in relation to our unique selves.

The other day, I was driving to a wood shop in my 1987 jalopy F-150 with no radio, no AC, no side-view mirror, and a half-functioning gear box. My smartphone was busted, so I was using a dumb phone that had YouTube.

It suggested to me, based on my algorithm, a video called, "The Psychology of the Man-Child (Puer Aeternus)" on a channel called "Eternalised."[1] The video discusses an archetype called the Puer Aeternus, Latin for "Eternal Youth."

I shifted down gears. The road turned to forest and I wrestled my half-working steering wheel through the turns, lumber and tools sliding behind me in the bed of my truck. I was astonished at how much this Puer Aeternus character embodied myself and my experience. I felt a little embarrassed by its accuracy.

The video explains that the Puer was mentioned in Ovid's Metamorphoses and has been represented by Dionysus or Peter Pan. It embodies someone who carries the light of their adolescence into adulthood. Someone who is charming, affectionate, creative, in perpetual pursuit of his dreams, full of life, yet can apparently become draining to those they spend time with. Someone who stays in a provisional life for as long as they need to, to prevent what to them is a prison of routine, responsibility, and stability. The provisional life is that life that is a place-holder, a dress rehearsal for the life that will soon be beginning.

There are positive aspects to the embodiment of the Puer Aeternus. There is enthusiasm, wonder, a fresh perspective, and the potential for growth into new things. Hope for the future. The other side is a man-child who refuses to grow up and take on the challenges of life, waiting for something or someone to come solve his problems. Living in potential all the time. What could happen if only this and that out-of-my-control thing would happen. A great imagination, a good mind, a deep sense of inner development that never comes out. A saturated sponge, reluctant to wring out a drop.

The Puer tends to depend on their mother and not grow up. Maternal relationships can be complicated. I did rely on my parents for help. The nest that was built for me as a child had amphetamines strung into it. I think there was some comfort and familiarity in being on amphetamines imprinted on me from youth. It was home. It was a place I felt safe.

I knew what would happen when I took it, and as chaotic as I may have appeared from outside, I felt in control. It made me feel whole. With each return to the habit, each time I took an amphetamine, it was like a light was on, full of creative potential that I just wanted to bask in. Yet, each return was slightly dimmer than the previous.

No job was ever right for me. I didn't think about money, growth, or qualifications. I looked for something with purpose.

"He is prone to megalomania," the video says into my headphones as I ride out to build some cabinets. On Adderall, I looked more at my previous self. Someone the world wasn't ready for. "Someone who could." I saw the world as "un-natural" and convinced myself I needed drugs to adapt myself to the flawed planet. A "hidden genius."

I had nothing to show for it. No movie, no album, no gallery show. I had skills, ideas, some notebooks, and a lot of talk. I had fallen victim to daydreams of success without experiencing the realities of failure. I was allergic to time. I avoided rigidity, structure, and Type A thinking.

"Such a person is missing a sense of identity, which results in disquieting feelings of fragmentation and worthlessness. The Puer compensates in his behavior by pursuing the ecstatic "high" in drugs, alcohol, sex, sport, and daredevil escapades that transcend the inner depression which threatens fragmentation, granting an illusion of selfhood, which underlies his restless search for that state of stability and harmony," the voice continues as I monitor the length of time the engine light blinks to gauge the condition of my aged chariot. The oil level gauge is erratic.

The Puer is in close contact to their unconscious. They are agreeable and charming. They engage in full, riveting conversations. The Puer embodies high levels of insight and intelligence but is unable to apply them toward anything but the circulating knowledge of the self and inner interpretations of meaning about the things that meaning represents.

I used to think about working at a fast-food restaurant for a few months and write about it. Not to get a job for the stability but for the spectacle of the experience. The spectator of life. The Puer and I both value independence and freedom and may struggle with lack of boundaries.

After three years as a teacher, musician, artist, comedian, and side hustler, I withdrew from all the gigs. I stopped recording music, I stopped making art, I stopped doing stand up comedy open mics, I stopped teaching music, I stopped chasing my tail. I chose not to be a teacher or a student but a person operating in the world. I pursued woodwork. I appreciated the tangibility of it.

The useful nature of the work I was doing felt meaningful. I started making cold calls to businesses and people I heard of to offer myself as someone who does woodwork. I put in long hours of manual labor and exposed myself to powerful doses of failure, mistakes, and confrontation with my greatest inner weaknesses.

I practiced things like measuring, cutting, sanding, table saw technique, jig making, routing, carving, sharpening, finishing, and much more. I was immersed. I decided to just get to work. It was a challenging and rewarding change.

I feel I am now recovering from the overcorrection of the integration of the Puer Aeternus. I may have taken things too seriously and gotten myself in a bit of trouble as I entered "real life."

I took a lot of it on and suffered the unique consequences of actual adversity, financial obligations, business challenges, client relations and expectations, large coordinated efforts with several parties and logistics, schedules, deadlines, and satisfactory work.

These lessons had been waiting. As the pendulum swings from this to that, one can hope that with patience, its back and forth swinging settles plumb on center.

The other side of the Puer Aeternus is an archetype called the Senex, also called the wise old man. He works hard, which was a big lesson for me to change. Hard - work. When I quit Adderall and decided to study hard work, I began my walk from the Puer to the Senex.

Between the big dreams of the Puer and the hard work of the Senex, there is the balance. Dreaming big always came easy to me, but a good idea is just a seed that doesn't grow unless you plant it and take good enough care of it for it to bear fruit.

Hard work gets things done. Without hard work, big ideas are just scribbles on a page. Conversely, to be without ideas leads to toiling in labor without purpose or meaning behind the work.

I took on an apprenticeship with a master craftsman who taught me more than how to work wood. Perhaps he was a Senex. He shared with me the techniques of how to use tools to turn trees into furniture. He also taught me much about being a person in this world we live in, as well as a way to carry oneself toward work.

"To integrate the Puer Aeternus, one must bring themselves down to earth, not by having a one-sided view on a life of fantasy but rather by exposing oneself to daily life, chores, and hard work." The Puer must transcend the individual and allow themselves integration into the mass of the crowd. They must lose this idea that they are different or special.

I have asked this of myself many times during the healing of my addiction. Just go to work. Be simple. Carl Jung believed the cure for the Puer's neurosis was hard work. Fantasy becomes reality and a conventional life becomes fulfilling.

Even in woodwork, I began with a fantasy of creating elaborate, artful masterpieces of magnificent woods and materials but, over time, have come to appreciate the mastery involved in doing a decent job with a drywall patch in one family's bathroom. It may not be ADD or amphetamines, it may be coming of age, but for me they happened upon each other as I developed.

It doesn't matter if my ADD has gotten better. I've gotten better.

Still, I forget my keys, I lose my wallet, I break phones. I can't solve problems if I avoid them. These are muscles that would atrophy not being exposed to the failures I have endured and the challenges I face that would fall into the classification of ADD.

The Puer denies the heroic quest until he doesn't. Meeting the dragon, and either slaying, training, defeating, or retreating from it, and ultimately integrating it. Psychological death and rebirth is necessary to break these patterns, as was the case for me and my addiction and my struggles with attention, focus, and work.

EPILOGUE

"Every action has an equal and opposite reaction"
— Isaac Newton

It has been a privilege and an honor to host some of the most powerful plants on the planet into my body to interact with my consciousness. There have been invaluable lessons and guidance toward growth through these experiences. The opportunity to take all those prescriptions from the chemical plant feels, at times, like a burden I have had to endure.

I don't believe those pills healed me of anything. I believe they delayed my process of becoming, yet inevitably became an obvious part of it. I can never get back whatever the medicine took from me. On the other side of the same token, I cannot clarify what gifts it may have given me.

As much as life is an experiment, your life is only one sample. None of the variables you introduce have a control; you only get one life. I believe in the freedom to take any substance one wishes to take for oneself.

It gets complicated with children. It's not recommended to give kids caffeine before the age of twelve.[1] Yet I was all but forced to take amphetamines at seven. It was my path. I was part of an experiment on how children will do in school and in life growing up on amphetamines. Long-term data is still unavailable, as we are all living it out.

I am doing all I can to reset, rejuvenate, and heal my body and mind of the effects that medicine had on me during those formative years.

———

HAVING ADD is like being in a sailboat. To sail, you need the wind, and you need knowledge of how to use it. When I took Adderall, it was like I had a motor on my boat and I quickly rolled up the sheets and sails, and some of the lines hung overboard, rotting.

Once I stopped taking the meds, the motor fell off the boat. I was left with these sails and ropes, adrift at sea, not knowing how to get along with them. A ship without a sail. And then when it rained and the wind blew, I got lost and scared.

Day by day, I untangled the ropes, found help, learned about sailing, and eventually had some good days with the sails full of wind. Some days are no good. Some days I can't seem to make much out of the weather, or things just aren't right.

The better a sailor I become, the fewer of those days happen, and the better I handle them. It is listening to the wind that allows for this ship to sail. I control the ship, not the sea.

I don't just flip a switch. I face challenges without amphetamine, knowing that some things may be easier with them. I have chosen to take the challenges as perpetual opportunities for growth.

———

AS I WRITE THIS NOW, I'm in a cluttered room in the basement of our home. There are fourteen books on the L-shaped plywood desk. Twenty-nine notebooks on top, thirty underneath, and twenty-one more in a box on the floor. Hundreds of papers.

There is stuff everywhere. Much of it is the infinity of journals I have kept for writing this book, the oldest of which I've hung onto for twenty-four years. I've thought about torching them all in a fire when this is done.

Today, I had a rough day. I work for myself doing renovations and woodwork. I slept in late. I rolled out of bed and got dressed and drove to my jobsite. It was freezing. I was installing drywall and a subfloor, and my helper called out, so I was unloading it myself onto sawhorses. I put in the subfloor and the first drywall panel. I felt sad.

I worked through the weekend with woodworking projects and in between times was a husband, father, author, and person. Being in business for myself is hard. Somehow getting in breathwork at sunrise and/or at sundown keeps it all together, yet I skipped today. It's still hard, but I keep at it.

Faced with challenges, approaching them, making strides, making mistakes, I continued to build and show up to build.

When it's on, it's a different focus than I ever had on Adderall. It's better, but I have to get into the right state on a deep level to access it. Every moment has to lead to the next. Scaffolding benefits. I have to turn it on. When I do, the sun is up and hot.

I am a kinetic woodworking machine. Measure, cut, fasten, and install. The heat and light from the sun are stimulants. Add in concentrated breathing, cold water, medicine from the soil, and a home and family to live with, and it all feels not just manageable—but valuable.

Maybe all I ever needed was the sun—along with fish, vigorous exercise, and water.

Acknowledgments

I acknowledge that it has been of therapeutic value for me to get this out. So thank you for allowing that.

Thanks to my parents, who were committed to providing every opportunity for my success as a human with happiness in their heart.

The amount of people to thank for this story to happen are enumerable, and my gratitude is here for you. Thank you.

For this book to be real there are many people who have helped me.

Anne Dykers. The fire for this book almost went out, but you turned over a coal that touched a log. Your encouragement and guidance has been a warmth in my heart. Thank you for reading, seeing, guiding, talking, and helping.

Jody Berman, Gina Hagler, Eric Lichtblau, and Alan Rinzler. Thank you for your time, inspiration, critical advice, sage wisdom, knowledge, and opportunities to speak and work with you all.

Thanks to everyone who comments on my videos or participates with me on the internet. Thanks to everyone who let me talk with them about this book.

Dr. Alice Lee, for your support and contribution to introducing this work.

To my courageous readers who provided crucial, honest, and supportive feedback: David Abelman, Sarah Beck, Heather Braxton, John M. Bros, Dad, Clark Day, Marie Day, Ed Deas, Daniel Feldman, Lesley Greene, Ralph Guinta, Charlie Hoover, Jimmy Hoover, Pat Hoover, Asia Hwan, Zack Kerxton, Ansley Kincaid, Adam Kramer, Christian Parra, Karen Prosen, Penny Roth, Emily Scheer, Darrin Somma, Tim Sommers, Dani Stormes, J. Theron, Ben Tiptonford, Bill Torrey, and Rachel Torrey.

A bottomless well of gratitude to Susanna Schollum, for editing and creating the space for this work to become materialized.

Annie, Atlas, and Melon. Thank you for waiting patiently for me to finish this. Your perpetual support of me as I am allows me to freely express myself.

About the Author

R. L. Kramer currently is a carpenter who enjoys fly fishing. He lives at home with his wife, child, and dog. He loves them all. He has ADD and often leaves cabinet doors open and loses his keys.

Despite this, he still doesn't take amphetamines.

www.rlkramer.us

instagram.com/r.l.kramer
youtube.com/@R.L.Kramer
tiktok.com/@adhdmedfree

About Dr. Lee

Alice W. Lee, MD is a holistic and integrative child, adolescent, and adult psychiatrist.

Since 2002, she has focused on helping her patients with medication withdrawal and restoring mental health by integrating functional and energy medicine techniques.

Ultimately, her goal for each patient is freedom from being a patient. She obtained her MD degree from the University of Utah and completed her adult psychiatry training at the University of Maryland Medical System, and child and adolescent psychiatry at Children's National Medical Center.

For more information, please visit her website to view her podcasts, presentations, holistic articles, social media links, and contact/practice information.

holisticpsychiatrist.com

Notes

Introduction

1. https://www.cdc.gov/nchs/products/databriefs/db380.htm
2. https://www.ncbi.nlm.nih.gov/pmc/articles/PMC2670101/
3. https://www.mayoclinic.org/diseases-conditions/adult-adhd/symptoms-causes/syc-20350878

1. Water, Fish, Exercise, and Research

1. https://chadd.org/adhd-weekly/more-fire-than-water-a-short-history-of-adhd/
2. https://ajp.psychiatryonline.org/doi/10.1176/ajp.155.7.968
3. Bradley C. The Behavior of Children Receiving Benzedrine. Am J Psychiatry. 1937;94:577–581
4. https://www.ncbi.nlm.nih.gov/pmc/articles/PMC3064242/
5. https://www.ncbi.nlm.nih.gov/pmc/articles/PMC3000907/
6. https://www.invivomagazine.com/en/corpore_sano/chronique/article/235/every-molecule-tells-a-story-ritalin
7. https://www.additudemag.com/treatment/the-feingold-diet/
8. Mayes, Rick, et al. "Suffer the restless children: the evolution of ADHD and pediatric stimulant use, 1900–80." *History of Psychiatry*, 18:4, pp. 435-457. December 2007.
9. https://www.smh.com.au/national/keith-conners-the-godfather-of-medication-treatment-for-adhd-20170717-gxciq2.html
10. https://link.springer.com/referenceworkentry/10.1007/978-1-4419-1698-3_216
11. https://www.psychologytoday.com/us/blog/saving-normal/201603/keith-connors-father-adhd-regrets-its-current-misuse

2. Set and Setting

1. https://khn.org/morning-breakout/study-links-c-sections-to-autism-and-adhd-but-experts-say-the-research-relies-on-correlation-over-causation/
2. *https://jamanetwork.com/journals/jamanetworkopen/fullarticle/2777034.*
3. https://www.psychologytoday.com/us/blog/moral-landscapes/201112/dangers-crying-it-out
4. https://pubmed.ncbi.nlm.nih.gov/32155677/
5. https://www.sciencedaily.com/releases/2004/04/040406090140.htm
6. https://www.pbs.org/newshour/health/could-being-born-in-august-make-an-adhd-diagnosis-more-likely
7. https://www.ncbi.nlm.nih.gov/pmc/articles/PMC3277258/

9. Amphetamine

1. Much of the information in this chapter is from the following book: Rasmussen, Nicolaus. On Speed: The Many Lives of Amphetamine. New York and London: New York University Press, 2008.

10. Childhood on Dexedrine

1. https://emedicine.medscape.com/article/289973-overview
2. https://www.ncbi.nlm.nih.gov/pmc/articles/PMC2735437/
3. https://www.ncbi.nlm.nih.gov/pmc/articles/PMC2518387/
4. https://www.sciencedirect.com/science/article/abs/pii/0736467989902631

13. High School

1. Mate, Gabor. Scattered Minds: A New Look at the Origins and Healing of Attention Deficit Disorder. Toronto, Canada: Vintage Canada, 2000.

2. https://www.nytimes.com/2008/01/14/opinion/14kalish.html

26. Woods

1. https://www.sciencedirect.com/science/article/pii/B9780128002124000261
2. https://wellnessretreatrecovery.com/amphetamines-accelerate-aging-process/

31. Adderall Researches Itself

1. It appears this language was mostly taken from a book titled *Obetrol*, written by Lambert M. Surhone, Miriam T. Timpledon, and Susan F. Marseken, published by VDM publishing in 2010.
2. Category C means "Animal reproduction studies have shown an adverse effect on the fetus and there are no adequate and well-controlled studies in humans, but potential benefits may warrant use of the drug in pregnant women despite potential risks." https://www.drugs.com/pregnancy-categories.html#catc
3. In this context, fetuses.
4. And Australia.
5. One of several active ingredients.
6. Although I wrote this under the glow of the internet and computers, I cannot verify that Adderall causes bradycardia.
7. I was confused what a psychosomatic disorder was. It is a psychological condition that manifests physical reactions in the body. Psychosomatic disorders do highlight the mind–body connection, but not in a positive light. https://my.clevelandclinic.org/health/diseases/21521-psychosomatic-disorder
8. This is a generalization and a reaction to being made aware of studies that show higher likelihood of developing schizophrenia when taking stimulants https://www.ncbi.nlm.nih.gov/pmc/articles/PMC6890973/
9. https://daily.jstor.org/the-raf-on-speed-high-flying-or-flying-high/

10. https://academic.oup.com/cid/article/42/9/1305/315936

34. Journals

1. I wondered for a long time if I was guessing their age. It clicked just now. I was at a cafe and these were their numbers to receive their lunches.

35. Dished Out

1. https://wellnessretreatrecovery.com/amphetamines-accelerate-aging-process/

37. Clots and Castor Oil

1. https://www.reuters.com/article/us-amphetamine-abuse/amphetamine-abuse-tied-to-heart-attack-at-young-age-idUSCOL36291920080623
2. https://pubmed.ncbi.nlm.nih.gov/18496266/
3. https://n.neurology.org/content/90/15_Supplement/P6.079

41. Psych

1. https://www.globaldata.com/global-sales-of-psychiatric-drugs-could-reach-more-than-40bn-by-2025-due-to-coronavirus-says-globaldata/

42. Guinea

1. https://www.ncbi.nlm.nih.gov/pmc/articles/PMC2873712/

47. Vine Juice

1. https://www.ncbi.nlm.nih.gov/pmc/articles/PMC6343205/

55. Puer Aeternus

1. https://www.youtube.com/watch?v=9A7GTGSfrIU

Epilogue

1. https://www.aacap.org/AACAP/Families_and_Youth/Facts_for_Families/FFF-Guide/Caffeine_and_Children-131.aspx

www.ingramcontent.com/pod-product-compliance
Lightning Source LLC
Chambersburg PA
CBHW050854150626
46549CB00013B/1624